CUTE HOORS AND PIOUS PROTESTERS

Traits and Characteristics of Irish Politicians

JOHN DRENNAN ～

Gill & Macmillan

Gill & Macmillan Ltd
Hume Avenue, Park West, Dublin 12
with associated companies throughout the world
www.gillmacmillan.ie

© John Drennan 2011
978 07171 4827 1

Typography design by Make Communication
Print origination by O'K Graphic Design, Dublin
Printed in the UK by MPG Books Ltd, Cornwall

This book is typeset in 11/13.5 pt Minion.

A CIP catalogue record for this book is available from
the British Library.

5 4 3 2

CONTENTS

SECTION 3: THAT'S NOT HOW TO DO IT: SAD TALES FROM THE
TAOISEACH'S OFFICE

SECTION 4: AH THE WOMEN, FAIR PLAY TO YE!

SECTION: 5 STRANGE CREATURES

ACKNOWLEDGMENTS

Thanks must initially go to Fergal Tobin of Gill & Macmillan. When we originally met, neither of us would have expected what was then quite a vague project would be completed so swiftly.

That it was can be ascribed to the skill of the staff of Gill & Macmillan.

In particular I would like to thank Fergal, Deirdre Rennison Kunz, Tess Tattersall, Ciara O'Connor and the rest of the team for the speed and professionalism with which they responded to rapidly changing circumstances and, worst of all, my handwriting.

Amongst my professional colleagues I would like to thank Eoghan Harris, who many years ago took time out of a busy life to foster my career in journalism.

Other figures I would like to thank for the support, and sometimes challenges, they provided over the years include the *Sunday Independent*, Eamon Delaney, Harry McGee, Vincent Browne, Matt Cooper and Dáil colleagues such as Miriam Lord, Michael O'Regan, Jimmy Walsh, the great Mairtin McCormaic and Jason O'Toole.

There is a cast of others, mostly politicians, whom I have left out for their own sakes whilst the patience of my wife Ciara, the delight provided by Timothy and Michael, and my mother Alice, who is responsible for my interest in writing, should be mentioned.

In conclusion, and perhaps most importantly, I would like to thank the cute hoors and pious moralists of our political class.

Though I always preferred the company of a slightly different wing of the political landscape, without your contributions this book would never have been possible.

INTRODUCTION

Chapter 1

THEY DO NOT MEAN TO BUT THEY DID

We may claim our politicians are vile creatures but any fair dissection of these strange animals should consider Philip Larkin's great lines about how 'They fuck you up your mum and dad, They may not mean to but they do, They fill you with the faults they had, And add some extra just for you.' Of course, like Larkin's parents our mostly well-meaning politicians may not have meant to 'fuck' us up but ... well ... we are where we are.

As with all modern family dynamics, our relationship with these dysfunctional beings is a strange one. One of the biggest difficulties is that our politicians are both of and yet not of us. If we want something, we encourage them to be venal but should they fail to provide us with what we desire, or if rather like the fabled three wishes of the genie the result goes entirely against our expectations, then we call them corrupt.

Our politicians are also different because these strange maligned creatures are a larger version of our own dreams and desires. They are poor Gullivers cast onto a hostile shore whose every vice and virtue is magnified.

In spite of the national obsession with politicians one of the other curious features of Irish political life is that so many people claim politicians are boring. Sadly it is hard to avoid the impression that Pat, again, is speaking with a forked tongue for politics has always been our great national soap opera. Indeed, some would argue that Bertie Ahern took this to its logical extreme by spending a decade being photographed beside 'Coronation Street' actresses at pub openings.

In fairness, Bertie was of his age, for the conventional politician was a peripheral creature in a Tiger that was all a-throb for the making of money. Nothing epitomised this more than the strange politics of Saipan where Roy Keane almost became the new Parnell as the country went ablaze over the walk-out of a soccer player from a football tournament. Gone indeed are those days.

Instead, as we pick our way fearfully through the acrid debris left by the bonfire of the Fianna Fáil/PD vanities, suddenly our politicians are important again. It represents a truly amazing reversal of fortunes for less than half a decade ago we were the complacent society. Like America under Clinton, we had entered a zenith of perfection where the end of history had been reached and nothing bad could ever happen again.

Now that we realise everything we 'knew' was wrong Ireland is a country that is awash with questions. We may still listen to Ray D'Arcy each morning but in the secret part of ourselves we ask just how a Republican party like FF could become so mired in acts of venality that veered towards the boundaries of active corruption. And even Ray is talking a lot about politics these days.

This book aims to explore the public and secret traits and characteristics of the Irish politician and there are a lot of questions to be asked. Some of these include how FF's special relationship with the people turned into a mutually destructive affair. We need to know why Bertie was the alchemist's stone of political success and what this says about us.

Of course, now that Bertie's rattling around the dustbin of history we are more concerned about how we managed to replace our insouciant sun king of a Taoiseach with a tortured soul who seems sometimes to desire a similar fate to Pearse. There is also a growing edge to the questions about our aspirant rescuers but, whilst the electorate increasingly chafe against the unbearable lightness of Enda, could it yet be the case that he has the resilience and the character we actually need? And is pink but perfect Eamon Gilmore a national Sir Lancelot or a Sir Talks-a-lot?

We will not, however, just be looking at the kings, for if we are to fully understand how politics got us where we are today we must explore the entire architecture of miserable Ministers, hapless Junior Ministers, cute hoors, fallen and rising deities, lovely girls, political archetypes, Anti-BIFFOs, scarlet women and strange creatures of the great Irish political game.

Perhaps, most importantly of all, we will be looking to see if any of them offer us the possibility of hope, for in our uncertain world the one sure thing we can say of our politicians is that, whether we like or loathe them, they are the characters who will either save us or send us to the bottom of the ocean wearing a pair of concrete boots.

Chapter 2

TOP OF THE WORLD, MA! PADDY IS FINALLY RICH

If there has ever been a moment of perfection in Ireland's troubled history it surely arrived at midnight on Christmas Eve 2006. There may have been some dissident voices about the excessive materialism from Bertie and a strange man called Mr Putnam but, as Miska from Poland prepared the children's organic chocolate-shredded muesli breakfast, Paddy was at peace. It may have taken millennia of oppression but Pat finally was rich. Surveys showed we were the happiest country in the world; foreign economists came to coo and gape at our little economic miracle, whilst the most popular Irish leader since Parnell could even take some time off from the minor task of keeping the Tiger ticking over to unite Europe in a manner not seen since the age of Charlemagne.

It may seem incredible now but back in the day we were kings to such an extent that the former begging bowl of the world could look Europe in the eye when she came asking for a small favour regarding that old referendum thing and tell Frau Merkel, the frogs, Brits and the rest of them to shag off. Paddy would do things his way now and sure why wouldn't he when our normally bankrupt Exchequer was taking in so much money it could not even count it right? At last Ireland was not only at peace, she was also, to paraphrase Jimmy Cagney, 'top of the world, Ma!'

Of course, it had not always been like this. Less than two decades had passed from the time when Ireland was a strange medieval place where the lips of a girl turned white with cyanosis as she died giving birth to a secret child beneath a sad-eyed statue of the Virgin Mary in a Midlands grotto. In the 1980s there may have been ritual public burnings of articles by British hacks about how the Irish economy was based on the pig and the potato. However, in a secret part of his soul Pat had to admit the Brits were right, for in an economy that was closer in its structure to a Soviet Eastern Bloc state than our twin cultural influences of Britain and America, often it looked as though the only difference between us and Albania was that we at least had the British TV channels. And we even had to rob those.

In years to come our historians will use phrases such as 'the great chimera' to describe the wonderful soft age of Blair, Clinton and Bertie. However, during the era of the three political tenors even Harvard intellectuals such as Fukuyama claimed we were living at 'the end of history'. And the miracle of it was that Ireland had not been left out, for all of the old terrors of emigration and unemployment had been consigned to the coffin-ship.

Even that gruesome failed entity called Northern Ireland forged a new mould as Trimble, Bono and Hume danced together on a Belfast stage. The show was so wonderful we scarcely noticed Adams and Paisley as they lurked in the shadows waiting to claim the peace.

It has to be said that Pat adapted easily enough to the life of a wealthy libertine. Up to the 1990s he might have struggled to hold on to one house but now Pat had become the house-owning equivalent of a nineteenth-century colonial power with his properties in Bulgaria, Spain, South Africa, China, Abu Dhabi and London plus, of course, the four Irish properties rented out to his Polish friends and the two new flats he had just purchased near the Darndale Hilton.

Pat was a bit concerned about the latter two, for even he suspected Darndale and the 'Sex in the City' style marketing about brownstone townhouse living didn't really match, but his new status as a share-holding capitalist meant he reckoned any possible losses there were covered.

It truly was a wonderful world. In the 1980s the only dining experience that had been available for Pat was Supermac's or the new local Chinese where he would go when drunk to peruse the menu suspiciously before ordering the European meal. Suddenly under the new dispensation Pat became a gourmet and chefs became celebrities.

Of course, Pat missed the bacon and cabbage but he put up with all this new wasabi pigeon stuff for you could always have a tasty breakfast roll with three rashers, four sausages, two fried eggs, four hash browns, three black and white puddings, butter, tomato ketchup and mayonnaise to wash the taste out.

Ironically, in spite of the new cult of the celebrity chef, it was the breakfast roll that became the signature dish of the Tiger. This was less surprising than you might think for the essential nature of the Tiger was homage to excess. Our arteries may have been silting up but there was no time to worry about that when you were busy spending on everything from decking to houses.

There were simpler dreams too for one of the features of the Tiger was the exposure of a whole new range of people to the world of work and opportunity. The morning trains were filled with what might loosely be called the 'country girls' talking about their dreams of a house, a fiancé and a life that would not be dissimilar to the heroine in the latest Cathy Kelly novel. There was something sweet about the candy floss nature of their hopes but you wondered how well these would survive the fire and sword of a recession.

Of course, even on that Christmas Eve there were shades of doubt. Pat had noticed his invoices were being paid more slowly whilst the 'in brief' news section of the *Star* had started talking about a strange thing called a subprime collapse in America. It also troubled him that whilst we were still the fiscal masters of the world, everything our government did went wrong. Happily, when Pat started to fret, someone like Charlie McCreevy would pop up like a chortling Jack-in-the-box and tell Pat to go away with himself for all the ordinary fellah should be thinking about was 'a few pints and the GAA'.

In truth, it didn't take that much to persuade poor Pat to give the old thinking a rest for that sort of stuff was for recessions and, well, life was good. When he finally nodded off and Miska picked a hundred-euro note from his wallet, Pat was smiling, for even as he dreamed of the rolling ski slopes of Bulgaria and of the not too dissimilar slopes of Miska, he was wondering just what new adventures the coming year would bring.

SECTION 1

Welcome to the party

Chapter 3 ～

| CULTURE AND ANARCHY

How Fianna Fáil's special relationship with the people broke the country

T he ceremony to mark the 90th anniversary of the first Dáil should have been a moment of mild national celebration where, at a minimum, a few national school children would have been bussed in for a day of compulsory flag-waving. Instead, though the full terrible stripping away of the decent drapery of the Celtic Tiger had just begun, the streets were bare. Outside of a scatter of politicians who scuttled past like court defendants, the only other signs of life consisted of the excessive security detail that has become such a feature of the Cowen regime.

As Brian Cowen arrived, glowering in a manner that brought Auden's famous dictator and the crying of small children to mind, the bleak affair bore a weird resemblance to the signing of some unwanted Anschluss. Later, as our unloved Taoiseach lumbered back through the scudding rain to the walled safety of the Dáil, it was hard not to avoid the sense that the strange event was laden with a piquant irony.

Were Bertie still there, the commemoration would have evolved into a celebration of Fianna Fáil's role in capturing the new Irish state. Sadly under Mr Cowen it had evolved into a weird emblem of how the most successful party in Europe is now detested in a manner their milk and water enemies never dared to dream of.

It is, of course, a peculiarly Irish form of loathing for both Bertie and Mr Cowen can still appear on the 'Late Late' and be applauded. Sometimes their jokes may be laughed at but that is simply a clever disguise, for like all post-colonial peoples we are experts at using good manners to hide.

The truth is that nothing epitomises the desolate state of our Taoiseach more than Mr Cowen's nickname of BIFFO. Some brave souls still argue that BIFFO is an affectionate, manly sort of a nickname. However, you would not have to be a psychologist to understand that the venom with which the ordinary citizen spits out the word is the most visceral symbol of how poor Cowen inspires a level of hatred normally associated with figures such as Pinochet.

Cynics will say our disenchantment with FF is simply linked to the money running out the door. But it is hard to avoid the suspicion that something more fundamental is at play. Conor Lenihan once argued that FF's success was centred on its status as a brand. Rather like Cadbury's, who in an ironic mirror of our own fate have now sadly been taken over by foreign interests, FF's strength lay in its familiarity.

As is so often the case with Conor he was nearly but not quite there for sometimes familiarity in a brand is not an entirely good thing. But when it comes to the FF party of the BC (Before Cowen) generation, uniquely amongst political parties the image was entirely positive.

Labour might have been an impotent mismatch of urban intellectuals and rural contrarians whilst a Fine Gael party that is perennially beset by begrudgery and self-doubt were simply the political equivalent of Guinness Light. FF, in contrast, were like an attitude of mind crossed with a Joycean stream of consciousness.

As with the best Guinness ads they conjured up a montage of celebratory images incorporating the GAA, the gallop of the horses' hooves in Galway, All-Ireland Sundays, mothers in aprons baking homemade bread, Michael O'Hehir, Bertie winking at you, cheering crowds, a bit of entirely safe cute-hoordom, drink, laughter, song and, in latter years, ambitious young Tigers conquering the world.

The success of FF BC in subsuming these images into their self-definition meant they could confidently say they were a national movement who most perfectly reflected the anarchic culture of the people. It was a status that provided them with an almost impregnable political bulwark, for the quasi-fascistic duality of the relationship between FF and the *volk* meant that if we condemned them we were finding ourselves guilty.

Some date the decline of FF back to the last two decades where the party became a franchise. According to this argument a great national movement was taken over by an ambitious coterie of careerist politicians, whose presence diluted the purity of their original vision to the point where FF became the political equivalent of bootlegged whiskey. But did the fault actually lie in their genes from the start? For though we apparently live in an age where history is dead, no one should underestimate the role of tradition in Irish politics.

One of the more fatal consequences of our colonial experience was the warping of Irish political development. Since the rise of O'Connell Irish politics has been dominated by the big tent school of politics, where a monolithic party, led by an authoritarian great national leader, devoted itself to the single objective of securing Irish independence. The long-term consequence of this was the evolution of a school of politics where vices like graft were accepted—for you were taking from the British—and virtues such as dissent or ideas about the structure of the state were not tolerated since they were a distraction from the great national objective.

The evolution of FF's definition of itself was informed by another toxic influence, for one of the many curious features of FF is the ongoing anxiety of the most successful political party in Europe to portray itself as a grouping of revolutionary outsiders. Intriguingly, despite their current success, the genesis of FF lies within the defeated wing of the Irish national movement. In so far as it has a genetic profile the party sees itself as being the inheritor of the tradition of 1798 to such an extent some faithful still fervently believe Wolfe Tone was the first FF leader.

The ideological line continued with the Young Irelanders, the Fenians, the men of no property who stayed with Parnell after the split, the 1916 faction and the defeated forces from the civil war. However, whilst this played a huge role in their success, it also left them dangerously open to acquiring the worst traits and characteristics of the Irish race.

The trouble with these ancestral voices was that they fostered a uniquely dysfunctional relationship with the state they have governed for so long. Our urban intellectuals may have condemned de Valera's fostering of a cautious national identity centred on the GAA, the Church, a farming economy, John F Kennedy, lovely girls, no dirty books, the Pope, *Ireland's Own*, the parochial hall and the parish field, but ultimately the real problem was to be found in FF's relationship with the state. Like so many other scenarios where the disinherited finally secure power, the long-term status of the state as their enemy meant they felt they owed it nothing. The bad news for us was that this absence of loyalty was alarmingly similar to the African post-colonial experience. As with Africa, for a time the asceticism of the first post-revolutionary generation held back the wilder impulses of the movement. However, as the ancient regime began to wither, TACA signalled the rise of new FF whose ultimate triumph was marked by the accession of the Emperor Bokassa of Kinsealy to power.

Ironically their detestation of the apparatus of government facilitated the success of FF, for it kept them intimately tethered to the mindset of a people whose national psyche had been branded by the concept of the state as the enemy. Of course, governance still had to function but it is a creature to which we owed no real allegiance. This meant that, unlike the obedient Germans, the anarchic Irish believe the role of politicians is to act as fixers between the dishonest poor citizen and the hostile force they are theoretically in charge of.

The difficulty with this concept was that for FF the state was merely something that simply existed to be despoiled for the benefit of their supporters. Sometimes the party called this theory of politics redistribution but it was really graft. This was grand and harmless, in an economic sense at least, whilst we were poor. But then Paddy got his hands on the treasure chest of European credit.

It was not by accident that our better-behaved European friends called Ireland the 'Wild West' of crony capitalism, for even if our carefully chosen regulators had barked, FF under Bertie were like a collective of rogue sharecroppers whose only priority is to turn a profit now, devil take the hindmost and let tomorrow look after tomorrow. The problem, of course, is that when tomorrow finally arrived, Ireland was the economic dustbowl of Europe.

Sadly the sloppiness was not confined to economics, for the endemic indifference of the anarchic Irish and our party of choice to the concept of good governance allowed so many other things—from our environment to the lives of our abused working class children—to have been destroyed. In a piercing study of Charlie Haughey the journalist Olivia O'Leary walked past the gaudy incidentals such as the houses, the bank drafts, the yachts and cut to the core of his great flaw with the poignantly acute observation that ultimately Mr Haughey simply didn't believe in himself enough.

Ironically it can be argued that this was also FF's greatest flaw. They didn't believe enough in themselves and, worse still, us to have the courage to replace our old anarchic culture with something better. And sadly by the time we and they realised that building the good society is about putting politics before people, it was all way too late.

Chapter 4

FINE GAEL'S DYSFUNCTIONAL KILKENNY CATS MAY YET LET GILMORE INTO THE TAOISEACH'S OFFICE THROUGH THE CAT FLAP

If there is one moment that captures the farcical nature of the most curious political organisation in Irish life it is the little-known Battle of Baggot Street. The spectacle of two groups of drunken middle-aged men almost coming to blows at 3am in the centre of Dublin was odd enough. But when the personnel consist of the distinguished front-bench members of the nation's top Opposition party, then we are in the territory of Swift.

Sadly, though the initial cat-calling was quite vigorous, age and the portliness of the combatants meant we were spared any headlines about the Fine Gael front bench 'arrested after late night brawl'. Instead, as is so typically the case with FG, after a short bout of the 'hold me back' stuff both sides embraced the politics of Slattery's Mounted Foot and ran away to fight another day. Coming as it did, shortly after the second heave against John Bruton, it was, however, yet another example of business as usual amongst the fighting Kilkenny cats of FG.

When it comes to the status of being the most dysfunctional party in Irish politics, one would have thought Fianna Fáil, with its vast retinue of corrupt leaders, would be the favourite for that role. However, outside of noting that like the Mafia FF are quite at ease with the corruption 'thing', the success of the party has fireproofed their members from any such concerns. Instead, like all natural born aristocrats, they are so insouciant that if Mr Cowen were to race around Dublin setting cats on fire, the most that FF would concede is that their leader had become a little eccentric.

Labour, meanwhile, are so at ease with their lack of success the faction fighting resembles some cunning plan that has been devised to keep the brethren safe from having their vestal consciences disturbed by responsibilities of any sort.

The madness of FG man is all the more curious for one would have to go back to the Ottoman eunuchs to find a body of men so at ease with impotence. FF's contempt for these courtly fops is summarised by one scathing comment: 'Carlsberg don't do Oppositions but if they did they'd choose Fine Gael.' However, if you are to truly understand why FG is mad, we must explore the soul of the petite bourgeoisie.

It might be expected FG's designated status as the representatives of middle Ireland means they should embrace the politics of normality. But history alone suggests no other class of society does dysfunction better than the petite bourgeoisie.

Our aristocrats and the working classes are at ease with their existence, for one class exists without hope whilst the aristocracy know nothing of fear. But, caught as they are by envy and unfulfilled desire, those members of a petite bourgeoisie that drove such disparate movements as the rise of fascism and Marxism need the exhilaration of secret vices to escape the tepid chains of respectability.

By day the petit bourgeois tries to understand the tumescent prose of Kevin Myers as he commutes and his Stepford wife chooses icy colour schemes of the 'antique white would be nice' variety. However, once the curtains close then the swinging and the opium pipes begin. Of course, the same petite bourgeoisie are the main cheerleaders of all our moral furies but their anxiety to join the mob is informed by middle class man's hatred of the self, which means he is always keen to fashion the whip with which he can beat his own back.

As with so many things the fault for FG's current status lies with Garret FitzGerald. Up to the arrival of Garret the Good, FG was the unimaginative voice for those solicitors, accountants, small shopkeepers and big farmers whose existence was informed by the desire to spoil the party for FF rather than any real desire to rule. Occasionally they accidentally gave FF a breather from the excesses of power and though nothing much changed during these brief interludes it did at least take the one-party gloss off the state. It was a limited existence but at least FG knew where they stood.

But under Garret suddenly the party became a riddle of contradictions as it attempted to graft an alien social democratic petit bourgeois liberal mindset onto the old blueshirt roots. It was, to put it mildly, a struggle to keep Oliver J Flanagan and Michael McDowell in the same tent. For a while the charisma of FitzGerald meant the Knight of St Columbus could walk, hand in hand, with the liberal secularist lion of the Bar Library. Inevitably, however, the departure of Garret to the sanctity of an *Irish Times* column meant FG splintered into a rump as the brains of the party took flight to the PDs and the Greens.

It was bad enough that the party was neither right, left, nor centre or that they have never, since Garret, secured a sufficiently charismatic leader who might unify the unlovely collection. Ultimately the greatest problem for FG was that under FitzGerald, they became the party of the petite bourgeoisie, and from that moment the madness of that class insinuated itself into the DNA.

In their case the bourgeois vice they picked was murder. The decision of FG to engage in a frolic of political infighting was also a classic case of how the devil makes work for idle hands, for when it came to the main theatre of political warfare these plankton stood no chance against a benevolent whale called Bertie. Seeing as, even during the age of Bertie, the FF theory of governance resembled Christy Moore's famous man on the surfboard after 15 pints of stout, one would have thought FG might have put up a bigger fight. That, however, would have required application and the one element of their core ethos FG remained true to is their dilettante instincts.

So it was that they were reduced to playing the preying mantis upon themselves.

Initially the war was between the Bruton and Dukes factions but they then split into the Kenny, Dukes, Mitchell, Noonan and Bruton clans. Ironically the more intense the fighting became, the less clear it became as to what they were actually fighting for. But like the Kilkenny cats that fought and fought until the only thing left was a tail, FG fought and fought until all that was left was a rump.

In fairness, during this 'family at war' era FG were at least entertaining. This was epitomised by one leadership crisis where four of their finest burst into Bruton's office to tender their resignations. Sadly before they uttered a word, Bruton, who had already been informed of the incipient coup d'état, beamed broadly and said, 'Aw, you've no need to resign, lads, you're already sacked.'

Such was the asinine nature of the internecine warfare on another occasion the Noonan faction leaked an internally commissioned profile to the media that had said that Bruton needed to get his teeth cleaned and lose 2 stone. Subsequently when Noonan replaced Bruton it was noted with some merriment the same could be said of the bright new leader.

Ironically, despite all his faults, the worst thing that happened to FG was the loss of John Bruton, for this was the moment FG finally lost its soul. You see, the one thing real FG man wants is to be on solid ground and Mr Bruton was the living representation of that desire. Like a sort of old-style Captain Mainwaring, the Brut was a stolid, unimaginative soul who sat in the office pondering great thoughts and bothered little with the necessary evils of meeting the people. He was, if you like, the political equivalent of a thick meaty steak. Enda, in contrast, is a soufflé.

Of course, by the time he left they were well fed up of 'the Brut'. But when one considers his successors consist of the man who brought us 'the Baldy Bus' and a nodding, winking caricature of Bertie, it was hardly an improvement and the party is, alas, still in a right old mess. For a time after 2007, the party that does not know what it stands for, under a leader it has no faith in, managed to hang together. However, in the aftermath of the failed coup of the innocents, FG are now led by a man who failed to take out Bertie when he was political road kill and Michael Noonan, who visibly blanched at the prospect of taking on a Bertie who was admittedly at the peak of his curious powers. It is, when one adds in Cute Oul' Phil Hogan and James 'Bottler' Reilly, a gristly sort of dream team that has left FG dangerously exposed to yet another Nightmare on Kildare Street.

On this occasion the threat is not that FF might slip in through the back door. Instead, the even greater horror is that whilst the FG cats are yowling on the Leinster House lawn, pink but perfect Mr Gilmore will become the first Labour leader to enter government buildings through the front as distinct from the servants' entrance.

Chapter 5 ∾

SITTING BY THE RIVER WATCHING SINN FÉIN FLOAT AWAY

The Chinese promise that if you sit by the river long enough you'll see the bodies of all your enemies float by certainly appears to apply to Sinn Féin. When they established a Southern beach-head in 2002, the kindest thing that could be said of them was that they had finally unified the civil war parties of Fianna Fáil and Fine Gael. Sadly the unity was informed by fear and genuine contempt over the questionable morality of the SF habitués of the high moral ground.

For a time they were correct to be fearful but by 2007 the defeat of SF's picture postcard candidate Mary Lou McDonald in the Stalingrad of Dublin Central was indicative of how the feared SF advance had been held in check. However, far from this representing the bottom of the barrel, the decay of the reputation of the party is so stark, in 2010 Gerry Adams was accused, at a minimum, of covering up a culture of sexual abuse against children. Suddenly a Republican movement, which still takes its orders from the ghost of Pearse, appeared to have as much moral credibility as a dissembling bishop from the Catholic Church.

Many within SF are privately relieved that the revelations about the party's 'issues' with child abuse have attracted so little attention in the South. But it could be argued this is a measure of their decline for were SF still a threat, the mendacious behaviour of the party would be bruited from the heights. However, once you've bowed the knee to the RUC to get a Ministry, you really are history.

It is strange that the children did for Gerry in remarkably the same way that they finished off the apparently all-powerful Catholic Church. After all, the context set by their other traits and characteristics means it is difficult to understand how anyone could be shocked by SF/MI5's indifference to child abuse. Still, when he makes brief sorties to the South to dissemble on the 'Late Late', before joining the disappeared again, even Mr Adams must sometimes wonder just how SF became so peripheral.

There was, after all, a point up to 2005 where we could stick nothing on the new Teflon party of Irish politics and there was a lot of stuff to be thrown. The discerning Irish electorate, however, appeared to have no problem with the murdering, the tarring and feathering, the bank robbing and a new form of cultural tourism in Colombia called narco-terrorism.

The SF/IRA movement were even taken at their word when they claimed the holiday homes in Donegal were the fruits of their literary endeavours. They almost received a round of applause for the Northern Bank robbery, and ironically now they would almost receive an overall majority for a similar action, whilst the movement's other political activities in the field of diesel and money laundering were praised for the new entrepreneurial spirit.

Once upon a time, and it wasn't such a long time ago either, the movement could have dreamed of Adams being ensconced in the Park for 2016 and of achieving real unity by stealth courtesy of being in government on both sides of the border. You could hardly blame them, for a broken FG party had been taken over by a man who looked and sounded like a village idiot. Labour were a little more solid but all that party of Irredentist underachievers had to offer was Dáil quips from funny-man Pat.

In retrospect maybe it was the modern equivalent of the curse of *VIP* what done for SF, for the peak of the project occurred during that fantastical *VIP* interview when Mr Adams admitted he occasionally hugged trees. Suddenly, a man closely associated with the murder of Jean McConville was being portrayed as a cross between Buddha and Ghandi. Afterwards Michael McDowell fumed about how Adams was more similar to Mugabe than Mandela but it was as effective as, er, the last sting of a dying wasp.

As the political establishment realised that Mr Adams had achieved the unique fusion of the sulphur of the gun with the more seductive scents of celebrity, the great panic began. Sometimes it was almost entertaining as appalled conventional politicians spoke in hushed tones about the hordes of SF community representatives who were engaging in dreadful acts, like representing the disenfranchised communities of the state.

So what was the fatal flaw that stymied the great advance? Ironically the fault may lie in their genes, for their most serious weakness was the great cultural divide between North and South. We may sometimes, though increasingly rarely, say we want a 32-county Republic but in our mendacious

Southern hearts we do not really believe the Northern person is one of us. Instead, as we see it, the archetypal dour little DUP bigot and the sanctimonious SF moraliser have a great deal more in common than our civilised latitudinarian politicians. Such was the intensity of 'la difference' that even during the heights of the property boom Pat was more inclined towards the purchase of a little *pied-à-terre* in Bulgaria than a redbrick house in Belfast.

The problem was that if you are not one of us, you don't get the votes, and SF were so not one of us, in one of his few acts of service to the state Michael McDowell destroyed Gerry Adams in the 2007 pre-election debate of the half leaders. SF may have been stunned by their electoral failure, but when Michael McDowell is closer to the Irish sensibility, then SF is always going to be doomed.

There was another problem, courtesy of the slight innocuous person of our former Minister for vegetarian recipes. SF's heartland consisted of the disempowered working class communities, but there were too few of those to achieve the political credibility that would come with 15 rather than five seats. This meant that, as with its destruction of the SDLP, the next phase of the SF blitzkrieg had to focus on the soft underbelly of the faux-radical liberal middle classes.

SF needed to acquire primacy amongst the sociology and Third World Studies graduates of DCU, and those SUV-driving mummies of Dublin South who yearned to embrace some form of radicalism that might bring a certain cachet. It seemed like an easy ask, given the speed with which significant numbers of the press corps were prepared to swoon when graced by the exciting presence of a reformed terrorist. And yet the little miracle whereby our Sancerre-sipping socialists could chatter between air kisses about their support for SF's progressive new policies on climate change, abortion, protecting seals, euthanasia of the elderly, a charter of animal rights and an amnesty for Osama Bin Laden never quite happened.

Gerry attracted the odd unfaithful flutter but whilst those who are bored of staid old partners may fantasise about sleeping with a piece of political rough, when the tramp turns up with a toothless grin at your door it is a slightly different game. And no amount of spinning could wash the coppery taste of blood off the freshly manicured literary hands of the SF leadership, or the fact that, well, to be blunt, they were a tad unsavoury and stupid.

The biggest problem of all for our SF carpetbaggers was that when it came to the High Cosmopolitan politics of cool, there was an alternative—for the Greens and SF were fishing in the same pool. It might have seemed to be an unequal match, for one side had treble hooks laced with dynamite, whilst the

others appeared to be using barb-less hooks baited with tofu. The reason for the Greens' surprise triumph was, however, quite simple. Ultimately politics in the Ireland of the Tiger was infused by the same designer ethos as the rest of society. There might, of course, have been a slight dissonance between the suvs and the Greens' holistic policies, but it was much easier at those dinner parties to murmur about how you were thinking of voting for Eamon Ryan as distinct to Nicky Kehoe.

How ironic it really is that at the end of it all the muesli-eating vegetarian pacifists were the ones who really did for Gerry. But when it came to middle Ireland, there really wasn't a choice. The Greens were like that nice graduate from ucd who would travel with your daughter to India and bring her back. In contrast, those unsavoury sf types were more likely to get her pregnant and move her into a Pro-Palestinian commune in Fatima Mansions.

Chapter 6 ∿

LABOUR, THE PARTY THAT WORKS IN THEORY BUT NOT IN PRACTICE

Olivia O'Leary once famously wrote about how the dapper, dandy leader of the Labour party, Michael O'Leary, was in a state of despair about how bored he was in the job. The astonished journalist wondered how O'Leary, who was also at that time the Tánaiste, could be bored and it was a good point. But there was something quintessentially Labour about Michael O'Leary's ennui. Since they politely decided to wait for power in 1918, the permanent Labour adolescents of Irish politics have always preferred the fractious excitement of Opposition over the tedium of power.

When it comes to our regular denunciations of the failure of the Opposition, the permanently forelock-tipping blueshirts may have got the majority of the criticism. But surely the real measure of political underachievement is provided by a Labour party that won more seats in 1992 than Fine Gael secured in 2002, has been the effective leader of the Opposition since 1997 and now has 30 fewer seats than the outdated blueshirts. You can blame the civil war all you want but it is hard to decipher what role it has played in the great Labour failure.

Of course, some still believe the hour is about to come when the benighted Irish electorate will reach the Zenlike perfection of a Fintan O'Toole column and do the right thing. In general such moments occur after the election of each new Labour leader, after each new election defeat and then swiftly disappear two years into the reign of the bright new leader.

Nothing epitomised this more than the experience of Pat Rabbitte after he took over in 2002. In truth, our faith in Pat started to deteriorate when we began to see Rabbitte sauntering contentedly around Leinster House on

Friday afternoons. We are sure Pat was thinking fine and lofty thoughts during these strolls. But as Enda toured the country trying to heal his broken party, Pat resembled a farmer dreaming of the delights of organic farming whilst the fox is stealing his geese.

In fairness, Rabbitte's prescient observation on taking office that his job was to capture the votes of 'those who think Labour and vote Fianna Fáil' perfectly summarised the difficulty he faced. Sadly the fine elegant phrase captured the essence of his party for, rather like Rabbitte's promise, Labour is a fine elegant party that has utterly failed to capture its appropriate share of the market.

The greatest irony, of course, was that the man who diagnosed the cure for Labour's malaise continued with the same policies of all talk and no graft that had contributed to their ongoing status as the sickly child of politics. It all came to the inevitable bad end, for Rabbitte took over and left a small sleepy party of 20 seats. In contrast, the gamine Enda Kenny wrested back 20 lost FG seats.

The true extent of the Labour defeat in 2007 wasn't just that they had stagnated for yet another half decade. Instead, what should have been more alarming was that they didn't appear to be at all demoralised. In election 2007 Labour was opposing a Taoiseach dogged by accusations of sleaze and a FG leader that huge swathes of the electorate believed to be nothing more than a happy idiot. But when the white heat of the real battle began, a party that was once again critically short of foot soldiers resembled some small neutral country in a war between two superpowers.

After their unnoticed failure the party should have been seething. Instead, they seemed to be simply relieved all that unseemly electoral business was over, and that most of the old rump had returned. The absence of any struggle by Rabbitte to stay or by Labour to remove him provided us with a telling portrait of Labour as a party that was really not worth fighting for.

All of the other parties, and those elements of the media who like to ensure our political system is as unchanging as a bee trapped in amber, thought it was a pity to see Rabbitte go. In fairness, he certainly was the perfect leader for his party of schoolteachers and university lecturers. FF have the support of our builders, workers, entrepreneurs and chancers, or at least that used to be the case, whilst FG were the party of the entrenched insiders such as lawyers, big farmers, consultants and the occasional terribly lost dreamer.

But Labour only ever had the love of the nation's teachers and they really are good only at talking. And this ultimately is the greatest vice of the party. All those elegant quips that we forgot within the hour may have meant that for the media Rabbitte, in tandem with Joe Higgins, was the popular leader of the Opposition. But after the electoral shake-out Joe lost his seat and Pat lost his party. There is something surely there for all of us, and especially Labour, to consider. And in particular, the new media hero Mr Gilmore should be paying close attention to the route map of his predecessor's fall.

Mr Gilmore should also consider that, outside of verbosity, the greatest flaw Pat suffered from was that he was as at ease with ordinary citizens as the poet Yeats. In fairness to Rabbitte, unlike Yeats who famously entered a public house once to see how the common people lived and fled after a minute, Pat always liked the bar.

The Labour leader did not, however, like any ordinary old pub. He was instead a witty urbanite who was happiest when in Doheny & Nesbitt's or the Dáil bar mixing with what Pat considered to be equals, such as Brian Cowen.

But one of the more alarming features of his campaign for the Labour leadership was how, once he was outside the Hy-Brasil of Doheny & Nesbitt's, Rabbitte became uneasy. After the debates when the delegates adjourned to the pub, Pat's lesser rivals would plunge enthusiastically into the canvass. Rabbitte, however, would stand away from the mass like a rotund distant bishop waiting to have his ring kissed by the more daring members of the flock.

Like his party, there always appeared to be somewhat more of show rather than substance about Pat. In the Dáil after each bout of questioning Rabbitte would stand for a moment before sitting down. It was as though Pat, in his own head, was acknowledging the invisible waves of applause that his contribution merited. In reality Ahern handled the elegant dilettante with an ease that was almost contemptuous, for Bertie versus Pat was the political version of rope a dope and, sadly, as the hard currency of the election proved, poor Pat was the dope.

As they settle once again into their much-loved familiar Opposition armchairs, it is hard to avoid the impression that we are actually using the wrong name for Labour. For a period of time there was great talk of a new united party of the left that might be called New Agenda or even Democratic Left. But the cruel truth of things is that Irish Labour is the equivalent of the British Liberal party.

Like the old British Liberals, Labour may well be the repository of fine thinking and, for that matter, fine dining. But outside of an urban metropolitan elite, the eponymous teacher with patches on his elbows who reads the *Irish Times* for fun and the more privileged castes of the public sector, the party has since Independence been an even more dismal failure than FG.

The party now has the bright new fifty-something Mr Gilmore. In the aftermath of the election there was some puzzlement over the decision, for the second time in a row, by the cautious old Labour party to choose a leader who had served his apprenticeship within the revolutionary territories of Sinn Féin the Workers Party. In truth, we should not have been too surprised, for there is nothing the Irish left cherish more than the sort of youthful radicalism that has been safely confined to the nearest ecologically friendly dump. Youthful radicalism is, after all, a fine signal of good intentions and Lord knows that no other party has ever had more good 'intentions' than Irish Labour.

For now the polls and the omens are good. But it has to be a concern that over time our hero has acquired a new moniker of Sir Talks-a-lot. If Mr Gilmore is to avoid the awful fate of going down in history as being just another clever talker, he needs to step out of the shadow cast by the Rabbitte and take some lessons in realpolitik from Enda.

Chapter 7 ∿

WHY THE GREENS BECAME THE BESPOKE ITALIAN KITCHEN OF IRISH POLITICS

In early 2006 as awestruck children and yummy mummies swooned around Eamon Ryan at the launch of a Green policy for children, it was clear the Greens were the coming force of Irish politics. Most Irish parties did not know children even existed except for photographic purposes. But here was Eamon, and Trevor too, billing and cooing at the kiddies and none of them were crying.

Even the location, amongst the vines and tendrils of some enclosed square in Temple Bar as distinct from the fusty function rooms of Buswell's, was symbolic of a certain modernist *je ne sais quoi*. The Greens, you see, were on the rise because they were the bespoke Italian designer kitchen party of Irish politics.

At the end, the election did arrive a year too late for, as concern about the economy intensified and the old political dogs put on the big squeeze, the electorate ran back to Cinderella's bigger sisters. However, after years of gentle mockery they had certainly attracted the attention of the biggest parties.

Just how much was epitomised by a vignette shortly before election 2007 where in the Dáil bar a Fianna Fáil Junior Minister, who currently enjoys excellent relations with his 'Green colleagues', was talking intensely to a group of rapt cloth-cap FF supporters. As our man solemnly informed the group that if the Greens got into power, they'd all be on bicycles within the year, there would be no shooting or fishing and that all killing of farm animals would be ended, we were relieved Trevor Sargent did not walk in the door. It was, in truth, unlikely the ever-moral Trevor would wander into such a den of suburban iniquity but, such was the risen nature of the blood, he would have been lynched on the spot.

As we watched this astonishing scene the ignorance of the poor yokels wasn't the most frightening aspect of the tableau. What in fact was even more disturbing was that the Minister actually believed it himself.

In fairness, the poor soul was not unique for the pre-election 2007 reputation of the Greens was a testament to the power of cliché in politics. There was something genuine about the FF detestation of the Greens, who were always attacking attempts by decent builders to corrupt an all too willing group of FF politicians.

However, Trevor Sargent's decision to wave a hundred-euro cheque from a builder in a council chamber was simply bad manners, which could always be counteracted by patriotic Senators such as Don Lydon, who punished Sargent's unmannerly behaviour with a steely headlock.

FF could even cope with the fact that the Greens were the sort of souls who read Fintan O'Toole for fun. And the Greens' curious love of An Taisce, or their equally odd opposition to the human rights of farmers to pollute the environment at will, was actually useful, since the deliberate blandness of Fine Gael under Enda meant there was no enemy for FF to attack. Happily the prospect of the Greens in power with hapless Enda, where they would enforce Green policies on stag-hunting and dog breeding, gave the more 'earthy of the soil' FF TDs an enemy they could sink their false teeth into with abandon.

But the all too enthusiastic Green embrace of morality in politics should not have generated the heat that it did, for FF have been repelling their moral superiors with affable contempt for decades now. However, there was something more visceral behind John O'Donoghue's infamous tribal attack on those prating Green slugs, and his observation that 'the country needs Green economics like lettuce needs slugs'. And 'tribal' indeed was the correct word, for FF suspected there was something of the Fifth Column surrounding those ever-ethical Greens. They instinctively realised the Greens were FG in disguise. Worse still, they feared the Greens were a stickleback, who could puncture the FF soft underbelly by persuading those who were thinking of dumping the FF brand but couldn't vote for Enda to go Green instead.

This concern meant the party's top designated gurriers such as Dermot Ahern were sent out to wail about the sort of instability that must accompany a FG, Labour and Green party 'dolly-mixture Coalition'. Thankfully, as it turned out, we instead got a grand stable FF, Independent FF, Green, Independent FG, Independents miscellaneous and Independent PD administration.

The possibility of a Green ambush also consumed the PDS' brilliant (not that we ever saw it) but terminally erratic (now that we did see) new leader Michael McDowell. This fear informed McDowell's brash but utterly unconvincing claim that the toughened Bash Street Kids of the PDS would rout the muesli-eating, hippy-loving Walter the Softies in the Greens.

Inevitably, as with just about everything else, McDowell got it wrong. The PD leader may, according to his own mythology, have turned over Bertie in 2002 with his 'single party government no thanks' démarche. However, the Green leader John Gormley is a gritty little street fighter. The PD leader might have started the war but it was the gentle Green hippy who sent the PD Gautier barking all the way back to the law library. And there were greater surprises to come.

There was some truth in the FF suspicions about the fifth columnist status of the Greens, and the clue lay in the ferocity of exchanges between the PDS and gentle Trevor. The intensity of the conflict between PD and Green was informed by their shared heritage as the lost children of Garret FitzGerald. They may have tiptoed away from the FG desert but to this day Eamon Ryan sounds like Garret's secret political love child. The PDS, in contrast, were the disappointed red in tooth and claw wing of the FG party who could no longer stomach the limp-wristed nature of the lesser brother of FF.

FF's premonition about the stickleback tendency of the Greens was almost correct. They did take out the soft underbelly of the government in 2007 but Garret's lost children confined their attentions to their sibling enemies. In the final definitive battle of the two lost tribes Eamon Ryan defenestrated Liz O'Donnell, Ciaran Cuffe ended the brief entertaining experiment that was Fiona O'Malley and John Gormley put a final stake in the career of Garret FitzGerald's former political nemesis. Amazingly, the Greens did what FG had been threatening for 20 years and took out the PDS.

Subsequent events would show the revolution was informed by style rather than substance. It wasn't so much that the Greens were different from the PDS but they seemed to be new and concerned about nice fuzzy things like trees, mountains and cycle lanes. In contrast, the PDS were hollowed out by the responsibilities of government. They could barrack and berate but there was nothing of joy or excitement to be found amongst their ranks, and sometimes politics needs hope rather than experience.

Ironically, when Bertie initially entered into negotiations with the Greens, it was seen as being a slightly mad frolic. Rather like Michael D Higgins, it was patronisingly observed that if they were not already mad then Trevor, Dan and Paul would surely go insane in government. This, however, was informed by the fundamental misapprehension that because of their views on climate change the Greens are anarchists. The opposite, in fact, was the case, for the

Greens were as left wing as the Irish Labour party. In economic terms they are the creatures of the South County Dublin liberal, who were entirely at ease with low taxes and even more in love with the delights of free fees for their upper middle class electorate.

Of course, going into government has posed the ever so nice Greens with a new challenge. Paul Gogarty, the party's official wild child, has most acutely summarised the state of play in that infamous *Hot Press* interview where he described a relationship that was not dissimilar to a scene from the rape of the Sabine women. In fairness to FF, they were open about the relationship for, during the negotiations, Seamus Brennan famously told the Greens 'you're playing senior hurling now, lads, and these fellows have medals'.

Since then, however, the Green apprentices have secured the whip hand over the FF sorcerers to such an extent they regularly sigh about the amount of Ministerial time that has to be spent rectifying the damage done by those FF amateurs.

But the amateurs may, however, be about to pose the Greens with one final insuperable conundrum. There is one curious similarity between the 'Republican' soul brothers of FF and Sinn Féinn/MI5. Over the years in the North the various partners of SF/IRA—be it the SDLP, the UUP or even the cunning backwoods men of the DUP—learned that only one winner ever emerged from these made marriages. In the South the PDs and Labour also discovered that no one who enters the marital bed of FF escapes unscathed. It all means that as the next election gallops towards the government bearing all of the nice intentions of the Four Horsemen of the Apocalypse, the great battle the nicer siblings of Garret's lost children face is to avoid the scenario (which the nasty kids in the PDs learned) of assimilation by FF, which inevitably leads to annihilation.

Now what did happen to all those Italian designer kitchen showrooms?

Chapter 8 ∾

WHEN TWO TRIBES GO TO WAR

One of the few moments of real pathos we have seen during Brian Cowen's premiership occurred during his first Ard Fheis in Citywest. Earlier that evening, as small beads of sweat slowly gathered on his forehead, Mr Cowen had treated the hated media to the usual looking-at-a-fixed-point-in-the-wall performance. Yet in spite of his unyielding hostility, you had to pity a Taoiseach who is as popular as a lost Black and Tan in West Cork. It is not as though one would want to give him a consoling hug for he is not that type of creature. But though he displayed nothing of the emotions that must churn beneath the cold public persona, the slitted eyes that twisted and turned like a coursed hare from microphone to microphone revealed a man who was surely living a nightmare.

Then, as Mr Cowen moved sedately onto the stage to receive the spotty applause of those few of the faithful who had gathered, astonishingly for one brief moment the mask slipped, and there was a second of what looked like genuine emotion. Suddenly, amidst the crumpling of his face, there was a discernable lightness of being that resembled the joy of some rheumy-eyed emigrant who, after years of being cast adrift, finally sees the first outline of Paddy's green shore.

In a real way, after a year of exile amidst the cavilling and public anger, this most tribal of creatures had come home.

One of the many great misconceptions the Irish liberal left suffer from is the belief that the only thing holding back the arrival of a state of perfection in Irish politics is the inability of Fine Gael and Fianna Fáil to realise they are essentially two sides of the same uncivilised post-civil war divide.

But whilst there are some within both parties who, if their own personal ambitions could be salvaged, would have no great objection, our bearded liberals are wrong, for the war between FF and FG goes far beyond the competition for political perks.

The subtlety of the thing is best captured by the open enmity that exists between Mary Coughlan and FG's Michael Creed. You would expect both of these relatively young figures to get on for they are essentially sociable politicians who come from rural political dynasties.

Yet when it came to their political exchanges, there was always an edge of genuine detestation, for both are pure-bred members of their respective political tribes. The difference is evident even in their physical appearance for 'merrie' Mary Coughlan is the very image of the buxom milkmaid from the peasant classes. In contrast, right down to his Roman-style nose and haughty straight-backed carriage, Creed is the incarnation of the all-conquering big farmer.

Intriguingly Mr Creed has quite a similar effect on the Taoiseach. Mr Cowen has been assailed over the last number of years by the finest masters of rhetoric the Dáil can provide but Creed was the catalyst for the only moment of transparency we have seen from Mr Cowen since he secured the Taoiseach's job.

It occurred when Creed launched an attack on Mr Cowen's crony Frank Fahey over the Lost at Sea scheme. The response of a Taoiseach who shares the same pure tribal blood as Coughlan was telling as he snarled, 'Look at the big farmer.'

For once we had to agree when, in reply to a query by Creed as to what the Taoiseach's rationale was, Cowen told the FG TD 'you know what I mean'.

And, in truth, Creed did. It was just the rest of us who didn't.

Ultimately, as is so often the case in a society that has a more subtle caste system than India, the difference between the FF and FG tribes comes down to class. Ireland may not have a conventional left–right divide but the division between FF and FG is centred on the agricultural equivalent of that split.

FG is, though many may not realise it, the party of the big farmhouse or the local shopkeeper where one son inherits the family fortune, another becomes a priest and the third became, if lucky, either the local teacher or the Irish Parliamentary Party MP. This status explains why, in spite of the fact that it has never been safe to be an intellectual in Irish politics, FG have been most susceptible to the odd flirtation with the intelligentsia.

Sadly such affairs never last for too long since FG's desire to be seen in the company of intellectuals is more about the desire to cultivate some perceived level of superiority over their FF tribal enemies than any real love of knowledge.

Outside of art and philosophy nothing epitomises the difference between the two tribes more than their shared love of 'country pursuits'. The FG man is an aficionado of fly fishing and fox-hunting who hunts with pedigree dogs and shoots his pheasant by daylight. In contrast, as part of their White-boy and Rapparee antecedents, FF prefer to dynamite their fish out of the rivers and to lamp pheasants, in woods they should not be in, by night.

Oddly enough, even the attempt via the election of Kenny Lite to emulate the success of the FF tribe has not worked, for the connoisseurs of tribal politics know that Enda is a fake. Oh he may try with the nodding and the winking and the bucklepping to pretend he is earthy of the soil. We, however, know that whilst no one could ever accuse Enda of being a fag hag to the intellectuals, he is the soft son of the village schoolteacher who had a boiled egg for breakfast every morning.

It is a strange conflict for the difficulty with tribal politics, and the reason the *Irish Times* dislikes it so much, is that there is no easy rational way of analysing it.

Instead, like two dogs who detest each other, the division is instinctive. Once they see each other, even if there is no immediate reason for battle, old hatreds and memories of previous scraps cause the fur to rise and the lips to curl back across bared teeth.

The bad news for the good people of pious new moral FF or the urban wing of FG is that the conflict is poised to continue indefinitely. All logic suggests it is time for Cain and Abel to settle their differences. But like two warring brothers, the intimacy between the two adds to the intensity of the divide and leaves the rest of us wondering with the puzzled incomprehension of all outsiders just why these two similar creatures simply can't get on.

There again, if we recall correctly, the Lilliputians had a similar problem that they never resolved and that was only over what side of a boiled egg you are supposed to open.

SECTION 2

So this is how you become Taoiseach

Chapter 9

THE DAY THE POLITICS OF PLANET HOLLYWOOD ALLOWED BERTIE TO BECOME THE NEW DEV

One of the unique features of politics as she was practised during the Celtic Tiger was its obsession with Bertie Ahern. We did, after all, still have an Opposition, though it was difficult to remember that sometimes. Within Fianna Fáil occasional comets such as Charlie McCreevy flashed across the political universe—and like the comet ultimately the only legacy Charlie left behind was a trail of noxious vapours—but Bertie was the colossus of the age to such an extent no one dared look at his feet.

Mind you, seeing as the era of the Tiger was one of greed crossed with a cynicism that trod gently at the edges of corruption, this was not necessarily a good thing. However, fairness also says that the most any democratic politician can aspire to is to be the quintessence of their age.

Bertie's capacity to be Everyman meant that, in the end, despite the fact that like all of us he went before his chosen time, our Taoiseach still managed to exit the stage in a blizzard of tea and sympathy. In one sense, in spite of all his flaws, the nation's sadness was apt, for Bertie's departure from politics was not unlike the premature death of Buddy Holly. In our case, however, it was the economy rather than the music that made its debut in the obituary pages of the paper.

Of course, like so many other things, the claim that the day Ahern turned his pinstriped broad shoulders away from the nation's cameras was the day the Tiger died has to be qualified. When Bertie left at the point of an invisible sword the Tiger was essentially a creature of illusion. Logical analysts swiftly claimed Ahern's resignation was another classic example of 'going whilst the going was good' for, like the set of a cheap spaghetti Western, Ireland was already a façade without an interior.

But in a very real sense the departure of Bertie officially marked the end of the Tiger. Up to that point whilst even the simplest of us could see the rats were running across our feet, there was always a hope that, like Prospero, the great illusionist Ahern could conjure up some new trick that would hold off the shipwreck for another day.

Ultimately there is no clearer moment of reality than a funeral and Bertie's month-long requiem was the state funeral of the Tiger. Ireland's brief Indian summer was about to be replaced by the cold age of Cowen.

As this 'sociable loner' left in a manner that was as ornately choreographed as the funeral of a Viking king, and we are probably lucky the leave-taking did not include flaming ships on the Liffey, it was easy to forget that when he first became leader, the man who defined the essence of his age was very new to us.

Though he had been on the political stage for over two decades, Irish politics had been dominated by giants like Garret, Haughey and Spring, a supporting cast of macaws such as Pee Flynn, subtle comedians like PJ Mara and men who carried a hint of sulphur such as Albert, Ray MacSharry and Ray Burke. Bertie, in contrast, was eternally at the edges throwing sheep's eyes at the media as he apologised for disasters such as Pee's infamous 'she with her new hairdo' remarks about Mary Robinson.

In a sense this may have provided him with one of his most critical qualities, for the man whose enemies even called him 'Bertie' had a unique capacity to secure the pity of the nation with a single suffering sigh over the latest crown of thorns he must place upon his furrowed brow. It served him well during the famous Bryan Dobson 'dig-outs' interview, which would have sunk any 'normal' politician, for all 'our Bertie' had to do was raise those defensive submissive eyebrows and a nation melted.

God, but we were suckers.

The ability to attract pity and love is a potent one but over the years other qualities emerged. The most obvious one of all was his youth, for this was a country that was used to leaders of a more elderly vintage. Whatever else can be said about Ahern, even to the end he remained youthful no matter what the cost was. And as the years went on, it certainly rose. However, this was not a callow youthfulness, for though few ever saw it Bertie was the most feral of creatures. The mouth was always smiling but his eyes were as dark and fathomless as a shark rolling in the ocean.

He was, as all the disguises suggested, the cutest of foxes. When he first became the leader of FF, the media innocently believed the pressures of office would inevitably unveil the real Bertie. Instead, like an experienced belly dancer, the Taoiseach knew mystery is the first child of eroticism, for if everything about you is known then why would anyone pay to seduce you? So right to the very end he retained a secret self that left us vulnerable to the desire to give everything of ourselves to him, in the hope that he might repay us in some currency.

Of course, Bertie was new to us in another way, for he did not have the taint of corruption about him. Here at last was a genuinely self-made man who was independent of the big builders and all the other parasites that had rotted Ireland's great Republican party away from within. Under Bertie, FF had at last returned to its simple roots, for what could be complicated about a man who had operated under the PAYE system for all of his life? It was nice to be respectable again.

Ultimately his defining political characteristic, however, was captured during the 1997 election when Bertie snatched victory from almost certain defeat in a manner that would have impressed Napoleon. In a scenario where the Rainbow had produced Ireland's first budget surplus in two decades, and were creating a thousand jobs a week, Bertie's decision to spend some valuable campaigning time engaging in a photo-call with Sylvester Stallone was unexpected.

The faded star of *Rocky* and *Rambo* grabbed a hurl, let the future Taoiseach put a Planet Hollywood jacket on his capacious form, and stumbled off the stage in a fugue of puzzlement. In contrast, Bertie's eyes shone like a child experiencing his first Christmas as he exclaimed, 'Did ya see dat, did ya see me giving him the jacket and he taking it offa me?'

Other grander, more historic events were to follow and the innocence of the new would in time crumble to the dust of a final defeat in the Mahon Tribunal. However, in a real sense the day Bertie met Stallone was as seminal as any moment in his political career. Afterwards we sneered about how Bertie would do anything for a photo. However, once again we had missed the point, for Bertie intuitively knew the value of celebrity. He understood that if a politician could wrap that enchanted gauze around himself, the normal rules did not apply.

Instead, that politician was a human being with a human interest story. And once he achieved that, 'our' Bertie colonised a tabloid world of the *Star*, the *Sun* and VIP. This alchemy was the political equivalent of discovering a precious new continent, for this was territory occupied by no other Irish politician. It was instead—and most critically of all—a world that was central to the very existence of our Breakfast Roll Men and their country girl fiancées.

During his decade in power the Taoiseach was continuously mocked about this supposed Achilles' heel. But, perfect chameleon that he was, 'star struck' Bertie's preference for the company of supermodels and 'Coronation Street' actresses over that of professors and economists meant he was in tune with the mood of the times. It ensured he became the most successful Irish political leader since the very different era of de Valera and the country maidens. Bertie's 'birds' may have been cast from a different template but, like Dev, 'celebrity' Bertie mirrored the obsessions of our society. Indeed, such was the perfection of the marriage between the Taoiseach's persona and the world of celebrity that Breakfast Roll Man did not distinguish between the real Taoiseach and the one on 'Gift Grub'.

The problem, of course, is that the show-time age was as ephemeral as the boy bands that dominated the age. Happily, well, for Bertie at least, by the time we discovered that particular truth, 'our' Bertie had disappeared as swiftly as any Arabian genie in a second-hand lamp.

Chapter 10 ❧

HOW THE MAN WHO DID NOT WANT THE JOB BECAME THE KING

It might be strange to suggest the best way to become Taoiseach is to not want the job at all. However, when it comes to Brian Cowen, who was handed the office in the sort of casual manner you might get a cup of tea at a wake, it is hard not to avoid the suggestion that this was the case.

When at the wake, as we gather around the modern equivalent of a turf fire, the one thing we shall all agree on about our poor Potemkin Offaly Prince was that he was the man who did not want the job. In truth, some of us knew from the start. There is some wisdom in the belief that the best route to becoming the king is like gathering apples in autumn. You can throw sticks up in the air in the attempt to dislodge the ripe ones but why run the risk of injury when you can just wait for rot allied to gravity to secure the golden prize?

But in the dying days of Bertie, even the oldest of sages had ceased to natter about how he who wields the knife never secures the crown. Instead, in an eerie prologue on the future state of the country, the great ward boss had turned into a political zombie.

However, as the Tribunal worms burrowed away, it was agonisingly clear the man we now know as BIFFO did not want the job.

Sadly the malign difficulty Mr Cowen faced was that he could not be seen to be the man who would not come onto the field of play.

It is all too late for poor BIFFO is now the original one-man political bubble. We expected very little from Bertie, appeared to get a lot more than we thought and in the end got absolutely nothing. The sad Mr Cowen, however, is a case study in how we invest our dreams in people against their will and then destroy them for failing to live up to what we wanted from them.

Ironically it was the politician he most admired that branded the mark of Cain upon Mr Cowen. And no, we are not talking about Bertie Ahern, who famously granted Mr Cowen the semi-official leadership status of being the 'anointed' one. If we are looking for the guilty party, it is in fact Albert who should be in the dock, for within the warring Fianna Fáil tribe he originally 'anointed' Cowen to be his designated successor with his prophecy that 'this man will yet be Taoiseach'.

It was a claim that decided Cowen's fate far more definitively than Haughey's famous 'cutest, most cunning of them all' remark. Bertie may have waggled those doleful eyebrows but a sole trader like Ahern was always going to decide his own destiny, irrespective of whatever mad prophecies Mr Haughey would throw into the ether.

In contrast, like any Beta male, Mr Cowen was not on the hunt for greatness. But once Albert beckoned his crook, a poor follower like Brian became irrevocably entangled in the great FF divide.

It was, of course, a terrible old situation for a man who, deep in his soul, did not have the slightest desire to be the leader, but the flaws of others—and most particularly of all Mr Ahern—saw it being thrust upon him.

It should be said that originally being Albert's Prodigal Son was not a heavy burden. If anything, it was hard not to be seduced by the responsibility-free status of being the little prince of the deputies from the bog. All that, however, was to change when Bertie confirmed the line of succession.

Even from the start in 2007 the ides were sinister. When Napoleon became the illegitimate Emperor of France, he seized the crown from the hands of the bishop and put it on himself. In contrast, for Cowen to even become the Dauphin, he needed the approbation of two powerful men.

And Mr Cowen was not 'anointed' by Bertie out of any kind regards for Prince BIFFO or the country. Instead, Mr Ahern's choice, as usual, was more about Bertie than BIFFO, for the Taoiseach's priority in that regard was to acquire a non-threatening human shield.

The strange thing about it all was that the closer he came to the throne, the more Mr Cowen's political performance deteriorated. But no matter how he twisted and turned, the chalice would not move. In retrospect it can now be argued that Mr Cowen's long leadership of the Falstaffian bar lobby was a despairing attempt to escape the real consequences of Albert's casual remark. If so, it was an attempt that was doomed to failure, for within the hidden codes of the FF party, the Prodigal Son of Albert was the political last chance saloon for all those who had not prospered in a manner they deemed appropriate to their abilities during the long reign of Bertie. And there were many.

These desires meant poor Cowen's attempt to evade his execrably certain fate by becoming the boy king who never grew up was doomed from the start. Mind you, he did do his best, for whilst Cowen was feted by a unique coalition of FF TDS and hacks it was often hard to see the rationale for the praise. During the FF Opposition interregnum of 1995 to 1997 he was a peripheral force for, outside of Bertie, the dominant politicians behind the drive for power were younger figures such as Micheál Martin and John O'Donoghue. In contrast, Mr Cowen's most noticeable contribution consisted of a spectacular sulk after an unconvinced Bertie exiled him to the foothills of Agriculture.

After 1997, presumably because he was already there, Mr Cowen got the Department nobody really wanted. Sadly, in what set the template for what was to come, unlike Micheál Martin who at least brought much activity but scant direction to Health, Mr Cowen was a ghost. The one definitive legacy of his spell that still resides in the public mind was the infamous comparison of the Department with 'Angola' and he even claims he did not say that. But the relish with which Mr Cowen believed you should be free and clear of the Department for the weekend spoke of a none too subtle love of the 10 to 5 working lifestyle and off by 4 on a Friday. The contrast with an obsessive such as Charlie McCreevy, who would have to be dragged out of the Department, was acute.

Cowen at least didn't get into the same trouble as any of his predecessors or successors. But this was hardly the sort of profile that was compatible with imagery of a man intent on uprooting trees. The fact that the avoidance of any disasters was down to luck rather than prescience should also have been a warning to us that this guy was flying by the seat of his pants.

In truth, the same could be said for Foreign Affairs, where our man was as sidelined by Bertie as Mo Mowlam was under Blair. Of course, wherever he has gone that school of anonymous civil servant, who is always quoted in the more worthy profiles of the great, was ecstatic about our man's capacity to master a brief. We have learned, however, to be wary of such praise for civil servants love politicians who have the qualities of the good schoolboy.

In spite of the pats, it was hard to avoid the impression that Mr Cowen had the sort of qualities more commonly associated with the perfect bureaucrat. He had a great capacity for the amalgamation of vast masses of useless information but his capacity to do anything of worth with it was questionable.

Happily, even as time went a-passing and the young Prince was getting fatter, his faithful retainers were unconcerned by notions such as the death of promise/or the compelling need for the formerly Bonnie Young Cowen to acquaint himself with a gym. They instead believed that, like King Arthur's Knights who are supposed to be slumbering beneath the Dover cliffs waiting for England's call, Mr Cowen was merely waiting for the hour of crisis to prove his mettle.

At the appointed time frolics like the great post-Budget Foley's lock-in would also be safely interred in the narrative of youthful aristocratic japes and the fun-filled exploits of a gorsoon. Mind you, by the time Foley's occurred, the gorsoon was in his late forties so it was perhaps getting a little late for these japes.

In retrospect it is hard to avoid the impression that, like Enda Kenny, the Taoiseach was yet another Playboy of the Western World-style false hero. The reluctance with which our Potemkin Prince undertook the top job was redolent of a Synge play where the fake champion of the village is conscripted to fight an all too real rival from the neighbouring county.

As the locals cheer, our panicky hero looks for a side exit from the pub but it is too late. No matter what he desires he is borne out to do battle by the cheering villagers.

Like our Synge hero, there was, alas, nothing Mr Cowen could do to save himself, for he and Bertie were sharing the same hourglass. So it was that Mr Cowen became Taoiseach and with that the last flickering glimmer of light went out of his eyes. The anointed one had entered Calgary.

The critics will, of course, say he did it out of his own free choice. That, however, we suspect is a contention that is open to question.

Chapter 11

WHY EAMON SIR TALKS-A-LOT GILMORE NEEDS TO ESCAPE THE POLITICS OF PONTIFICATING UP THE REAR END OF COWS

It might seem strange, seeing as he has become the most popular Irish leader, to ask what has gone wrong with Eamon Gilmore. There again, since the competition consists of a Cyclops of a Taoiseach, Fine Gael's Forrest Gump and Gerry 'where is that brother of mine?' Adams, the achievement is not what it might first seem to be.

The issue he must particularly confront is that there is a growing sense of the Pat Rabbittes surrounding Gilmore. Sadly this is not necessarily good for, like his fellow student Prince, a great flaw is gradually being unveiled. It is a strange thing for a people who are renowned for having the gift of the gab but the Irish are uniquely suspicious of talkative politicians. The unease about fine speaking was epitomised by the warning some years ago by a wise soul to a vocal young deputy that 'many a man who has talked himself into this place has talked himself right back out of it'.

It would be disappointing if the wily Eamon Gilmore became another victim of this phenomenon, for the Labour leader has brought a new vitality to the Dáil. Gilmore's predecessor Pat Rabbitte may have been the petted child of that element of the political media, who are so well informed they never debase themselves with the horror of actually attending the Dáil. However, the truth of things was those humbler types who actually watch the floor show had become somewhat jaundiced about the overweening cleverality of Pat Rabbitte.

This meant it was essentially a relief to get a straight-talking, straight-shooting, plain speaking new sheriff. Unlike Enda, who was treated with doughty contempt, it was clear that even Mr Cowen saw Gilmore as being somewhat of an equal.

There was concern that the prize had come too late, for the cross-fertilisation of politics and celebrity means leadership is increasingly a young man's game. And Labour's penchant for late-blossoming fifty-year-olds has not been a successful tactic, for Pat Rabbitte and Ruairi Quinn, having served their time, departed with the ease of old lags who wished only to return to the familiar comforts of the radio studio.

Of course, Eamon Gilmore found himself in a very different dispensation, but it did help that the young fifty-something leader eschewed Ruairi Quinn's 'Mr Angry from Sandymount' school of politics, which had turned the formerly urbane Quinn into a slightly plumper version of Victor Meldrew. The avoidance of the excessive Ronaldo-style rhetorical step-overs of Mr Rabbitte came as an even greater relief.

He was, of course, helped by a government whose capacity for incompetence saw the new acronym of the politics of GUBUYBBA (Grotesque Unbelievable Bizarre Unprecedented Yes its Bloody BIFFO Again) being invented. It was also hard to look bad when the other alternative is nodding, winking and shouting 'pick me it's my turn' with all the élan of an over-enthusiastic five-year-old schoolchild.

Not even Gilmore, though, could have predicted the surge in support that now means the leader can credibly claim the party is poised to become an equal player with Fianna Fáil and FG. But as Ireland bent below the gathering storms, ironically old weaknesses have now become strengths. One of the classic examples of this is how previous afflictions, such as the greying nature of Labour, can be entered into the credit side of the ledger, for we are now in the market for security rather than partying.

But just at this critical point a subtle change began to occur in Mr Gilmore's personality. One of the most useful figures in history was the slave who would ride in the imperial chariot with Roman Emperors, and remind them of their own mortality if they became too arrogant. Oddly enough, when the imperial classes grew tired of this trick and outsourced the slave, the Empire swiftly went into decline.

Sadly it is now increasingly looking as though Mr Gilmore could do with a slave of his own. The change in the Labour leader's persona was initially subtle, as suddenly the short snappy questions that harried Cowen so effectively were replaced by lengthy dissertations. We had hoped it would never happen but it was clear the Labour leader was falling prey to the unwise yet common failing of all Opposition leaders. This is not so much that they have nothing of worth to say, but rather that they think every word they say is of importance.

As Mr Gilmore developed an additional penchant for simplistic clichés, where every crisis from global warming to stopping a soufflé from collapsing could be solved by the 'knocking of heads together', the tragedy of it all was that we genuinely are at a moment where the Labour dream is achievable.

It will not be easy, though, and for more complex reasons than history or the absence of candidates to pick up all these loose FF seats. The extent of the crisis we face means we need the government to behave like an Opposition and the Opposition to behave like a government. By this we mean that what is required to deal with our great disruption is a government that acts in a radical way and an Opposition that has the courage to take tough public stances. The tragic incapacity of either FF or FG to play this role provided Labour with a unique opportunity. There was, however, one problem, for if Labour were to behave like a government, like every great leader, Gilmore would have to be toughest of all on his own core vote. However, just around the point where this needed to happen, the more questions Mr Gilmore was asked about the need for public sector reform or budgetary cut-backs, the more Mr Gilmore talked.

As our Sir Lancelot evolved into a garrulous Sir Talks-a-lot, the Labour leader resembled the sort of soccer player who, if he puts his head in amongst the flying boots in the penalty area in the final minutes, will score the winning goal but at the likely cost of a few slaps to the head.

Instead, our cautious leader has to date engaged in the equivalent of taking a decision to keep his head where it was, trot out to the edge of the penalty box, hope to curl one into the top corner and if that doesn't work sure then we'll play for penalties.

For our sake we had better hope Mr Gilmore is better than he sometimes appears to be.

But if it is to happen, he must tear himself away from that most beloved of places, known to all cute politicians as the Ministry of De Fence. This may be a wonderful safe place where you can be a bystander and stand aloof from the heavy tackles, oaths and cursing. But whilst you keep the togs nice and clean, and won't Mother be pleased about that, on the fence you are a commentator rather than a participant.

To date, the omens are not good, for when you lose your stroke it is hard to get it back.

And sadly on the rare occasion these days when Mr Gilmore leaves the comfort of the fence, he has been surrounded by a certain air of desperation. There was rather too much of the old Pat Rabbitte school of rocking the foundations of the state around the claims that Mr Cowen was guilty of 'economic treason'.

There again, perhaps we are being too harsh on our new pink, perfect and properly cross Mr Gilmore, for his determination to threaten or offend no one has inspired more than a few recent admiring FF comments of 'Jaysus, that fellow would remind you of Bertie.' And isn't it good to know there's another one of those coming down the tracks to save the country?

It would be a heavy blow for politics if we find out that the Labour Emperor has no clothes too. However, too often these days we are reminded of the tale told of Michael Smith, the former FF Minister, during the time when he was doubling as the local Artificial Insemination Man and ambitious county councillor. Smith was a man who was fond of the sound of his voice to such an extent that he was inclined to offer the local farmers his views on world events, such as the dangers posed to their simple ways by the rising tide of communism.

One day, as an old farmer watched suspiciously whilst Smith struggled to inseminate a rather truculent cow, he was joined by an equally elderly somewhat more short-sighted neighbour who asked the identity of the fellow struggling behind the cow. Our Sir Talks-a-lot of an increasingly loquacious Labour leader can only hope that the dismissive reply of 'It's only Smith pontificating up the rear end of a cow again' is never applied to him.

Chapter 12

ENDA KENNY AND THE CRITICAL IMPORTANCE OF BEING RESILIENT

Shortly after his unnoticed election as the leader of Fine Gael, I met Enda Kenny by accident in a city centre pub. As the then new FG leader sat clad in a grey gabardine coat and we talked about irrelevancies, he resembled a man who was anxiously looking for something to do but nothing was happening.

The change that has occurred since those early uneasy times was most clearly epitomised by Kenny's valedictory speech about Ahern, where he cleverly defined the Taoiseach in terms of being a 'social loner'. As Bertie gazed over impassively, we were left to wonder just what Ahern was making of Enda's own achievement, for he was the first of nine political leaders to usher Ahern off the political stage.

In his time Bertie had outlasted giants like Dick Spring, Ruairi Quinn, Pat Rabbitte, Mary Harney, Michael McDowell, John Bruton and Michael Noonan as party leader. Oh and Trevor Sargent had also gone too. How puzzling it must have been for the great Fianna Fáil pilot that, as he left the ship of state, poor 'Lite' disregarded Enda had stayed the course beyond even the most cunning one of all.

In fairness, Enda deserved the praise his speech received, for the acute nature of his analysis secured the rare achievement of pinning the Ahern butterfly to the canvas. But perhaps no one other than Bertie would know more about the soul of the sociable loner than Enda.

One of the more intriguing features of Irish political life before Cowen was the clarity of Bertie Ahern's dislike of Enda Kenny. Of course, Bertie never really liked anyone unless they were of use to him. However, he generally managed to mask his dislike in a fog of confused bonhomie where the former Taoiseach would claim he had no idea in the world why a left-wing socialist like Joe Higgins had issues with poor conservative (with a small 'c' of course!) Bertie.

The reason the Taoiseach could not hide his secret soul when it came to Enda was that the great old fox of Irish politics saw danger. Ahern knew Enda was a lighter doppelganger of himself and in an age of facile politics, which he played no small role in creating, Bertie understood there was a real danger that Enda might sneak into power in a remarkably similar manner to Mr Ahern's own achievement in 1997.

The lightness did eventually catch up with Enda, for whilst the FG leader went on the run during the campaign, the point came where he had to turn and fight. Such was the tension and anxiety of it all, astonished witnesses noted Ahern was visibly trembling before the debate. The fear did not, however, last too long for it swiftly became evident this high noon was a leap too far for an Enda who had spent the previous five years talking about the plight of a variety of women he had met outside crèches, supermarkets and schools.

The ongoing survival of Enda is all the more surprising for, outside of the former Manchester United manager Tommy Doherty, no other individual has been dismissed so often. Kenny was dismissed the first time he ran for the leadership of FG; he was definitively dismissed from the front bench of FG after he lost to Noonan; at one stage he came within 5 votes of being dismissed from politics altogether by the electorate of Mayo; and he was dismissed when he ran against intellectuals like Richard Bruton in 2002.

And even when Enda did seize the poisoned chalice from his comatose party, he was promptly dismissed on a regular basis by the pundits for being a Playboy of the Western World, a busy fool, a simple fool, the Mayo version of the wild colonial boy, a lightweight and, occasionally, an imbecile. Then, just as he thought he might be safe, three years after the voters effectively dismissed him in 2007, his own trusted front bench and half of the FG parliamentary party tried to give poor Enda the sack again.

If there is an explanation for his ongoing survival, it may lie in Enda being a classic case study in the Importance of Being Resilient in Irish politics. Though there sometimes is a fine line between stupidity and resilience, the latter is one of the underestimated political virtues.

In theory, of course, we want our leaders to be generals on horseback, charging into the fray to inspire us with some old-fashioned 'where's your fucking pride?' rhetoric. However, as we twist in the wind under the fitful reign of FF's dilettante Prince Cowen, the more prosaic virtues such as resilience are coming back into fashion.

And, like his nemesis Bertie Ahern, the extraordinary resilience of Enda is Kenny's finest virtue.

The first evidence of this was seen in the aftermath of the Noonan putsch against John Bruton. After that defeat the status of poor Kenny was eloquently captured by Noonan's post-victory Mansion House press conference. On the ceiling what appeared to be a thousand points of light shone as Noonan outlined his vision of a social contract. Halfway through the speech the challenger flitted into the back row of the audience in yet another grey nondescript coat. As he sat there, the cruel description of John Major being as interesting as a pair of drawing room drapes came to mind.

It was, in truth, bad enough to have lost but Enda had suffered the additional humiliation of being described by a 'Prime Time' focus group as even less charismatic than Bernard Allen (a long-term back-bench TD who scarcely anyone outside of Cork has heard of). That, we thought, was the last we would hear of Enda and we came damn close to being correct.

After all of that 'nigger' commotion, we thought that was the last we would hear of Enda too and we probably came damn close to being right on that occasion too. But like the cat they couldn't kill, Enda kept on going for reasons we do not fully understand. And, in truth, we sometimes suspect Enda doesn't fully comprehend it either as, like a one-man Joe Duffy show, he crosses the country to listen to that eccentric wing of the people who voluntarily go to town halls to listen to politicians.

Nothing epitomised the nature of the task Kenny had taken on more than a night he spent in a place called Cloneygowan. In summer it is a delightful spot but this was mid-winter and it was steeped in the sort of darkness more commonly found in Elsinore. Such was the desolate nature of the place we struggled to find the venue until our instinct that a plump, curly-haired, forty-something farmer in a Jeep might be of the requisite FG stock was validated.

On being asked where the meeting was, he beamed like the beacon on top of the Spire in O'Connell Street and, oblivious to the fact that his hero has now been deceased for more than 20 years, bellowed, 'Ah ye're welcome to Oliver J [Flanagan] country.' Inside, as Enda took modest priestly sips from a pint of Guinness and listened patiently to inanities, a strange thing happened during the speeches.

As one aspirant TD tore into the many failures of FF, the ruddy-cheeked farmer became increasingly dismayed. Eventually, as our man shook his head emphatically and indulged in a series of hollow moans, curiosity got the better of us and we asked what he was finding to be so appalling about what appeared to be a perfectly fine speech. Not even we, however, were prepared for his response of 'Ah bejaysus, you see, it's very quiet in Cloneygowan so the people here go to everything but all of them here with the exception of myself votes Fianna Fáil. Yer man up there will have them rightly insulted if he doesn't calm down.'

Well, no one said it would be easy, for Cloneygowan was only one night and over the last decade Enda has visited a plethora of even more desolate spots that might be called one-horse towns were it not for the fact that even the horse had left.

It could well be argued that the FG leader would be better occupied in reading abstruse philosophical texts or the collected writings of Paul Krugman. The cruel reality is that even Enda knows that putting ideas from intellectuals like Richard Bruton into his mouth is a bad idea. And in a very real sense, like the Rolling Stones or any rock band, Enda is only ever really happy when he is on tour.

The reason Enda gets solace from ordinary people is because that is how he defines himself. Though the public are less than receptive to Enda's claims to be one of them, the very appearance of humility may have taken him a very long way.

It is, of course, a faux humility, for no man who thinks he can be Taoiseach is short in the ego department. Sadly, though it has taken him to the very ante-room of the Taoiseach's office, the great question he has not yet answered is whether we do not now need a national leader who has more traits and abilities than the simple capacity of staying power.

Chapter 13 ∾

| SUCCESS AND SEXUALITY

The Joy of Bertie

If there is any consolation for Bertie Ahern during his current travails it must be that no politician since Parnell ever won the unequivocal love the former Taoiseach once secured. Indeed, the fact that we can use 'travails' to describe the fiscal status of a former Taoiseach who is trousering a few hundred grand a year from the lecturing, the book deals and the *News of the World* indicates how, like the Irish mother, our capacity for forgiveness is endless.

There again, perhaps we should not be too surprised, for the voters always adored Bertie with the guileless innocence of first love. If we had looked more closely we might have seen Ahern was the sort of hound who was hard to keep on the porch. However, when it came to Bertie, such was the fearful level of the enchantment, our focus was always on the wagging tail and the soulful eyes rather than the political fleas that were hopping around on the Taoiseach's fur waving at us.

Sadly, like all divorces, it's now all about accountancy rather than kisses. But even when the Tribunal reports Bertie knows he will still possess that secret part of us that no politician can reach. Oh, we will, of course, complain and throw the crockery and do the rest of the hysterical stuff. However, 'our' Bertie will know, damn him, that at night when we are full of desire and alone, the only person who will ever be in our heads will be the man who stitched his initials onto the soul of a nation.

It might be over now but he is carved into our DNA in the same way those ancient hearts proclaiming the long lost love of couples who are now dead can be seen branded into flowering summertime chestnut trees.

It was always you, Bertie.

No one else.

Just you.

Nothing epitomised the strange nature of this love affair more than a vignette in which the pig-farming millionaire TD Ned O'Keeffe is celebrating his twentieth year as a TD. Suddenly, as Ned is courteously ferrying plates of potato and 'lovely bacon top bacon' to the media, there is a hubbub. We are not too offended when Ned drops the plates and scarpers, for 'the special one' is here.

You might expect there to be bad blood between Ned and Bertie Ahern, for the Taoiseach had recently sacked O'Keeffe over what was essentially a technical offence. However, when Ahern arrives, Ned sprints over to be beside him with all the delight of a blushing bride. Of course, no Fianna Fáil man is ignorant of the uses of being photographed beside the Taoiseach but something more innocent is also at play here, for Ned's delight is sincere. He too is in love with a politician who once inspired the pungent admission from one TD with less cause than most to love our former Taoiseach of 'Jesus, if you found that fellow in bed with your wife you'd nearly apologise for disturbing the man.'

It should be surprising that little has been written about the sexuality of Ahern but there again, in another example of his unique capacity for dissimulation, Bertie played the role of a man's man to perfection. But those tales of a long-haired Bertie shambling around the disco with the lads, clutching his anorak protectively to his bosom as he stared, puzzled, at dose exotic strange tings called women, were an elaborate disguise. Like all great electoral politicians such as Clinton and Blair, Bertie understood the importance of women, for they do comprise over half the electorate. Or perhaps, to put it more accurately, he knew of the critical role of desire in politics.

He was also highly aware of the importance of his sexuality. Some years into his reign as Taoiseach, the English *Mail* featured a photograph of Bertie sporting a little pot belly underneath a white tracksuit. The belly was, alas, booming as swiftly as the economy and there were many ribald chuckles about our little Drumcondra Buddha. However, when he returned to the Dáil a month later, the bump was gone. Unlike our poor Mr Cowen, the former Taoiseach intuitively understood how important it is for the king to dress like a monarch rather than a mom in a maternity smock.

Sadly, as political journalism is dominated by men of the anorak class, few of us understood the importance of Ahern's extraordinary connection with women.

However, had we been more intuitive, we would have realised women 'got'

Bertie in a way that men simply could not. Some simply wanted to love him in a mothering sort of way. Others looked into those cold, calculating eyes and wanted the status of being the one to 'turn' him. It was, of course, impossible but the challenge of being able to take this quintessential 'man's man' away from the pub, the party and the lads simply added to the attraction, for women love the impossible task.

Unlike the rest of us, who needed to spend half a billion on a Tribunal to understand the obvious, women could see more clearly he was a bad lad. The brigade of clever anoraks might have thought Ahern was a harmless, bumbling sort of chap but the women knew Bertie was of the devil's party. Bertie being Bertie did complicate things, for those sad sheepdog eyes whispered to them of a man who also needed nurturing and of the possibility of reform. But women looked into those cold eyes and also knew Bertie would be a boss in the Cabinet table … and in the bedroom.

Of course, the old bumbling about 'the women, how curious they do be' stuff was also part of the cunning of Bertie. His mentor Charlie Haughey may, in public at least, have had a more salacious personal life but with the best will in the world only courtesans and salon queens found Haughey interesting. In contrast, like any boy band member, Bertie was far more democratic in his appeal.

In one way or another, though, women knew that Bertie was a sensual being and women of all ages wanted him. The most famous photograph in his first campaign was of a young student kissing the aspirant Taoiseach on the lips. It would never have happened to John Bruton … or Enda Kenny for that matter.

Though both the student and Bertie looked as though they were enjoying themselves, in a strange way the real template of the exoticism of Ahern was provided by the matronly women of Mitchelstown. They may well have been ruddy-fingered farmers' wives but, as Ahern glided through the tables like a cross between Sonny Knowles and Mick Jagger, their eyes dripped with desire. The Taoiseach's easy charisma had turned an otherwise stuffy FF function into a Ballroom of Romance and though some might demur, had Bertie crooked his finger at any of those staid peasant wives that evening they would have sprinted up the stairs.

The why of their desire will never be known for, rather like Updike's Rabbit, even the Iar Taoiseach may not know the secret source, and like Rabbit he is so self-absorbed a creature he may not even care too much about it. Instead, he may just think it is his due that all of the desire, the need in the world, just naturally flows towards him and, in truth, who could argue with Ahern?

After all, when, after the great fall, the former Taoiseach appeared on the

'Late Late' with Ryan Tubridy, he would not have been excessively surprised if the audience had started ripping up chairs and booing. Instead, like any sophisticated gigolo, all he had to do was waggle those defensive eyebrows and start off into the old shtick about being a modest man of the people and the audience were putty in his hands.

Time may have passed, like his fellow old roué Bill Clinton he is a bit redder in the cheeks, but even in politics, no matter how it ends, that part called the id always cherishes your first love.

And like any romantic cad, Mr Ahern knows all too well that in the long dark night of our recession we may say in public that we want Enda or BIFFO or that nice pink but perfect Mr Gilmore to be the Taoiseach, but, when no one is looking, for the women at least, their secret thoughts about Bertie will always be 'and then I asked him with my eyes to ask again yes and then he asked me would I yes and his heart was going like mad and yes I said yes I will'.

SECTION 3

That's not how to do it: Sad tales from the
Taoiseach's office

Chapter 14 ∾

HOW CAN WE LEARN TO
LOVE AN ABSENCE?

For democratic politics to work, a significant minority of the people should at least like our leaders. This is not just another media fiction, for even politicians admit they invest enormous emotional capital in the desperate pursuit of the affections of the public. Like some Roman tribune showering bread upon the unwashed masses, they appeal to our love but there is a certain futility surrounding their cries, for our affections last for no longer than it takes to consume the bread. After that the only man we have a stake in is the guy coming along with the next basket.

It is always the sad case too that when the equivocal love of the people ends, like a cuckolded husband whose virility is vitiated by the fear of loss, our politician cannot rescue himself. There is, you see, always something sickening about desire when it is poisoned by desperation, and once the end is reached, the fate of all politicians is to slink muttering about ingratitude into the shadows.

The unique plight of Brian Cowen, of course, is that except for a brief cameo of a lost weekend in Tullamore, as Taoiseach he has never managed to secure the love of his people. Or to put it more accurately, the tragedy of Cowen was that he was only liked by the people when they did not know him. It may be hard to believe now but before he was Taoiseach Cowen was popular. However, in that strange negative way that has been so characteristic of his career, this had more to do with his status as the anti-Bertie, rather than any real liking amongst the electorate for his innate qualities. That sent its own warning, for there was surely a need to be wary about a politician who, after 20 years as a national figure, was not known to his people.

Outside of that brief Offaly honeymoon he has been as close to the people as one of those nineteenth-century absentee Ascendancy landlords. It is a wounding and perhaps a slightly cruel charge but since that point he has been the absentee Taoiseach who rules us in name only.

Outside of the loaded question of legitimacy the problem, of course, is that it is very difficult to love an absence. Those of us, and we are legion, who were not part of the inner circle of the Fianna Fáil tribe never really got to know the eternally suspicious Mr Cowen before he became Taoiseach. Sadly the situation has not changed since the accession, for absence has been the defining characteristic of Mr Cowen's short inglorious reign. It began during his first summer in office, where he lurked in Ballyconneely like some modern version of the exiled Wild Geese, whilst the house of cards Bertie built collapsed around his successor's form.

And though Mr Cowen has bravely attempted to speak to the people since then, unless they are bankers in bow ties we know his heart is not in it. And when he does speak, there is nothing in the bureaucratic, speak-your-weight discourse that might pique our interest or attract our sympathy. Instead, such is the extent of the public hollowness of Cowen that we still do not know what Mr Cowen loves. We do not know, though we sometimes privately guess, where in the cold grey monotone world of a Cowen there is a place of sunlight or laughter.

Sometimes he seems to us to be like a man who just wants to be left alone by the world. His tragedy, however, is that they will not let him be. Instead, there is always some whore tugging at his arm trying to clothe him in the hem of greatness.

One of the more surprising features of our absent Taoiseach is just how small the man is. If one looks at those Ard Fheis speeches, he resembles some gargantuan apocalyptic figure. But when seen in the flesh, he is actually a small butty little fellow. Of course, he is running to fat but the detail is in the delicacy of those alabaster hands, which look more as though they belong to a pianist than a claymore-wielding slayer of political enemies.

The diminutive scale of Mr Cowen is of use in one regard, for it does provide us with a clue to his persona. The reason why loyalty to the tribe has been one of the few defining public characteristics of Mr Cowen is that he is a Beta male. This informed and sustained his most impressive political ability: being the enforcer for a more dominant mate.

The problem for us is the that reason Mr Cowen values loyalty so deeply is because he needs so utterly to believe in something that is better than his poor self. It is an understandable desire, but you will forgive us for noting that an abyss of self-doubt, however honestly felt, is not the quality of leadership we need right now.

The absence of leadership had certainly left Mr Cowen in a precarious position. In nature you should never become detached from the herd, for that is the point when even the jackals strike. But in Mr Cowen's case this has happened to such an extent FF's good soldier is now the hunted one, running spectacles askew like poor Piggy in *Lord of the Flies* as the savage mob chase him towards the seashore.

We hadn't a clue about the hidden soul of Bertie either but we had an accepted narrative of a humble pint-supping plain man of the people who would say the 'hard working man' to anyone. It wasn't a great deal but we got the false impression that Bertie cared for us in some way. And, in truth, we did not need much complexity for we like our politicians to be summarised in a sentence.

Albert could be filed under gambler, deal maker and keep her country.

Mr Bruton could be summarised as bumbling, well intentioned and slow but didn't make as much of a mess of it as we thought he would.

But, alas, when it comes to poor Mr Cowen, there is nothing but a collection of negativities.

Ironically, when it comes to Cowen and the politics of absence, it is Haughey, the great swooping hawk of FF politics, who casts the darkest shadow. Unlike Cowen, who is known only by his absences, Charlie Haughey built an entire treasure chest of personas. As with Mr Cowen, Haughey was not without knowledge of the bawdier side of the world but he was also a self-proclaimed public intellectual. There was, as with much else involving Mr Haughey, far more of style than substance to this persona but in fairness his relationship with the arts brought a sense of theatre to the office. In contrast, Cowen has never been seen in the company of a single intellectual.

If they were buildings, Mr Haughey would be a Gothic cathedral. Sadly Mr Cowen would, however, be a 1960s-style brutalist concrete-fronted edifice with a flat roof.

The lack of imaginative empathy even extends to the strange belief of this poor rough beast, who appears to think we should thank him for adopting his plain 'take me as I am warts and all' persona. But we have not taken him and in spite of this absence there appears to be no plan B where he might seduce us.

And, rather like our brutalist 1960s building, there is a terrible absence (sorry but that word again!) of imagination lurking in the soul of a politician who glories in the fact that he has nothing interesting to say.

It is hard not to think that the reason for this absence is that ultimately fear has been the defining theme of Brian Cowen's career. Even his reputation for 'winging it' in whatever job he took was informed by this emotion, for if he did nothing and failed that was because he had not tried.

Of course, his public reputation is that of being a bruiser. But whilst there is something of the Victorian dad about Mr Cowen that does not mean he is a strong man. Shakespeare's Toby Belch once famously mourned the absence of cakes and ale in Puritanical societies. Mr Cowen's unique campaigning style certainly suggests he is a latter-day cakes and ale man. There is, of course, lest our libel lawyers are starting to get excited, scant public evidence of any ale since the lost weekend in Offaly—and that unfortunate hoarseness in Galway!—but no other politician has so passionately absorbed Napoleon's view that an army marches on its stomach.

Being on the campaign trail with Bertie was like going on a WeightWatchers course. In contrast, with Mr Cowen it is quite the struggle to go for more than 400 yards without finding oneself in a café drowning in buckets of scones and tea.

When our man is out and about, it is only when he prepares to put the butter and the jam onto the gooey concoction that a radiant lightness of being appears on Mr Cowen's visage. It is as though he is thinking, 'Food is here. I am being rewarded.'

We are not quite here in the territory of Noel Browne's celebrated description of William Norton, the diabetic leader of Labour, lustfully spooning saccharine concoctions into his mouth with warm little piggy eyes shining with delight at the sweetness of it all.

But Mr Cowen's need for sweet things does speak of an inner Beta softness. It reveals a need to be mothered. Above all else it speaks of an absence at the centre that can never be filled by any amount of cake ... or ale.

Chapter 15

THE GREAT GATSBY MEETS HOMER SIMPSON

Sad tales of the political Brut

It is strange to think the last Fine Gael Taoiseach is an object lesson in the politics of how not to be Taoiseach. However, even John Bruton admitted, when he fell into the top job in 1994, that it was 'a bit of a shock' and he was right, for nothing John Bruton did had very much to do with John Bruton becoming the Taoiseach. And then, at the first chance he got to retain the post, he squandered it.

Though he might not think it, we all tried terribly hard with Bruton. There was no shortage of patient sighs about his qualities for he was supposed to be honest, hard-working, idealistic and, on occasion, even mildly perceptive. But, of course, during the age of Bertie, these were not really positive traits at all.

Sadly, if there was a moment that encapsulated the leadership of John Bruton, it was the narrowly avoided Fracas of the Lough in Cork. It would have happened to nobody else, for the scene beside a famous Cork lake appeared to be a safe one. But as Mr Bruton impatiently waited to launch some by-election stunt, though all the rest of the local wildfowl were flapping and quacking amiably, one goose had taken an instant dislike to the leader of the Opposition.

It was not even Mr Bruton's fault but as the hissing form began its approach at a rapidly increasing pace, it swiftly became clear that he had selected the one spot on earth the goose wanted to reside in. The even worse news for Bruton was that as the FG leader stood in the usual state of lofty disdain from the world, he was utterly unaware of the imminent threat to his distinguished person.

We could, perhaps, have shouted a warning but our heart was not in it. Instead, we decided to let the cruel fates have their way, only to be spared a diplomatic incident when Bruton moved out of the way and the goose belatedly aborted its take-off.

Afterwards, in thinking about our non-interventionist stance, we realised this was not informed by a dislike of Bruton, or the lovingly crafted headlines such an assault would have generated. The problem with John, though, was that the iron-clad air of superiority he brought to every aspect of his life meant any discomfiture he suffered was always terribly enjoyable.

Of course, the other problem with John Bruton was that no one knew where to start with the problems. He was too lippy for a start for, whilst the entire country agreed with him, it was bad enough that he would be caught referring to 'the fucking peace process' once. However, when a Taoiseach is stupid enough to repeat the trick a week later, add in the codicil of 'Is Charlie Bird in the bushes?' and be caught, don't blame us if we start chuckling about the man born with a silver foot in his mouth.

And like all awkwardly built men, he was terribly accident prone. This meant, much to our delight, that he was regularly caught in embarrassing situations. One such cherished moment occurred when, during another election, he is reputed to have noted that an unprepossessing soul handing out leaflets resembled 'Clarence the cross-eyed lion'. There was a tragic awkward silence before a mildly terrified press officer whimpered, 'That, Mr Bruton, is our candidate.'

Ultimately the biggest problem with John was that he looked like a cloistered child of privilege who had known nothing of the hardships of life. And he just did not look like a leader, for in 1997 the contrast between 'the Brut' and that nice young Mr Ahern was embarrassing. Mr Bruton moved with a duck-like walk and in a chaos of loose papers, ill-fitting suits and food stains. In contrast, once we got past the teething difficulties of the anorak era, Bertie dressed like a boy who was on permanent standby for a First Holy Communion ceremony.

When it came to poor Mr Bruton, his nickname of 'the Brut' said it all for, in spite of his supposed intellect, there was something irredeemably gauche in how he operated. He was like those German tourists who reserve the deckchairs each morning and then complain when the British steal them anyway.

As with so many of his political party, the most fatal weakness of all was there was always something of the gilded dilettante about his politics. For unlike the professional poker players of Fianna Fáil, the loss of power sat easily on his shoulders. The very soul of FF man would ache at the loss of a Ministerial Mercedes. In contrast, Mr Bruton brought down one government as Finance Minister over his inability to realise that in a recession the taxing of children's shoes might not be popular with its left-wing independent supporters.

In 1992, having been gazumped in the leadership stakes by Dick Spring in a manner that set an alarming precedent for Bertie, he lost an election to Albert Reynolds that was almost impossible to lose. The worst was yet to come, though, for in 1997 the big farmer's son did not have the stomach for the rough trade with Dick Spring that would have kept the Rainbow party going until the autumn and in doing so led his party into a 15-year electoral desert.

Ultimately it was his utter Fine Gael-ness that brought out the very best in FF, for Bruton was FG man incarnate. Every aspect of his frame spoke of his essential status as the soft-bellied big farmer's son who was utterly lost in town. The hardy lads in FF knew they could always walk over John, for when it came to the real cruelty that is needed at the top end of politics they knew there was an irredeemable softness at his core.

Others might call it decency, but whilst Mr Bruton was too moral to trick with Sinn Féin whilst they still held hands with bombers, the wide boys in FF had no problem.

When it came to the important art of connecting with the soul of the new Tiger, it also did not help that Bruton was possessed with an unreformable deference towards the establishment. Initially the new Taoiseach's inability to pass a barrister or a monsignor without bowing was funny. But by the time our man joyously burbled about how the visit of Prince Charles to Dublin was the happiest day of his life, it had become tiresome.

It is laughable in hindsight, given how enthusiastically they nestled amongst the fur of Ireland's vested interests, that FF were surrounded by a faint hue of radicalism. But in 1997 they, rather than the ever-deferential Mr Bruton, appeared to be in tune with the burgeoning iconoclastic tendencies of the new Tiger.

The other problem with John was that there was an irredeemable absence of sophistication in almost everything he did. There was the terrible legacy of the famous Bruton laugh, which was memorably described as resembling a cross between the death cry of the corn crake and a Honda 50 motorbike starting on a frosty November night.

It did not help that the Brut was filled with an insufferable certainty in his intellectual brilliance, for there was scant evidence to suggest this actually existed. Of course he could consume and regurgitate mountainous numbers of facts but even the myth of Mr Bruton the Christian Democrat intellectual was punctured by that FF corner boy Willie O'Dea, who famously noted of Bruton, 'he is the first intellectual I have ever met who has still to utter an original thought or to publish a single book'.

This did not stop Mr Bruton from being photographed on every conceivable occasion beside a bookcase full of what appeared to be learned tomes, but there was something strangely needy about his eternally unconsummated desire to prove his superiority.

All of these flaws created a creature that, in a democracy, lacked the most critical virtue of all. Try as he did, and on most occasions it was with great reluctance, he was not able to connect with ordinary citizens. This was epitomised by his ill-fated 1997 election tour when the FG leader was, after a week, finally persuaded to meet the people. Unfortunately after his debut walkabout was collapsed by a raucous shout of 'Here comes Homer', Mr Bruton spent most of the rest of the campaign on the train.

The awful thing for John was that for all the cleverness, the Homer Simpson cap fitted.

And it is in some way fitting that his happiest and most appropriate role was that of EU Ambassador to America, for whilst the post was outwardly important it was in fact an utterly harmless, impotent line of work. One supposes he had at least been trained up for it by leading FG.

They are an unlikely duo but the role Bruton played within FG bears a remarkable resemblance to Tom and Daisy Buchanan in *The Great Gatsby* who were 'careless people ... they smashed up things ... and then retreated back into their money or their vast carelessness ... and let other people clean up the mess they had made'. The bad news, alas, for FG was that the couple who ended up sorting the mess out were the less than comical duo of old 'Baldy' Noonan and a Kenny 'Lite'.

Chapter 16

MICHAEL NOONAN AND THE CORNER BACK THEORY OF POLITICS

Sometimes in politics it just doesn't go according to plan. Nothing epitomises this more than the time Charlie Haughey addressed a Munster rally for the European elections during the 1970s. The candidate, Chubb O'Connor, may have been in his seventies but our man was still willing. It was a grand occasion with the burning sods of turf and the finest of rhetoric about Fianna Fáil's vigorous dynamic team and the party's relationship with Europe from the days of the monastic settlements.

Then the candidate tottered onto the stage, fumbled with the microphone for what appeared to be an age, before a thin reedy voice finally hesitantly croaked, 'People of Killorglin, I have a vision for a new Europe.' In the background Haughey was heard to mutter, 'Well, that's that fucked anyway' and he was right.

It certainly did not go to plan for Michael Noonan either. When he was elected to the leadership of Fine Gael in 2001 the expectation was that Master Noonan would sort out Bertie Ahern with the élan of a large Christian Brother who has seized by the ear a small gurrier robbing apples.

Instead, the Michael Noonan of 2002 provided us with the most distressing campaign anyone involved in politics has ever seen since the implosion of Adi Roche. Paradoxically, the collapse of Noonan was all the more excruciating because of his status as the roughest, toughest, meanest son of a blueshirt the Dáil had ever seen.

But some were more prescient. As songbirds gathered around the newly elected FG leader, Eoghan Harris warned that it wasn't going to work because Noonan did not have 'the bottle for the battle'. Harris was dismissed because he had past form as a Bruton supporter, but the columnist grounded his views in a promise by Noonan a decade before he became FG's latest bright new balding fifty-something leader that he would be taking 'leadership positions' on national issues.

This and his subsequent failure to fire any more shots were forgotten in the flux that is Irish politics. But the failure was significant for it opened up the possibility that Noonan was deficient in the 'blood and bandages' front. He might be a good man for the fanciful phrase but did not have the stomach or intensity for the long campaign.

For a time it didn't really seem to matter for Noonan enjoyed a pleasant career anyway. He was a witty urbane Finance spokesperson who enjoyed the delights of being constantly told that it would be the better day for Ireland when he finally replaced that dullard Bruton. There was the trauma of Hepatitis C, where, in a typical example of Irish politics, Noonan was savaged for his response to sins committed by a series of FF governments, but it seemed this had been surmounted when the metropolitan elite got their wish.

Little more than a year later one afternoon captured the essence of Michael Noonan's utterly bizarre election campaign. For those of us reared on the *blitzkrieg* style of Bertie Ahern, this had already been a curious day. It started at the unusually late time of just past 10, after which we took a leisurely trip to two locations where the aspirant Taoiseach met about 20 members of the electorate.

In truth, it had all been a tad weird from the start of the campaign, for on the day when the aspirant Taoiseach had embarked on the compulsory walkabout down Grafton Street a busker with uncanny prescience started into an acoustic version of David Bowie's 'Space Oddity'. As the eerie notes rang out, they were strangely appropriate, for as the leader and a ghastly-looking front bench plodded down the thronged street, he did not greet a single voter.

The worst was yet to come, for an appalling apparition waited at the top of the street. As the infamous 'Baldy bus' shimmered in St Stephen's Green, it was bad enough that it was coated in a luminous colour that left it resembling some hostile alien spacecraft. But as a spectral Noonan grinned despairingly amidst the promises of a social contract, even tourists moved away from the wheeled vision like nervous fawns spooked by the taint of incipient death. Sometime later, we did take our courage in our hands and spent a day travelling on board the bus of doom.

Happily the interior was a far more pleasant place, where dozing members of the media were supplied with copious amounts of confectionery and travel games to pass the time as the leader's campaign wended its way past the thousands of Bertie posters. On our restful day the oddest moment occurred when the entourage stopped for lunch. With Mr Ahern one would have been lucky to grab a Mars bar but it soon became clear that even in the white heat of this campaign the refreshments would be a civilised Ascendancy-style affair. By the time the soup had been enjoyed, then the main course, a pleasant dessert and finally, of course, coffee, an hour had passed without any sign of Mr Noonan being ready for the road.

For a moment we wondered if, in some mad prank, Noonan had driven off on the bus and left his media torturers stranded, for we would have deserved it. But an anxious look out the window consoled us, for the metal monstrosity was glinting vilely in the sun like the Irish version of the mini-bus in *Priscilla Queen of the Desert*.

Some 20 minutes later, fretting at the absence of activity, we decided to take a post-dinner stroll amidst the rolling fields of newly mown hay. As we basked under the gentle shade of the trees and were lulled into sleepiness by the slumberous murmur of bees, the scene made for some bucolic contrast with the chaos of Mr Ahern, where a thousand hands would be shook and a thousand blessings of the hard-working man would be bestowed in less than an hour.

Then, suddenly, a dark rolling shape disturbed the pastoral tranquillity. As it neared we got quite the shock, for who did we see strolling in solitary splendour beside the gentle water of the Barrow, where the only sound to be heard was the gentle plop of the rising trout, than the leader of the Opposition. For a moment we were going to shout 'Come on, Mr Noonan, there is an election to be won', but we stayed our voice. It was just that it seemed to be such a pity to interrupt him, for this was the first time in a year he appeared to be at ease with himself.

It was not the first time during that campaign that Noonan was spotted on his own, for on the evening of the first day of the election campaign we spotted the FG leader walking through the corridors of Leinster House with all the vivacity of a man approaching a gallows. Normally during an election a party leader is surrounded by a flying column of spin-doctors and advisors. They may not be doing anything that is of use but it creates the impression of dynamism. Yet in that corridor of a spookily empty Dáil Noonan was utterly alone. And in a very real way he remained alone for the rest of the contest.

But what really did go wrong with Michael Noonan? The claim that he didn't have the bottle to get stuck in and get a bit of blood on the shirt may be unfair, for he was a clever man who was no coward. The best explanation may come from a wise old FG TD who talked about the corner back theory of politics. Our man noted that 'you have a fellow who is a brilliant corner back. There he is pulling, maybe even biting, his man when the referee isn't looking and the manager decides to put him in centre back. But it is a different world out there. Everything is faster, the ball is fizzing past him, our man first gets disoriented, then cranky and before you know it he's pulled on his opponent, is caught, he gets the line and it's game fucking over.'

One of the oddities of election 2002 was that though Bertie Ahern was at the peak of his popularity, Michael Noonan was far more liked by the media. This had very little to do with any sound-bites from Noonan. It was instead about character, for we were starting to sense there was a lot more tin than gold involved in FF's cynical construction of our Celtic Tiger golden calf. In contrast, though he was a visible wreck, we suspected the outwardly cold Noonan was a more humane man.

Our sympathy didn't really matter, for in that tormented time the FG leader experienced really only one triumph. During the leaders' debate with Bertie he told the Taoiseach he was like the 'cock who gets up crowing each morning about how he has got the sun up when it has nothing to do with him at all'. Though neither we, nor perhaps even Noonan, realised it at the time, the FG leader was absolutely correct. But even if we had, it was far too late for him, and us, for it to make any difference at all.

Chapter 17 ∾

ENDA LITE LOSES HIS
LOVELINESS

He is not normally the sort of figure one would associate with the Twilight Zone but something curious has started to happen to Enda. These days when he appears on the national news it is almost as though the Fine Gael leader's skin is starting to peel. Before the lawyers pounce we don't think Enda has been at the Botox but increasingly he looks as eerily false as one of the mannequins from 'Tales from the Crypt'.

The problem this change is causing is all the odder for we normally associate FG politicians with middle-age spread. And as they speed towards their sixties, lusting still for a final sip from the fountain of power, this version of FG are starting to show their age. Outside of the return of Noonan and Sean Barrett, when, you see, that eternal Robin, Richard Bruton, is acquiring wrinkles it is clear the new Rainbow are poised to become the most elderly 'new' administration since de Valera's civil war veterans in 1957. Still, at least they should be 'ball hungry'.

This does not matter so much for Noonan, or Bruton if Enda takes pity on him, since we like our Finance Ministers to be somewhat weathered. It smacks of safe hands at the tiller and wise old carbolic-scented nurses. But the ageing process is having certain unanticipated consequences for the FG leader. Sadly as we look at the alabaster skin, the petulant crow's feet gathering around the eyes and those lips that purse like the rear end of a duck, it now sometimes looks as though Kenny is experiencing the public equivalent of the fate of Dorian Gray.

It is a serious transformation for a politician who has been, from the start, marketed as being a golden-haired piece of political booty. Such was the importance ascribed to creating an impression of youth during Enda's initial time as leader, much play was put upon the capacity of the nation's aspirant alternative leader to climb mountains in Africa. In truth, the electorate might have preferred if he spent his holiday swotting up on economics for dummies but those were the times we lived in.

Unfortunately the sight of the FG leader losing his mojo is just the latest example of how it is all going slightly skew ways for Enda. As he struggles to keep above Brian Cowen in the national tar pit of the unpopularity stakes, it is hard to remember that Enda was originally chosen to end the endemic indifference towards FG leaders. He was, as the party handlers noted with a certain uncouth cynicism, a Bertie Lite figure who would be popular amongst women and the young.

In fairness, taking on Bertie in a national love-a-thon was always going to be a difficult ask, but when you are barely a neck ahead of Brian Cowen, we are in 'Houston, we have a problem' country. And in yet another example of how, in politics, the best-laid plans of mice and men will always go astray, it is amongst women and the young that he has his greatest problems. For some, such as one female TD who whispered coldly that 'when he touches me I shiver'—and she didn't mean it in a pleasurable way—he is almost a crepuscular figure. The women can, of course, be odd but like spooked horses they are accurate predictors of character. They sense something is not quite right with hail fellow well met Enda.

And strangely enough, the feeling is also endemic amongst the rather more emotionally obtuse male sex, for when the FG leader does the Bill Clinton thing and indulges in the intimate grasp and half caress of the elbow, even grown men wince.

We are not yet, of course, in Michael Noonan territory but what precisely is wrong with Enda? He is to a certain extent a victim of the curse of television for, in a very different way to Richard Nixon, the FG leader does not suit a medium uniquely tailored to unveiling falsity. On television when Nixon smiled the beaded sweat and the narrowing eyes told us he was a fake. In contrast, when it comes to Kenny, the problem is authority, for even when it may not actually be there some politicians such as Gilmore at least create the appearance of it. Enda, on the other hand, has always looked like an over-promoted primary schoolteacher playing at being a national leader.

He can try as he will—and bless him, he does—but it is impossible for poor Kenny to ever move beyond the territories of pastiche for the core is hollow. This, alas, means that once Enda tries to crank up the engine beyond anything more than winking, nodding and acting the goat, the whole thing begins to rattle and overheat.

Sadly the even worse news for Enda is that the lost battle for authority is no longer the only issue he must deal with. Instead, the critical issue Enda must confront is the growing list of claims that far from being nice he is actually a bit nasty.

On one level the open claims by his enemies that he is not loved should actually be good. Few TDs in FF loved Bertie, for the ruthlessness necessary to secure power, and the ego required to believe you are the best-qualified individual to hold it, means party leaders are rarely instilled with the chivalrous ethics found in *Tom Brown's Schooldays*. And in the current dangerous times there is a lot to be said for a bit of the politics of nasty rather than nice.

The issue with Enda, however, is that there is something effeminate about his alleged dark side. In the aftermath of the comical putsch of the FG aristocrats the victors tried to script a narrative centred on Kenny as a Haughey-style man of steel. Outside of noting that Mr Haughey is not perhaps the most appropriate role model—well, for the decent skins of FG at least—the problem is that the ongoing FG civil war has resembled a knife fight between courtly eunuchs.

Some may wonder why it is that the hidden dark side of nice Enda has emerged so late. This may be closely linked to the nearness of the political prize our man believes he is about to secure. The problem with Enda, you see, may be that, like the unloved boy on the dance floor, he is becoming too desperate. Just as nothing causes Paddy's heart to sink more than well-merited praise, we become equally uneasy when someone wants something too much.

Sadly the real problem with our nice-but-Lite FG leader may be more fundamental. The worst politician is one filled with a hankering desire to possess that which they are not worthy to seize. Though such creatures are characteristically filled with an envious disregard for the talented, they are normally harmless, unless they get into power and succumb to the desire to bring the smart guys down to their level. And when it comes to Enda, it is the unguarded Dubya Bush type smirk that gives away the game.

As of now, the main concern about 'Lite' is that if he secures the prize he is insufficiently qualified for, we may get a leader who may be secretly envious of talent. If this fear is true, should the patronised, despised, poorly regarded Enda ever fall into the Taoiseach's chair, he will be a very different creature to the happy-go-lucky soul who arrived at the audition. And the problem for us is that countries led by weak, vindictive men never prosper, for self-preservation dictates they must reduce everything to their level to survive.

Or perhaps it is just the case that we are inventing a dark side to disguise the cruel fact that we are now simply fed up of Enda. It's been fun for a while, but like a sponge that's been left in the oven too long, the centre has sunk, leaving a bitter taste at the edges and a big hollow in the middle.

Whatever it is, Kenny is now starting to resemble the ghost in the wonderfully sinister poem by Hughes Mearns where the narrator says, 'Yesterday upon a stair, I met a man who wasn't there. He wasn't there again today. I wish, I wish he'd go away.'

He may have had one narrow escape but Enda can only hope the election comes soon enough, before his cowardly party properly responds to the increasing desire of the spooked Irish electorate for the 'man who wasn't there' of Irish politics to simply 'go away'.

Chapter 18

SO WHATEVER DID HAPPEN TO MICHEÁL MARTIN AND THE LIKELY LADS?

His Cabinet colleagues talk about him now with a kindly contempt normally reserved for lost old age pensioners. On the rare occasions when they are asked about his views on some crisis, they chuckle, 'Musha, Micheál, sure he's very windy about it all. You know what he's like.'

It's not easy to be a contender in Fianna Fáil when all your colleagues think you have too much of the rogue oestrogen gene. Still, at least young Micheál doesn't appear to notice his status. But as he wanders innocently around the Dáil canteen with his breakfast of fruit and muesli, the lads are looking.

Oh, they'll be very polite and delighted to see him if he sits down, for when it comes to aspirant leaders you cannot be too careful. But as they tuck into their full Irish you can almost sense the unreconstructed parts of their brains clucking, 'Look at him with that lady-boy bowl of fruit. Is he a man at all?' Then as he leaves they smile politely and say, 'Fair play to you, Micheál, you're keeping the old weight down.'

Still, he does try, God bless him. On weekdays, in a new development, which has absolutely nothing to do with Mr Cowen's dwindling support, young Micheál has acquired the new habit of appearing in the Dáil bar to sup healthy masculine pints of Guinness with the lads.

But again they are smirking, for abandon in the pursuit of alcohol is not Micheál's style. They know that as he takes careful bird-like sips, rather like them women at the WeightWatchers, Micheál will be itemising every single calorie.

Still, it might be worse, for Micheál could be in an economics ministry. Instead, Martin is grand and peripheral, now galloping around the world stage giving out to the Israelis and talking tough to whatever group has attracted the ire of the *Irish Times*. And though it's doubtful the ever-cute Micheál is pleased with those who chuckle about his status as the new David Andrews, it can only do Martin good to be the only fellow in the Cabinet who's not capable of harming friend or foe.

Micheál is, of course, not the only FF ghost rattling around the building. Indeed, sometimes of an idle hour you do have to wonder whatever happened to the Likely Lads of FF for a key factor in the triumph of Bertie in 1997 was a posse of able young FF TDs like Micheál Martin, Dermot Ahern and John 'the Bull' O'Donoghue. In the run up to the election, 'the Bull' secured a higher profile courtesy of his 'Carthage must be destroyed' style embrace of Zero Tolerance. However, those who have a far-seeing eye on political events believed smooth Micheál had the better long-term leadership potential.

In fairness, Micheál did as effective a hatchet job on Niamh Bhreathnach as O'Donoghue managed on the Fine Gael dowager Nora Owen. Young Micheál's contribution did for the most part merely consist of roaring, shouting and acting the eejit but Martin thought it was the real thing. In Education he continued to think this was the real thing as Micheál dashed around commissioning a lot of policy documents and making a lot of noise without achieving much. It all appeared to go very well, but the value Bertie places on education was epitomised by his decision to subsequently replace Micheál with Michael Woods.

Back then, however, Micheál's profile was so positive the astute Pat Rabbitte swiftly garlanded him with the status of Cork Dauphin. Our suspicion that there were cruel intentions lurking beneath this apparent act of kindness were swiftly confirmed by the joy of seeing Micheál quiver every time the phrase was used.

The politically wily Martin knew enough about the realities of life in FF to fear that under Bertie aspirant princes have a short shelf life. But though some 'astute' observers detected shades of a young Bertie in Micheál, it was hard to see the comparison for Bertie, even in benevolent mode, was accompanied by an air of stocky menace that suggested he could burst you.

Though certain female journalists, and out of pure kindness we won't name them, may coo over those photographs of Martin's bare torso emerging from the sea after his Christmas Day dip, Cork's wilting pretender is, in contrast, a willowy sort of creature. He is Jack Lynch minus the steel and we can put it no more kindly than that.

We never got to see who would win if the two stags of Bertie and Micheál had met, for Charlie McCreevy took Micheál out first. Oddly enough, as Micheál's star soared for no very good reason, Bertie decided the best location for the winsome young Dauphin of Cork was the Angola of Health. It took a while but the handsome Prince began to develop worry lines.

Initially, within Health Micheál had been performing in much the same way as in Education. However, as the Minister issued a Speer-like series of plans, the escalating cost of these dreams began to irritate Charlie McCreevy. For once, however, Micheál decided to stand up for himself and came to a fatal spot called Ballymascanlon armed with a new vision for health.

Unfortunately Micheál's decision to take on Charlie McCreevy was hamstrung by one fatal flaw. When the arm-twisting began, Bertie disappeared and without Bertie ... well, the laughing Kildare man, who knew the secret thoughts of Bertie better than any other Minister, took a claymore to Martin's notions and that was the end of the 'Micheál the new leader' story.

The wonder of it is really that we would we be surprised by the failures of Micheál.

Is he, after all, merely an over-promoted secondary schoolteacher with a talent for facile oratory? Political friends also say he has a great capacity for uncaring empathy, and in the new politics you certainly can go far if you can empathise and dispose in a matter of minutes.

In truth, the moment that completely captured the essence of Micheál Martin occurred in the foyer of Buswell's whilst he was still in his prime. With their busted livers and AIDS-infected bodies the survivors of the haemophilia scandal were hardly a terrifying lobby group. Since the country was spending billions for sport, their request that lawyers be paid to examine files in America, which might allow them to sue some of the American multinationals who had poisoned them, did not appear to be excessive. But in a state that will always prioritise the American multinational over the citizen they had managed to irritate the then Attorney General, Michael McDowell.

So it was that poor Micheál was facing quite the awkward dilemma. Like the good child he is, Micheál wanted to help the dying people, but more powerful voices had spoken and a good boy always listens to his betters. However, it was astonishing to see how the Minister melted under the none too ferocious pressure imposed on him by the nation's ever so polite health correspondents. As Micheál's entire face was infused with the sorrowful mien of some wounded rabbit being lifted up by the ears, he did not strike one as being the sort of guy you would want beside you in the trenches. The haemophiliacs never got their legal team but Micheál continued to look terribly sad throughout the squalid affair.

His supporters talk of a legacy in Health courtesy of the infamous smoking ban. The actual truth was that when it came to this decision, the only interest group Martin took out was the poor oul' fellas shivering in the rain. In contrast, the other, well-feathered, plump-vested elites escaped unscathed.

When it comes to the leadership Micheál is, of course, still mentioned in despatches, but the references contain all the sincerity of the harlot's kiss, for even his own realise poor Micheál is the ghost of his youthful potential. He is only in the Cabinet now under the simple principle of squatter's rights.

Sometimes, like the narrator in *The Sixth Sense*, Micheál appears to be half aware of his fate. But when it comes to his stalled career, the most excruciating indicator of the extent of his fall is what would have to happen for Micheál to move from the current courtly impotence of his king-maker status and actually become the leader.

If FF is reduced to the status of a rump after the next election, then, like Enda's takeover of FG in 2002, the absence of alternatives means that Micheál could be the most credible alternative to Charlie O'Connor in the leadership stakes.

It is perhaps a less than enchanting prospect that Micheál's political future could be that of being a lighter version of Enda Kenny. The cruel truth of things, however, is that it is the most appropriate measure of the man.

Chapter 19 ॐ

LITTLE RICHARD THE FINE GAEL DEITY FALLS TO EARTH

It is early Friday afternoon at the very upmarket Four Seasons Hotel in Ballsbridge, and the ascetic barrister is unveiling his soul, in a manner that would almost be embarrassing on 'Oprah'. But surprisingly he is not alone, for an entire room of ruddy-cheeked baby barristers, their even more crimson-cheeked superiors and yummy Fine Gael grannies are experiencing the sort of communal ecstasy that would normally be associated with the arrival of Brian O'Driscoll in these environs. Happily, as we gaze across the flushed cheeks and trembling bosoms, at least the celebrated Celtic Tiger Ice Bar is nearby, for if things get any hotter we may need to organise a raid.

That certainly appears to be the case with our barrister, who reaches the point of no return courtesy of a final ejaculation, before sitting down with flushed cheeks and a spent appearance. Still, thankfully, it allows the star of the event, who is blushing modestly in the aftermath of the last bleak cry of 'He is a deity', to step forward.

Afterwards Richard Bruton admits with his usual commendable logic he is not keen on the whole deity thing, since the last particular occupant of that office was crucified.

He is, though he does not know it yet, being far more prescient about the dangers of divinity than he might think. Today, however, no one else, not even a bright-eyed Lucinda Creighton, is in a mood to be cautious about the greatness of Richard.

In some respects the love affair between FG and Little Richard is all a bit of a puzzle. It is perhaps not quite the compliment it might appear to be to suggest that, were he not in his current occupation, Richard Bruton would be an excellent heir for the British royal throne. He is, after all, impeccably polite, very well spoken, always on time and he never interrupts or loses his temper.

What really stokes the fire within FG is that, like the best of royalty, he is not in any way infected by the terrible virus of overweening ambition. Other politicians may aspire to become intense brooding figures out of an Emily Brontë novel. In contrast, Richard is more of a Mr Pooter than a Heathcliff for his template is formed by the quintessentially British belief in the virtues of respectability.

It is this strange characteristic—well, strange in FF eyes at least—that is the source of Bruton's status among the perennially timorous dilettantes of a FG party, whose collective ethos is centred on the desire to be seen to be more moral than Fianna Fáil. This 'living saint', who values being 'correct' far more highly than mere fripperies such as power, is the FG dream of itself as a polite, not too excessively idealistic, petit bourgeois party, which supports reform rather than revolution. Unlike the Bonapartes of FF, who would cut the crown from the head of a dead king if it was necessary, this most un-modern man of morals, who will accept power only if everyone thinks it is a good idea, also embodies the FG core virtue of reticence.

In truth, many of these qualities were admirably suitable for Bruton's former critical position and, no, we're not talking about being FG's Finance spokesperson. Instead, the very important job Mr Bruton held was that of being FG's official safety net should things ever go terribly wrong with Enda.

Sadly, as things began to go increasingly wrong with Enda, the lesser Bruton's place in the affections of his party did begin to slip. It was noted that whilst self-restraint is an admirable quality in Deputy Leaders, it is not perhaps the best quality for a boss. Real meat-eating leaders do not sigh wistfully about how it would be nice to be Minister for Education. Instead, a real red in tooth and claw FG man would be clamouring to keep those Labour communists out of Finance and give them the 'women's work' of Education.

But even before the coup of the political innocents was so cruelly terminated there were signs that the lesser Bruton was going through the sort of change in temperament more normally associated with the arrival of adolescence in boys. The first real moment of fire occurred when, on examining yet another calamity in FÁS, Bruton spoke tersely of the reforms he would have made had he retained the Enterprise job after 1997. It might seem to be a harmless sort of a comment but there was real frustration and anger in his voice.

The great wound that is chafing at Richard Bruton is that he is part of that generation of talented FG and Labour politicians who have been haunted by the defeat of 1997. Though they did not know it at the time it cost the two Brutons, Pat Rabbitte, Ruairi Quinn and the rest of that talented Cabinet 15 of the best and most productive years of their lives.

It had not been much better in Opposition for, despite his status as Finance spokesperson, he was constantly overridden by Enda on policy issues and the results were never good. Despite such indignities, for a time Richard continued his modest lifestyle of mixing the making of home-made jam with a policy document a week. Unfortunately by 2010 the idyllic existence of Friday nights at home watching 'Sex in the City' was starting to come under threat. It was increasingly said Little Richard was simply too much of an officer and a gentleman to ever take the side of any devil's party of mutineers. As the early months of 2010 saw a growing decline in support for Kenny, the mutters about Richard's 'fire in the belly' issues intensified.

It was noted that in terms of intellect Richard is everything that the Brut was and more but he has never really possessed the same 'presence'. When it comes to the odd couple of FG, John Bruton resembled Oscar in just about every way whilst Richard was the Felix element of the relationship.

In a strange way, like poor Mr Cowen, it was almost as though Richard the Lesser was too normal, for all party leaders are dysfunctional in some hidden fashion. The worst, however, that can be said of Richard is that he is a clever man who appears occasionally to fret. He possesses the nerdish tendencies of a Niles Crane crossed with elements of the Bernard character in 'Yes, Minister'. Outside of that, his private personality is one of a man who is complete and happy with himself.

Within FG the faith continued to slip away from those supporters of Bruton whose support was so passionate they never bothered to check with Richard to see whether he actually wanted the job. However, as the idle back benchers muttered warnings about how 'faint heart never won fair maiden', Richard continued to resemble the sort of Oxford don who is at his happiest when surrounded by his books.

But the complaints of Richard's 'team', about how Bruton had not been sufficiently 'upset' when he fluffed his chance in 2002 to secure the leadership against the none too demanding troika of Cute Oul' Phil Hogan, Kenny Lite and Gay 'you're a waffler' Mitchell, ignored one rather fundamental point.

The constant whisper surrounding Richard has been that any time he wanted it, the job was his. But perhaps cautious Richard was wise to wonder about the veracity of all those 'all the man has to do is ask' entreaties, for around here, as he had learned the hard way in 2002, asking and getting are two different things. The crown may have been trembling visibly on Kenny's head but wise Richard still, however, did not move, for he knows support whispered in corridors has a way of disappearing like snow in a summer's meadow once it is exposed to the white heat of a leadership contest.

And when he did, the support did melt.

Sadly, as in the aftermath of the children's coup d'état, the mauled aristocrats condemned Cute Oul' Phil for his behaviour and slammed Bruton for not behaving like Hogan, and it was evident that far from being a 'deity' Mr Bruton is from now on nothing more than a first amongst equals. Instead, and it is pretty unlikely now, were Enda to be toppled, the mane of Leo the Lion will be prominent in any future FG leadership contest.

It might, however, still be unwise to write off Richard. The alacrity with which he skipped across the dead political forms of his allies to get back into Enda's front bench suggests there is a certain steel behind the civility. The cute old enforcers and the great bearded ones in Kenny's all-male court believe Richard is a broken reed. But he may yet evolve into a turbulent priest, for the problem with Richard's refusal to ever do wrong means that if he continues to believe Enda is a false man he will move against Kenny without compunction. For now, however, that photograph of a limp-wristed Richard having his arm raised by the victorious Enda will serve as an eternal symbol of how not to become a Taoiseach.

SECTION 4

Ah the women, fair play to ye!

Chapter 20 ∿

LOVELY GIRLS AND NAGS
IN DRESSES

The lonely fate of the Leinster House women

The role and status of women in Irish politics is best captured by the famous photograph of the Labour party in 1987. At first glance nothing appears to be wrong but, if you look hard enough, one thing is finally apparent. There were old men, fat men, bearded men, bald men and even one accidental young man in the grisly crew. But there is not a single woman amongst them. On being asked about the curious absence, one veteran Labour TD sardonically noted that 'We did used to have a token woman TD, Eileen Desmond, but she retired that year.'

There should be something astonishing in the resemblance between what was supposed to be Ireland's sole progressive party and a Victorian gentlemen's hunting party. But nothing captures the strange nature of Leinster House more than the lonely plight of what the 'lads' nervously refer to as 'the women deputies'. In the rest of the outside world women may be breaking the glass ceiling with their graduation caps but, in spite of all the fine sentiments that are regularly expressed, the reality of their status is summarised by that scene.

And truth be told, little has changed since then. Labour might have a few more TDs these days but only seven of those are women. And of that number two are actually from the ancient Democratic Left regime whilst Jan O'Sullivan got her start in politics under Jim Kemmy's former one-man band (and sisters!) of independent socialists.

It is quite the puzzle. Women can be professors, scientists, barristers, judges, teachers and nurses but when it comes to the none too intellectually rigorous task of being a TD, or a Minister for that matter, there is an embarrassing absence of female voices.

Of course, women do participate at the higher levels of Irish politics, for our senior politicians are always telling us with patronising delight that our last two Presidents have been female. But this, however, is only a cunning blind, for the Presidency is nothing more than the Irish House of Lords.

Outside of the Presidency women are welcomed in a manner that is often quite mysterious for the women concerned. However, whilst we slot them into grand little jobs in Education or Social Welfare, we have never had a female Finance Minister let alone Taoiseach. And we have never had a female politician who has contended for the leadership of the top three political parties. And yes, we know about Ms Harney, but Florence Nightmare was really a sole trader who used a Fianna Fáil rump to gain some critical mass.

In contrast, amidst the real parties, when it comes to the top job it is as though the old civil service marriage ban never ended. Of course, the political system can highlight Mary Coughlan as an example of equality in practice. But it should be pointed out that within the FF family Deputy Coughlan is an associate male. She was seen as being different to the other women for, even though she was the party's designated 'lovely girl', Mary drank, clapped backs and cussed with the best of them. It also helps enormously that she was part of FF's line of dynastic families, for when it comes to 'the Republican party', the secret rules can be broken for those with royal blood.

There is one area, in fairness, where our political parties do try to nurture 'the women'.

Any party leader in a photo-shoot is always found casting his eyes desperately around to find a couple of good-looking chicks who can be placed around our hero in a despairing attempt to prove he is for the women. And whilst we may have originally concentrated on Labour, the other parties are no different. Fine Gael did have lovely Olwyn and Olivia Mitchell but, in the aftermath of the FG leadership heave, when Enda unveiled the party's bright new decomposing front bench, one onlooker noted that it almost reminded them of William Trevor's Ballroom of Romance were it not for the fact that the Ballroom was brightened by the odd member of the fairer sex. Rather like the balding Labour party of the 1980s, Sinn Féin has no women at all whilst Mr Cowen's studied air of indifference towards the fairer sex is matched only by five-year-old boys.

When it comes to the marginalisation of women, the talk in Leinster House is generally about the need for family-friendly working hours, crèches and quotas. In truth, the exclusion of women is a far more subtle accidental affair. There is no conscious discrimination but, rather like the parochial house in 'Father Ted', Leinster House smells, thinks and looks male.

This land of the Marks and Spencer hundred-euro suit is a final staging post where, safe from the invidious incursions of the Equality Authority, men can commune. Within this Shangri-la an excess of femininity would come as a positive harassment for those TDs who view the Dáil sitting term as representing the sort of necessary break all men need from the 'other side'. As with the old spit and sawdust Dublin pubs, letting women take over the place would simply spoil the essence of the thing, though they can still secure the associate membership status of advisors, journalists and, perhaps most importantly of all, secretaries.

Ultimately nothing epitomised this attitude more than the tale about the unfortunate fate that befell Mary O'Rourke after Donie Cassidy accidentally took her seat in 2002. In the somewhat turbulent aftermath it was believed that as part of the compensation package Ms O'Rourke would be given the Cathaoirleach's job in the Seanad.

It is not a particularly critical job, for the main role of the Cathaoirleach is essentially to slap David Norris on the nose when he gets too excited and issue the odd bleat of 'Ah lads' when the exchanges get too robust. Still, you do at least get a car and a few extra bob and around here that counts.

It should not even have been a contest.

In one corner O'Rourke, who had once contended, albeit harmlessly, for the leadership of her party, came burnished with the status of decades as a senior Minister and a higher national profile than most of her party bar the Taoiseach. She was even armed with a nervous Bertie's whispered support for what that was worth.

Her opponent, Rory Kiely, was a career Senator whose most high-profile political achievement was a capacity to deliver Munster hurling final tickets.

Those of us who knew it would be no contest were right.

Afterwards Mary said that she had not gone for the job and wasn't interested in it at all. One suspects, however, that the wise O'Rourke got wind of the likelihood that the lads were not keen at the prospect of being talked down to by the less than Belle Dame of Longford Westmeath for five long years.

Mary got the consolation prize of Leader of the FF group.

The post had 'status' and 'prestige' but there was no extra pay and no free car. As with every other institution within Leinster House, even within the harmless environs of the Seanad the politics of tokenism had reigned supreme.

Chapter 21

ENDA FAILS TO TAME A SHREW CALLED LUCINDA

If there was a moment that captured the uneasy relationship between the dominant male species and the women thing, it occurred during Bertie's election campaign in 2002. During his sweep through one of the nation's ecstatic towns the Taoiseach entered a hairdressing salon, backed away briefly, then took his courage in his hands, poked his head in the door, waved at everyone and left.

Once safely outside, Mr Ahern approached the agog media and, with the sort of look of awe more normally associated with someone who had just found the treasure of Ali Baba's cave, noted the place had been full 'of women getting their hair done'. There was a further dramatic pause before he added with some astonishment 'and their toes and hands'.

In fairness, Mr Ahern was by no means an exception within a system that believes women should be photographed and not heard. When it comes to this particular trait, the most modern example of the importance of being a lovely girl is Fine Gael's Lucinda Creighton. When she first began to make a stir in politics, Lucinda was a terribly cross mature student type whose obsession with obscurities like Christian Democracy meant she was somewhat terrifying.

The nervousness such treatises sparked was not merely inspired by her gender, for Gay Mitchell, the FG TD, held similar views with a vehemence that ignited a similar level of unease amongst his colleagues.

However, whilst Gay's passion was granted the fool's pardon of 'there's Gay going on about the Christian Democracy shite again', Lucinda's veered close to the territories of conduct unbecoming. Eventually Creighton realised cross girls do not get elected by the voters. So it was that a new Lucinda no longer concerned herself, in public at least, with issues such as European integration. Instead, she concentrated on seeing off any potential FG running mates in

Dublin South East and ensuring that she was in the prime position to secure the certain FG seat that was bound to come courtesy of Michael McDowell.

On the canvass she presented herself as a winsome girl rather in the manner of a nineteenth-century debutante seeking a husband. Lucinda, it appeared, had belatedly realised FG is a party that so idolises the concept of the Stepford wife, they still have a 'ladies who lunch' event each year.

Still, Lucinda was at least finally getting there. Nothing epitomised the change more than a *Sunday Independent* interview where Lucinda outlined her new political persona. On this occasion philosophy was replaced by a photograph of Lucinda smiling gently in a white cotton dress. It was an image that would have impressed Bree in 'Desperate Housewives'.

Of course, Lucinda still had ideas, and a set of values that are largely conservative, but at the start at least she did the decent thing, as all that previously indecorous flaunting of her intellect and those low-cut ideologies were covered over with a new Burqa of pleasantness.

Sadly Lucinda has not perfected the art of being lovely. There can be no doubt that if she were a little nicer to Enda she could be rewarded with a more prominent position amongst the chinless wonders of the biggest political amateurs in Europe. Instead, in a party that is in a state of permanent uncertainty about the capacities of a leader who has not brought them to the nirvana of Mercs, she has been incapable of disguising her lack of appreciation of Enda's mysterious better qualities.

In truth, from the beginning there were occasional departures from the politics of *Ireland's Own*, for on the morning after she was elected Creighton told one enchanted journalist that 'I didn't give up a promising career as a barrister to become a mere back bench TD.' As is the way of the world that, of course, is precisely what did happen.

It would have helped if Enda had followed the precedent set for Leo and appointed her to a front-bench position on her first day. But there again it might never have worked, for 'the lads' are well able to slap Enda on the back, tell him he's a great lad to his face and bitch away about him in private. There is, however, something visceral going on between Lucinda and Kenny for, in spite of the new Stepford wife thing, she visibly quivers with distaste in his company.

The first act of the revenge of Lucinda occurred when, as part of a desperate attempt to pretend FG is a party of radical reform, Enda's right-hand man Cute Oul' Phil Hogan attempted to bring in compulsory gender quotas for women. The best-laid plans of the elite of frontbenchers and spin-doctors were going well until they were confronted by a bush rebellion of the FG back benches. And *quelle horreur*: who was leading the revolt but the very bold Lucinda.

Such was the political chaos initially it appeared to be the case that the embrace by Cute Oul' Phil of the politics of Ailbhe Smyth had been accepted. However, one wise soul noted dryly that when the party's internal rebels saw an opportunity to bloody their leader's nose, 'a couple of them got a bit braver'. It was an occasion when no one could have blamed Enda had he sighed, 'That's women for you.'

Sadly, some months later, a whole lot of FG TDs, but still not enough of them, got brave and tried to behead the leader. However, when a drowning Kenny threw his hand out of the water, clutching the offer of that much-coveted front-bench position, Lucinda didn't just walk on by.

Instead, she stopped, considered the matter and calmly plunged a stiletto into her leader's head. Now that all the teeth are bared and it's out in the open, it is still hard to comprehend the full extent of the complex between Enda and his Mayo colleague. The hatred does appear ultimately to be driven by Lucinda's belief that Enda is a fake and Kenny's own self-doubt over whether she might actually be right.

As the summer of 2010 was dominated by the joy of the grand old FG 'soap opry', the simplest way to describe the extent of the cold war between them was the old Cold War phrase of Mutually Assured Destruction. The bad news for Lucinda, though, is that whilst she and Enda may both be engaging in MAD politics, in this duet there is only one superpower.

Sadly it is, one supposes, all too late to change things now. The new nice re-invented Lucinda should have been able to smile nicely, blush gently and laugh at Enda's priestly old jokes. However, one supposes that in politics, as in life, there are some things that even a Stepford girl in a white cotton dress cannot do.

In a sense we are actually relieved. We had fretted that, in spite of her acceptance of the political necessities of her world, Lucinda would become too nice, for it would be a pity if the Broom Hilda of the FG Christian Democrats was sucked into some amorphous maw of a winsome chuckling lovely girl.

However, after FG's summer of communal war in 2010, the one thing we can say with certainty is that Enda is never going to tame this particular Southside shrew. And, in truth, we don't want him to do so anyway for bad Lucinda is much more fun.

Chapter 22 ∾

COULD MARY NOT SO LOVELY TURN INTO FIANNA FÁIL'S ANTI-BIFFO?

The story may be apocryphal but it does cut to the core of the public persona of Mary Hanafin. A constituent who was, it being Dun Laoghaire, a member of the affluent classes once attended our Minister's clinic in pursuit of some minor favour. On entering, he was surprised to be handed a number for it wasn't the passport office, so he promptly put it in his pocket and forgot about it. Such indeed was his level of forgetfulness that as he perused his edition of the *Irish Times* he hardly heard the first call of '*Uimhir a h'aon.*'

After a brief silence a far more stentorian bark of '*Uimhir a h'aon anois, le do thoil*' caused our man to almost fall out of his chair. For a brief moment the constituent was distracted until he looked at the number and realised he was the delinquent one. With head bowed, our Senior Counsel entered the office, knees quivering in a manner he had not felt since the last time he was in the headmaster's office in primary school.

It is, of course, that very headmistress persona that has made it so difficult for Ms Hanafin to be accepted by the Fianna Fáil 'lads'. The party has, as Mary O'Rourke could testify, always had a difficulty in dealing with acerbic women who do not smile shyly and melt if one of the 'lads' does them the kindness of tipping her a wink.

They admit she is 'able' but there is something too much of the schoolteacher eternally clad in a prim, high-necked blouse about Mary. She reminds them too much of Irish summer schools and cold showers mingled with bracing walks, brown bread and porridge for breakfast.

And yet the caricature is perhaps unfair, for the great love of her life, Eamon Leahy, liked his cakes and ale. But he was blissfully happy with Mary and he hardly decided to go home to a virago each night.

The Leinster House media ratpack also have their difficulties with Mary 'quite contrary'. Nothing epitomised this state of affairs more than the response to her comment, after being appointed to the brief of Arts, Tourism, Sugar, Spice and All Things Nice, that she had some experience in the brief for 'Daddy had a hotel, well, until he drank us out of it. Isn't that right, Daddy?'

As the former FF Senator and now teetotal Hanafin Snr nodded ruefully, there was much tutting amongst the more sensitive doyennes about how unnecessarily cruel Hanafin had been. In fact, the Hanafin father–daughter relationship is uniquely warm, and Mary was being straight and honest and slightly wry about the vicissitudes of life with an alcoholic father. These surely are qualities any father would like a daughter to have.

They are also characteristics that Irish politics is sorely in need of. And in spite of her current lowly Ministerial state, we may be about to see a great deal more of them. For though it may be slightly indecorous to put Mary Hanafin into the same sentence as something as uncouth as a BIFFO, it may well be that the Big Intelligent Fellow From Offaly will be the defining influence on her career.

He certainly has for now been the only dark cloud in the almost too perfect political life of Ms Hanafin. Mary may have been too schoolmarmish for most of the 'lads' in FF, but something about her caught the roving political eye of Bertie. But though the demure Hanafin was, for the acutely critical ward boss, one of the special ones, all that stopped with Mr Cowen.

Like all unhappily married couples, in public the duo profess that everything is going terribly well and they are the best of friends, but in private it is a different story.

In fairness to Mr Cowen, the great dissonance is not entirely his fault. In so far as Mr Cowen likes women at all he prefers them to be comfortable in an apron. He is a poor needy soul who likes the sort of motherly woman whose first instinct on seeing a man is to butter the soda bread, whip up the cream for the scones and start brewing the big pot of tea for the lads. In contrast, nothing deadens the Taoiseach's smile more than an ambitious career-driven woman who only goes to the Dáil bar for morning coffee.

The sad news for Mary is that she is now experiencing her own ice age to such an extent that a Taoiseach who is not overburdened with political talent has consigned her to the Ministry that is associated with political death. In the aftermath of the reshuffle BIFFO and his increasingly frosty Anti-BIFFO could air-kiss all they liked, but it was impossible to avoid the whispered supposition that Mr Cowen had, in allocating Hanafin to the Ministry for

Fun, branded the glacial one with the mark of Cain.

However, though we, the accursed media, may hanker for a martyr to put as a burning necklace around the neck of Mr Cowen, to date Ms Hanafin has been putting quite the brave face on things. And she may not be totally wrong, for as the country implodes, outside of Foreign Affairs, just about the only good news Ministry is Arts, Sport and Tourism. Indeed, though she pretends otherwise, as Ms Hanafin glides to the nation's arts festivals like a serene swan that is far above the squabbling ducks of the Cabinet, she will know there is no better place in FF to be than outside of Mr Cowen's diminishing circle of friends.

Anyone who has had the benefit of a good religious upbringing will know of the great age of popes and anti-popes. Now, as the hopes of Brian and Micheál wither on the dry vine of their absent talents, should she play her cards right the decorous Ms Hanafin could yet emerge as the FF Anti-BIFFO of choice.

She is certainly blessed by her rivals for the leadership race that is not happening. Micheál Martin's uncertain star is imploding to such an extent he now may struggle to save his seat from the unruly encroachments of a loudmouthed Fine Gael Senator, Jerry Buttimer. And after that, well, should Brian Lenihan not be fit to take to the field, the only alternatives are misanthropes, eccentrics and political straw-boys.

A party desperately seeking for an alternative to Mr Cowen may swiftly realise the sober Ms Hanafin is everything Mr Cowen is not. However, before everyone gets overly enthusiastic there were more justifications for Mr Cowen's chilly disposition than Ms Hanafin's apparent preference for the Burqa over the apron. In Education, despite her popularity, Hanafin left a questionable legacy, for in politics there is always a latent danger in allowing someone to be in charge of the thing they love. Placed in her native heath, to paraphrase Tiger Woods, the schoolmarm 'went ghetto' and turned into the Minister who could not say no. But in fairness, when it comes to that distracted Cabinet, she was hardly unique.

Of course, once the prospect of putting a woman in charge of FF would have been as impossible as having a black man in the White House. But such now is the nature of the times that if the electorate behead FF and Ms Hanafin survives, the only other contenders may be Noel O'Flynn or Charlie O'Connor, and even in FF Ms Hanafin should have the beating of those.

There is only one problem with this vision and it is not just the chilling experience suffered by the equally formidable Mary O'Rourke who, in spite of her dynastic ties, struggled to outpoll Michael Woods when she ran for the great prize.

The state of FF is so desperate they might actually be prepared to indulge in the sort of tokenism where they can put a woman in charge of a post-electoral rump. But Hanafin is locked in a desperate battle for survival against the motley mix of Barry Andrews, Ciaran Cuffe, Ivana Bacik and the Celebrity Socialist candidate Richard Boyd Barrett. It would be ironic if the elegantly liberal burghers of Dun Laoghaire scuppered the possibility of FF acquiring its first ever female leader. However, it would almost be comical if the final curse of Cowen would be to deny Hanafin the leadership of FF by costing the Minister her seat. Perhaps it is that which has her so chary about giving up the teaching job.

Chapter 23

SO HOW DID MARY HARNEY TURN INTO FLORENCE NIGHTMARE?

There has been some puzzlement as to why Mary Harney appears to have perked up so much recently, for our politicians are not normally at ease with the sort of vicious cuts that damage the lives of the people whose love they need if they are to be re-elected. One explanation may be that after her own enormous pay, conditions and gigantic retinue of advisors were sorted, Ms Harney was never quite at ease with the Boom.

The evolution of our former Florence Nightingale into a political Typhoid Mary is, in fairness, genuinely surprising for those of us who are ancient enough to remember her first PD incarnation. During this revivalist son of a preacher man style affair no one could ever have expected she would evolve into a form of political dry rot who has managed to wither away two Departments of state and a political party.

It all represents some change from the time when 'our' Mary was seen as being a straight-talking woman of the people. We were frequently told about how there are 'no airs and graces' with 'our' Mary. She was moral and kind and talked often of how politicians needed to have more respect for the public purse. 'Our' Mary did look a little sad sometimes but that was because 'our' Mary had made great sacrifices to be where she was. The sacrifices were, sadly, never exactly clarified. Neither for that matter were we ever told what was so hard about working in one of the shortest sitting, most overpaid legislative assemblies in the world. Few, however, were of a mood to cross-examine a woman who was, after all, 'one of us'.

Well, but what a changed world we now live in. As we approach the twilight of her political career, everyone now admits that the true nature of no other politician has been so misjudged. The strange thing is that it all started so well for her; back in 1997 it looked as if Harney in government would live up to the great myth. During the initial months of the Fianna Fáil/PD Coalition there were many spats with Bertie over what Mr Ahern used to nervously call 'ettics'. But even when the future of the government quivered in a macabre tango with the trembling bottom lip of the Tánaiste, a closer examination of the 'domestics' uncovered a common theme. On far too many occasions Miss Harney's spats appeared to be informed by Florence Nightmare's own hurt feelings rather than any concern over the greater good of the country. And there was worse news to come. It came as a terrible surprise when our blessed Tánaiste was caught whistling up a helicopter to go down the country to open an off-licence at the expense of the taxpayer. This was only the first of many examples of how Ms Harney was to develop the habit of treating government like an all you can eat buffet.

It is a measure of the changed times that Mary Harney regularly berates the simpletons of the Opposition when they dare to raise any questions about the frankly terrifying goings-on in the Department of Ill-health. But there again, as she quivers with indignation over the appalling vista of being held responsible for the failures of what notionally is her Department, the Lady perhaps remembers all too well that she secured her current comfortable lifestyle via her embrace of the same school of 'oppose now, think later' politics.

Ms Harney might in Opposition have regularly complained about how if Dáil questions had been answered we would not have expensive disasters like the Beef Tribunal. Then once she got into government the Queen of FÁS set up a HSE that is the most secretive organisation in Europe since the fall of the Berlin Wall.

One supposes we should not be too surprised by Ms Harney's enthusiastic adoption of the FF ethos of taking diametrically opposed positions in government and Opposition, for Mary, you see, has been hiding a terribly big secret. Within government she has been FF's fifth columnist, for she is still in her soul a creature of the party of Haughey and that ilk.

But how did it happen that the current poster girl for the wanton self-regard, secrecy and greed of the Cabinet was once the most popular politician in the state?

In truth, from the very start the *modus operandi* of our Florence Nightmare was set in stone, for our heroine had that most critical ability of being able to attract the pity of the electorate. As in so many other aspects of political life, the capacity to play the victim card offers, even the worst of offenders, a cloak of invisibility.

The first great spectre Ms Harney conjured up was Mr Haughey. After many disagreements, there was finally a row over the failure of Mr Haughey to send Ms Harney a Christmas card. Mr Haughey was at that time quite busy what with the job of leading FF, managing the leader's allowance, sorting out Ben Dunne and dealing with the world recession. Anyway, after some further minor disagreements Ms Harney left FF and Mr Haughey didn't have to double-check his Christmas card list anymore.

The suspicion that had Mr Haughey thrown her the slightest bone of a Junior Ministerial position Ms Harney would have been onside was confirmed, for when the PDS went into Coalition with the ogre of Kinsealy, like Dessie she accepted Ministerial preferment without a murmur.

Outside of an ability to play the pathos card the other key to Ms Harney's political success is her skill as a communicator. Like any good convent girl, on the rare occasions when she is forced unwillingly into the public arena, she still sits in the Dáil chamber with her notes all carefully laid out on crib cards. But she, and we, have found out the hard way it takes more than just the capacity to be glib to reform a government Department.

When it came to Health, our antennae were raised even before the great fall by the spectacle of Ms Harney enthusiastically playing the well-worn pity card. She was, we were told by sources that were not at all connected to the Minister, very brave to be taking on such a significant challenge. In truth, we were more terrified by her track record prior to taking the job, for she had spent seven years in Enterprise and Employment without leaving a mark, except perhaps for the destruction of the old successful bank regulatory regime.

Our concern about Ms Harney's move into Health was intensified by the reality that this was a Department that needed significant reforms involving much labour and hard work, and very little time in Michelin-starred restaurants. Sadly for those blessed by any form of prescience, the notion that our heroine worked into the small hours of the night by a bedside lamp had been sundered by her shocking admission in 1997 that she did not even know the contents of her own party manifesto.

It swiftly became evident that there was no need for Bertie to worry about the possibility that Ms Harney would live up to her reputation as an iconoclastic reformer. The unique achievement of merging nine health boards into a single HSE, without the loss of a single bureaucrat, showed Harney was still Bertie's girl, for the surrender to the vested interests had been concluded before the reform had even started.

Ms Harney has continued to practise her patented politics of talking big and acting small. In fairness, she has talked tough to certain classes of people, for if you were a nurse you were lazy and slapdash. But if you were a well-heeled consultant who dines in the same restaurant as Ms Harney, then you are a valued public servant.

Those who are now surprised by the emergence of a happy Harney should not be surprised. Self-pity is a first cousin to misanthropy for it is the child of the egotistical belief that the ignorant world has failed to respect your talents. It takes therefore but a small twist for the belief to emerge that the world must be punished for its failure to properly appreciate the sacrifices 'our' Michelin star loving, globetrotting, junket-loving former Tánaiste has made for the state.

In our case, sadly it appears that we are being punished on the double. It was bad enough in 1997 that we got Bertie but the even worse part of our 'two for the price of one' offer was that we also got Harney.

Chapter 24 ∾

A LONELY BLUESTOCKING BECOMES 'ONE OF US'

The great reinvention of Joan Burton

If there was a moment that captured the secret views of Fianna Fáil on the unhappy role women should play in politics, it occurred during one of our many querulous NAMA debates. After a series of characteristically incomprehensible replies by Brian Cowen, where the only thing that was clear was that the Taoiseach either didn't know or didn't want to know the answer to the question, Labour's feisty Finance spokesperson Joan Burton testily informed the Taoiseach that there was no point in him trying to evade her questions for 'I am a qualified accountant, you know.'

The response from the FF benches was immediate and uniquely honest.

As the entire parliamentary party, including its women deputies, fell around the Dáil chamber howling with uncontrolled laughter, it was alarmingly similar to the famous episode in 'Father Ted' where the female solicitor dealing with Father Jack's will tries to convince Ted and Dougal that she is a genuine officer of the court.

Of course, the laughing refusal of 'the big thickos' from the Island to believe a mere woman could be a solicitor ends badly for poor Ted and Dougal, who are subsequently seen nursing bruises. Ms Burton is far too refined for that but the apparent incomprehension within the ranks of FF that a woman could be anything so complicated as an accountant said a great deal.

In these fallen times 'the lads' are now comfortable with women as nurses, teachers and possibly social workers whilst widows are also entitled to inherit their husbands' seat on the Mafia principle that they married the party as well as their spouse.

However, nothing stirs the night terrors more than the concept of a woman with a serious academic qualification. But perhaps the most intriguing aspect of the whole affair was the amused response of Burton. Her relaxed attitude was probably helped by her status as one of those rare political creatures that is utterly in command of her spokesperson's role. This ease is relatively unique for, rather like the media, most politicians are utterly clueless about the issues they hold forth upon.

If they are in government, they are at the mercy of the top mandarins who may themselves not know what is going on, and even if they do know the score, decide it is better the Minister doesn't.

The unhappy fate of our Opposition TDs is even worse, for their desire to look good is utterly dependent upon the cluelessness of their political opponents. Unsurprisingly, such a dialogue between Tweedledumb and Tweedledumber tends to promote insecurity and terseness in political exchanges.

In truth, we are still getting used to the sanguinity of Joan, for in her first incarnation in Leinster House Burton was one of the card-carrying members of an elite cadre of women known as the Labour bluestockings. It was always unlikely the bluestockings would be loved for these were women on a mission to improve us all and that is never really appreciated.

The situation was probably not helped by the decision of Dick Spring to appoint three of them to Ministerial office on their first day in the Dáil. At the best of times first-day Ministers are monstrous testaments to the rampant ego but when you appoint three of them together you run the danger of creating a political mini-Frankenstein. This was certainly the case with the cantankerous Labour bluestockings of Joan, Eithne FitzGerald and Niamh Bhreathnach, who embarked on an immediate campaign involving much lecturing, hectoring and cornering of the citizenry over issues such as the limpid delights of ethics.

Sadly, though they sallied forth with all of the pious certainty of a flotilla of vicars' wives on bicycles, the project did not go at all well. The first problem was that the three little bluestockings were opinionated, narky and, like many ethicists, appeared to be embittered by fortune. They quickly learned the hard way that all poor Pat wants from his governors is that he be for the most part left alone unless there is a burglar in the house and even then he would sometimes like to be left to his own devices in dealing with the matter. And he was not likely to be at all impressed by the spectacle of three little bluestockings visiting the house to tell him he was going to have to pay more tax so they could set up an ethics commissioner to improve him.

The even worse problem was that, being infected with a surfeit of ego, the three Labour bluestockings could not see round corners. This failing meant it was always going to end badly for them … and, to a large part, for us. In a desperate attempt to save her seat Niamh Bhreathnach brought, courtesy of free third-level fees, the most socially regressive piece of educational legislation the state has ever seen. Alas, she discovered even the South County Dublin electorate were not at all grateful for the five hundred million euro electoral bribe.

The voters took the cash, used it to buy Bulgarian skiing villas, sacked Niamh and let the Bert in the side door. Meanwhile 'Ethics' Eithne, the girl with 20,000 first-preference votes, got lost in a forest of Freedom of Information and Ethics legislation. FF put up a semblance of opposition based on the human rights of TDs to engage in a modicum of graft. However, it was mild enough, for the FF boys fish with a long line and they suspected there would be time a-plenty in government to reverse all of this. As it was, the tactic of 'softee softee catchee monkey' worked out perfectly, as Ethics Eithne was beheaded by the electorate too.

Joan, whose main contribution to this period was the sort of nagging voice that would frighten seagulls, suffered a similar fate but her loss was different from the other two. When it came to Nagging Niamh and Ethics Eithne, the execution by the electorate, who were fed up of mini-Robinson-style Savonarolas and wanted to party with Bertie, was almost personal. But in the case of Burton there was some dignity, for she was simply outflanked by the people's 'bin charges' campaign champion, Joe Higgins.

As so often happens in acts of personal transformation, misfortune was the catalyst for change. It has always been the case that the best politician is that wise soul who has finally realised they are not master of the universe. This was certainly so with Burton, for when she scraped back in five years later a transformed TD was unveiled.

Astonishingly we swiftly learned the new Burton had discovered how to flirt and play the *coquette* on the floor of the Dáil. Surprisingly enough it was Charlie McCreevy who began the seduction of Joan. The love affair was perhaps understandable for both are accountancy nerds. So it was that they exchanged *billets-doux* over the Estimates Committee debates whilst poor Richard was left to play the gooseberry as Finance Questions evolved into a strange menagerie of laughter and fiscal teasing.

Happily, even when McCreevy left, there was no return to the old Joan. It did, of course, help that Mr Cowen found the new Burton to be rather terrifying, for men of his ilk prefer to compartmentalise women as mothers or nags. There was, however, no way Mr Cowen could deal with a woman who could act flirtatiously over the Exchequer Borrowing Requirement.

There is, of course, still plenty of the old Joan to be found. She still talks too much and the Burton whinge is now as much a staple of Irish impressionists as Michael D once was. But the critical change is that, as with Michael D, the mimicry is tinged with affection, for Joan has managed the critical transformation that Enda has never achieved.

Suddenly she has become 'one of us'.

It is a measure of the great failure of Labour that it is odd for one of its frontbenchers to be the people's champion. But she is as loved by the cleaners who work invisibly in the Dáil as the Sancerre-sipping socialists of Sandymount.

As we attempt to cope with the scenario where Labour's former bluestocking has become 'one of us', there is perhaps a critical lesson to be learned from the reinvention of Joan. It is not that we want our women to be more feminine, but that rather we want our politicians to be warmer and more human in their public discourse.

The transformation of Joan Burton is the classic example of this.

Chapter 25

FROM NATIONAL 'LOVELY GIRL' TO CANARY IN THE COALMINE

The terrible fall of Mary Coughlan

The photograph of Mary Coughlan leaving her first teacher conference certainly said more than a thousand words. For the first time in her career, our acutely image-conscious Tánaiste looked like a canary trapped at the wrong end of the coalmine. Of course, 'lovely girl' Mary is far too tough, and self-regarding, to be dismayed for long. But it is still a strange experience for the designated 'lovely girl' of Irish politics to be unpopular.

There were always critics of the girlish chuckles and flirtatious eyes of our heroine. On one occasion we had the misfortune to meet a senior Labour politician who was still chewing his beard in anger after an encounter with Coughlan. Normally the gentleman in question is a sanguine soul but on this occasion he was 'fed up of this lovely girl act where there are no disagreements and everything can be decided with a joke and a laugh'.

On being asked what had sparked his outrage, the former Minister mentioned some abstruse ideological point about social welfare. We agreed with his hurt, sighed 'terribly dry' to ourselves and carried on worshipping at Mary's boudoir.

Now that it's all gone terribly sour, Mary thinks that, like *Carry on Cleo*, it is a case of 'Infamy infamy they've all got it in for me.' But the truth of things is that a lot of people wanted it to work for Mary. Back in the day, in Agriculture she seemed to be a breath of fresh air that could walk and talk by herself and, in a political culture desperate to prove its bona fides on the women front, that was enough for most of us.

At the risk of being sexist, we sometimes wonder was it the diet that did for Mary? She was, up to a couple of years ago, a hearty country girl, though by 2007 Mary may have been veering too much towards the hearty side of things. Then suddenly she embraced a fitness guru and a new healthy living style of life.

It didn't help that at around the time our heroine went on the dry bread the world economy went into flitters. But watching her mournfully dining on a breakfast of two slices of brown bread one day we instinctively felt no one could run a country on such arid fare.

Still, even as the world went into meltdown, it was expected Coughlan would bring a certain earthy charisma and a connection with the lives of real people that the two Brians at the top table simply do not possess. Mary, quite lovely, was a mother with a straight-talking sensibility whose capacity for humour and rough talk was crossed with life experiences that were poignant.

The only blemish on perfection occurred when the Tánaiste was caught calling some unlovely Meath farmer a fucker and, in truth, for some of us that merely enhanced Ms Coughlan's reputation, for many of us believe not enough politicians have used that sort of language about our farmers. Sadly, now that there are claims that the Tánaiste's 'earthy' language is upsetting the more sensitive wing of the world's capitalists, we are somewhat less tolerant of the cursing. It is not the only change either, for in a heartbeat Ireland's 'lovely girl' has become the Marie Antoinette of Irish politics crossed with certain trace elements of the poignant fate of Darling Clementine.

She is still in our Old Man River style Cabinet that's 'half afraid of living' and 'half afraid of dying', but it has become increasingly clear that Coughlan is a politician drowning in fear. As is often the case with fear, the Minister's vain attempt to disguise this weakness provoked only more irritation and derision. But only terror explains the archaic, legalistic and sometimes almost incomprehensible language the trembling Tánaiste uses in the Thursday morning Order of Business.

It is a measure of how out of her depth the Tánaiste is that she would be fearful of making a mistake at what is essentially a comical sideshow. This, however, was not the only location where Donegal's Darling Clementine has fallen down a linguistic mineshaft. In the critical Lisbon referendum she got the number of Commissioners Germany had wrong whilst by the time she managed to confuse Darwin and Einstein such had been the decline of her reputation some were relieved she had actually heard of them.

As she became the visible feather-headed emblem of a bankrupt state, the problem with Mary became terribly clear. She was as, our Labour friend stated, all too clearly nothing more than a clever talker. In fairness to Ms Coughlan, she is not the only politician in our Cabinet of teachers and solicitors whose merits do not extend beyond that false talent. However, she is at the centre of the firestorm and it is not poised to get any better. When he finally moved his limping political ugly duckling, Mr Cowen could have put her into some harmless Ministry for Arts, Sugar, Spice and All Things Nice. Instead, he decided to put a broken-winged politician carrying the indestructible taint of failure in charge of the critical Education portfolio.

You would wonder sometimes what we have done to deserve such punishment.

If there is a moment that defines all that is wrong with Coughlan, it recently occurred at a Fianna Fáil West of Ireland conference. On one level her speech was just another of these 'all on the pitch together, drive her on, Patsy' performances we are so, so familiar with. But what was astonishing was just how wrong Ms Coughlan was about absolutely everything.

The context of the speech was a week in which the Irish universities claimed they were bankrupt. Mr Gormley had just admitted a new system of water charges would be needed to replace our busted up water pipes, which have been functioning with the same infrastructure since the British decided to let Pat have a go at running the joint. The Taoiseach was under fire over his non-intervention in the Ritchie Boucher Bank of Ireland pension top up whilst our EU Commissioner, Maire Geoghegan Quinn, who had been chosen for the job because within FF no one else was available, was at the point of giving up the hundred thousand a year pension she was planning to trouser on top of the EU salary.

So what was Ms Coughlan's take?

In a society experiencing social breakdown she complimented the Taoiseach on the success of his '*Meitheal* concept'. There was a self-satisfied recitation of the 'legacy of great FF names such as Bartley, Beegan, Carty, Callanan, Geoghegan and Killilea' and 'the great names of the present Ó Cuív, Fahey, Kitt and Treacy' whose fine work means 'Galway has taken centre stage economically, socially and culturally on the Western sea board'. Sadly it was rather compromised by the unfortunate fact that most of the country hasn't heard of the great names but we can all dream.

The Tánaiste then decided to scatter her and the country's enemies as she claimed FF 'should be proud' about the great job they have done but obviously not in a, wait for this, 'arrogant or complacent way'.

It got even better courtesy of the claim that 'FF the Republican Party in the true sense of that term' is a 'party that protects the weak and vulnerable and stands up for the small guy in Irish society'. As it went on and on and on about facing 'significant challenges ... from a position of great strength' and FF's virtue in not 'blowing the boom', none of the harmless rameis could disguise the fundamental truth.

Our 'lovely girl' is now nothing more than the visible symbol of the destruction of FF. She may be as sweet as any spoilt Princess but at the end of the day, when the crown goes bust and she has to go peel spuds with the rest of us, that is not too lovely at all. The other cruel truth Ms Coughlan may have to face sooner rather than later is that, in spite of all our affection, when the next election comes, the simple politics of moral hazard means the only thing we can do with this poor feather-headed Marie Antoinette is to decapitate her.

Chapter 26

FINE GAEL'S TESS OF THE D'URBEVILLES LEAVES THE POLITICAL PITCH

The day I first saw Olwyn Enright she was draped seductively across the bonnet of one of what appeared to be a row of Toyota Corolla cars. Before you get too intrigued, it was a bright summer evening in the respectable Ascendancy town of Birr, and the location was the infinitely respectable one of a Fine Gael campaign launch. Still, even though no one besides the photographer can ever explain why Olwyn was sprawled across the car, we immediately knew we were in the presence of a future political star. Olwyn, you see, was something new and unique in a political party whose central image was 'old Baldy' Noonan.

In fairness, we were not alone in our response, for when Olwyn entered the Dáil even the driest political hacks immediately knew how Thomas Hardy felt when Tess of the D'Urbevilles first entered his imagination. Enright is, to paraphrase the poet Blake, a classic case of innocence crossed with experience.

This was even evident in her first major political outing. The acceptance speeches of most new candidates consist of half an hour of 'that's enough of me talking about me now what do you think of me'. In Olwyn's case, however, she started with a declaration of thanks to a long list of utterly unknown FG county councillors for their support in the lead up to the nomination.

It was clear Olwyn knew jam only arrives after you butter the bread and she would need these same fine gentlemen for the arduous tasks of putting up posters and knocking on doors in the harsh environs of Cowen country.

Of course, she didn't lick this cunning up from the ground, for her father Tom Enright had forged a 30-year career centred on the soubriquet of being known as 'poor old Tom'. The defining moment of Tom's little-known Dáil career occurred during a famous Dáil vote on contraception in the 1970s, when he was seen anxiously cocking his head fretfully to see which lobby his then leader Liam Cosgrave was heading towards. In a classic case of free expression of conscience Irish-style, once Tom saw the Taoiseach heading in to vote against his own government's bill, he swiftly followed.

Tom knew you could build a long career on the Jim Hacker 'these are my people. I am their leader. I must follow them' school of politics and he was right.

Back at the coronation of Olwyn, in spite of the youthful vivacity of our fawn-like candidate, it was expected she would happily adjust to the traditional secondary role the Enright political dynasty played to the all-powerful Flanagan Empire. But even on voting day in 2002, as a Flanagan campaign car engaged in hot pursuit of Enright in Portlaoise, it was evident that the times they were a-changing.

Afterwards it all came out. It always only comes out afterwards. Charlie had missed this funeral, had failed to send a card to someone else on the occasion of their graduation, he had been up in Dublin too much on that radio and legislating, the big FG farmers were unhappy, they ran to Parlon— the list was endless. Nothing, however, could evade the truth that Charlie lost his seat and breathless, naïve, happy little Olwyn scooped the pot.

Of course, as is so often the case, success brought its own crises for normally a new TD in Leinster House has a settling-in period. However, a FG party of bald men fighting over a comb embraced the vitality of Enright with all the enthusiasm of a parasite latching itself onto an innocent host. In a Dáil where many poor souls believed Liz O'Donnell was alluring Enright allowed the party to say 'Look, we have women, they are young and pretty, Fine Gael is not the latter-day equivalent of some dying Welsh coal-mining village.'

Such was the importance of this image our heroine was drafted into the none too easy task of proposing Enda for the leadership of FG. In truth, the media were no better—and who can blame us?—for there was little to report about FG at the time that was of the slightest interest. Some of us even suggested she might make a perfect leader, but again we should not be criticised too harshly since the alternative was another pretty, doe-eyed blonde and there is little enough to suggest Enda has been any better.

Sadly after a fine beginning we swiftly began to tire of Olwyn. She was, like any well brought up, educated convent girl, hard working and diligent. The neat and tidy Enright was a girl whom we suspected would do very well in calligraphy class. And Olwyn did not disgrace herself in any of her contests with the combative Mary Hanafin over education matters. But Leinster House is a cruel judge and she did not distinguish herself sufficiently to retain our attention either.

Too often the breathless schoolgirlish style of delivery spoke of someone who was feeling the effects of a steep learning curve. And there were other brighter comets, such as John Deasy, who were far more capable of attracting our attention. Olwyn, in contrast, was simply too much of an honest toiler. It was sad but rather like Alec in *Tess of the D'Urbevilles*, having used and made the Offaly milkmaid our plaything, we cast her aside in the wanton pursuit of more interesting toys.

And again you could not blame us for our lofty sighs about how it is simply not enough to be a lovely girl, for there was more than enough of old Tom in Olwyn to render her cautious. In FG's great comeback of 2007, where frontbenchers were needed to carry the fight to Fianna Fáil, Enright was peripheral. Olwyn could argue that she was engaged in a battle to the death in the designated Taoiseach's own constituency. But by this stage even as FF with characteristic modesty went for the big four seats it was cruelly apparent that Tom 'the Carpet bagger' Parlon was a busted flush and that Olwyn was safe.

This peripheral role meant that after all the dramas of the great comeback in 2007 Olwyn was overlooked. She might have in two elections seen off the Flanagan dynasty and the designated next leader of the PDs but, as with John Deasy in 2002, there were better and even more delightful toys to play with.

So once again Olwyn was discarded in favour of the tears on the plinth from James Reilly, Lucinda's stiletto and the ferocity of a Varadkar. But then suddenly quite the change occurred to Olwyn. She was still too nice a girl for all that Order of Business braying but that perhaps is to her credit. However, up to the great failed coup d'état of the innocents she was at least the equal of the designated shiny new FF Anti-BIFFO Mary Hanafin.

And when the recent motion of no confidence in Kenny came in, she took a stand for the future rather than safety. If Olwyn had supported Kenny, even had the aristocrats won, because of her rarefied status as a FG front-bench woman she would have been entirely secure. But Enright was no longer willing to be Enda or Cute Oul' Phil's dolly-bird.

Instead, she was blunt with her leader to the point where nice Enda dropped the mask, snarled and revealed a lot more of the real Kenny than he might have liked them to see. The subsequent departure of Olwyn from politics was unfortunate, for she had left the legacy of 'poor old Tom' behind her and moved decisively beyond her designated status as a walking photo-opportunity whose sole purpose was to create a sense of vitality beside the living corpse of the party leader. Olwyn was still no Lucinda; few are, but she had evolved a long way beyond her old status as the little girl with a curl in her hair and a dimple for each cheek.

In the aftermath there was much talk about gender quotas. The real tragedy of Enright's departure, though, was that it was simply another example of how our political system has become utterly irrelevant to the lives of the very generation that must reap the consequences of the myriad landmines our failed generation of fifty-something politicians have strewn around the country with such gay abandon.

SECTION 5

Strange creatures

THE STRANGE MYSTERY OF MICHAEL LOWRY, THE 'THICK' COUNCILLOR FROM TIPP

The curious demonstration outside the Moriarty Tribunal against the oppression of a millionaire Tipperary TD by the Bolsheviks of the Bar Library did not exactly have the appearance of the spontaneous revolution of the proletariat. Instead, it looked rather more like an attack of the ladies who lunch. But there is little that has been normal about the fabulous life and times of Michael Lowry. Our wild colonial boy from Tipp may have started life as a humble refrigeration engineer but he has since then befriended and almost destroyed Ireland's two most famous businessmen, become a Fine Gael Minister and now supports a Fianna Fáil government.

If the rise of Lowry was extraordinary, his fall was even more surreal for it began when a hogtied Ben Dunne was carried out of a hotel following a series of farcical misadventures involving copious amounts of cocaine, a bath and a plump escort girl.

Mr Lowry was probably at that time enjoying the tranquil sleep of the just in his fine Tipperary house, which would become an even finer house courtesy of the same Mr Dunne. But though he did not know it, the great unravelling was about to begin and after more than a decade it is still unwinding.

In its aftermath, he is in a place filled with strange creatures, surely the most curious political animal of all. Of course, the man known as Lowry is a bit of a ghost now. He is seen infrequently within the Dáil and the hair that was once a lustrous bottle black is now grey going on white. In truth, even before the great fall, there was always something delicate about Lowry but after 15 years of a Tribunal process that has been compared with 'a murder sentence' the pallor of the skin stretched tautly against high cheekbones is intense.

Lowry might once have been surrounded by the sort of sallow menace associated with Peter Mandelson. He now, however, carries the harassed mien of someone who is nearing the end of a fabulous journey without knowing exactly what the destination will be. And though he is not quite yet like Coleridge's Ancient Mariner, the toll on his spirit has been immense. No one except the toughest and most driven Citizen Kanes emerge from Tribunals unscarred.

The public awkwardness of his appearances means it might be strange to associate the word 'charisma' with this disjointed figure. But when you meet him in person an aura of intensity and, more intriguingly still, the sense of a man who knows and will never reveal extraordinary secrets radiates from the pallid form. And it is seen by his political peers for he is that rarest of creatures who is given the unique approbation of being known by his surname, 'Lowry'.

You see, within Leinster House, only the special ones are called by their surname and here, even amongst his friends, it is always 'Lowry'.

It is easy to forget now that he is a whispering ghost, that in his time of political plenty no other Minister has ever been as loved or trusted by his Taoiseach. And yet even when his name inspired whispered speculation about the FG leadership succession stakes, he was always strangely lacking in confidence. During debates his delivery was halting, his eyes flitted nervously and even those perfectly manicured hands shook. Curiously enough it was a trait shared by Ray Burke, for men carrying secrets often seem to be accompanied by a ghostly taint of unease.

Nothing epitomised this trait more than a vignette in the Dáil where the Minister produced a characteristically halting performance. It was a minor enough affair yet on looking up into the visitors' gallery we saw Bill O'Herlihy, the Minister's designated spin-doctor, gazing down anxiously at his star protégé. The presence spoke of a man who left nothing to chance because of hidden uncertainties about his own ability.

He remained a star in the making for less than two years, but when it came to the prosaic, efficient technocrats of the Rainbow, no one attracted more attention. For FF, Lowry was a menacing figure who warned of cosy cartels and commenced a whole series of investigations into semi-state companies such as CIÉ. There were frantic tales of surveillance and mysterious white vans following the cool campaigner against the great enemy.

Then slowly the façade fell apart. An investigation that must have been the worst inquiry in the history of the state found there were no cosy cartels in our semi-states and no surveillance of Mr Lowry either. In one of his rare shafts of humour Brian Cowen noted the surveillance was so good it didn't exist.

The problem with politics, of course, is that once one bubble bursts then a whole sequence follows. And so it was that in a denouement that delighted all political cynics, and most of all FF, Sam Smyth revealed Lowry's status as the kept man of Ireland's biggest grocer.

The fall of Lowry saw a number of unique phrases entering the Irish political lexicon. At the moment of his dismissal, Lowry claimed that he and Mr Bruton were 'best friends, friends forever'. He soon realised a pressurised Taoiseach, who wouldn't be trotting up to Ben Dunne anymore with his 'best friend' for tea and a €50,000 donation to FG, had a rather different definition of friendship. This was followed by the infamous weasel words declaration where Lowry's claim that 'if a man was trying to hide illicit payments surely he would have an overseas bank account' was swiftly confirmed by the discovery of Lowry's overseas bank account.

For a media that was by now almost blasé about corrupt FF politicians, the discovery of a dodgy FG Minister was a case of joy unconfined.

Indeed, we were almost disinterested when Lowry's travails sank the biggest shark of all courtesy of the dragging of Charlie Haughey into the maw of our avaricious Tribunals.

And in a strange way he also sparked the exit from politics of Bertie Ahern, for the culture of Tribunals eventually led to the establishment of the Mahon Tribunal.

It was some achievement for a man from a small rural village who used to fret that people might think he was stupid because he had 'a thick country accent'.

After the initial furore, surprisingly, Lowry swiftly disappeared from view. He did occasionally surface as a source of scandal to the nation's ethicists courtesy of the ongoing loyalty of the voters of Tipperary. But the public began to tire of a Tribunal that has inspired comparisons with the infamous Jarndyce versus Jarndyce trial in *Bleak House*.

The weight of it all saw Lowry sink into himself as he evolved into the political equivalent of the central character in Waugh's *Handful of Dust*. There was, however, to be one final fascinating denouement as the man who had formerly been at the heart of FG ended up becoming a key prop in the destabilised FF Coalition.

Michael Lowry is not without humour. He once famously remarked that the only bars criminals would see under FF were lounge bars, whilst in the aftermath of the local elections Lowry noted his Independent Alliance had more councillors than the Greens.

Now, astonishingly, he holds the future of FF in his hands. It is amazing to think that if the cards fall a certain way, Lowry could go down in history as the man who destroyed the reputation of two former FF Taoisigh, kept another FF Taoiseach in power, finished off FF, ended FG's long affair with probity and that's before we get to the consequences of his actions for former tycoon Ben Dunne, the Irish civil service and Denis O'Brien.

And should the tide turn in favour of Lowry, he could also destroy the whole Tribunal system that once caused an entire political establishment to teeter at the brink.

Ultimately, despite all of the forensics, the most intriguing feature of Lowry's career is that we still do not know why such a strange figure went into politics. It could, of course, be the case that there is rather less to know than we think, for maybe he was really just an over-promoted thick councillor from Tipperary who, like Forrest Gump, accidentally changed history without ever quite knowing what he was doing.

But we suspect such is his closed nature, the enigma of the man known as 'Lowry' will never be truly unveiled. And it might actually be a disappointment if it was.

Chapter 28

BEVERLEY THE SCARLET WOMAN AND THE BURQA OF HISTORY

When she screeches to a halt in the big suv that would put a black maria to shame and strides in that purposeful Wellington-wearing countrywomen's way through the doors, it might be strange to wonder where it all went wrong for Beverley. As she continues in that vigorous rolling gait through Leinster House, a couple of Fianna Fáil backbenchers look hungrily at the departing form, for in spite of her tough intellect she has an earthy sensuality that leaves men dreaming of purchases involving black lace.

Truly like her father she is a peacock in a farmyard of clucking hens. But though she is her Daddy's girl, there is a difference. The only place you would follow Pee Flynn, in the white schoolteacher's suit, as he talked incessantly about himself, would be to the edge of a pond sporting a free ducking stool. In contrast, rather like a latter-day Sally O'Brien, when Beverley gallops through the corridor leaving a scent of some very expensive perfume, elderly TDS who should be long past these sort of thoughts whisper longingly of how 'Jaysus, there's half a dozen would follow her anywhere. She's the only man here.'

Beverley, thank God, talks a great deal less than her father but when she does the phrases are short, clipped and, above all else, knowledgeable. And though there is roguery in those lively eyes, she looks like a politician from whom it would not be a pleasant experience to get a scolding. In short, she carries that air of authority that suggests this girl would be a serious Ministerial performer.

But though she is one of the best within a party of callow boys and wizened cynics, this will never happen. Her problem is perhaps best encapsulated by a marvellous vignette in Tom Humphries' history of the great Dublin–Kerry rivalry, where the laconic Dublin forward Anton O'Toole is confronted in a Leinster football semi-final by a tearful Offaly defender after the final notes of 'The Offaly Rover' end. In a rare display of sangfroid on the playing pitches of the GAA, O'Toole deflated the passionate wails of 'Do ya hear that, sonny?' with a response of 'All history now.'

She may still be on the political pitch but it's 'all history now' for Beverley to such an extent her actual survival as a mere TD is one of the wonders of the political world. In the whispering corridors of Leinster House they still puzzle over why she took on RTÉ People's Princess Charlie Bird in the libel courts. But figures as diverse as Wilde, Reynolds and Kavanagh could tell you pride and a whispering lawyer holding your hand and clucking about the hurt to your reputation 'my dear' can turn any head.

It was by any standards the sort of error of judgment that should have been fatal and in a very real way it was. Beverley may have secured the halfway-house style status of a FF backbencher. However, the dramas of her formative years mean a politician who appears to be far more talented than our current Tánaiste is merely in survival mode.

There were, when she returned to FF, dreams of a Junior Ministry, but whilst Bertie's seduction was sweetened by vague intimations of a Ministerial ring on her finger, FF's great political Casanova was already a spectre when the deal was done. In truth, even if Bertie were still there, the reality of things is that advancing Beverley was a political folly that belonged to the mad romanticism of the Tiger era, quiescent Greens and a 13-seat majority.

Anyway, the bracing arrival of frosty Mr Cowen saw a bolt gun being put to the head of that particular ambition. It did not help that, as is so often the case in this most interwoven of parties, Beverley and Mr Cowen have some history. Their relationship dates back to that strange day the Beverley Hillbillies marched on Leinster House. It was a beautiful evening when the bite of spring was tempered by the sort of belated warmth that hints at the arrival of summer. As the sun struck the granite plinth, casting everything in a luminous gilded hue, it was easy to understand why one would, once here, want to stay for ever.

Beverley was, however, at the edge. Her father Pee had become too much of an embarrassment, even for FF, and Beverley, in the wake of a speech supporting her father, had been summoned to a National Executive meeting to be booted out. Outside, the scattered children's crusade of toothless FF loyalists with their 'Up Bev' posters waited confidently for Beverley to sweep to victory. But the only attention these ingénues secured was the amusement of city slickers who genuinely thought they had stumbled upon an episode of 'Killinascully'.

Beverley was in trouble, for she was guilty of the great crime of disloyalty and the sombre prosecutor was Mr Cowen, the arch loyalist of the party. Inside in the party rooms Mr Cowen roused himself from his Ministerial slumbers for long enough to do the bidding of his political master. Beverley was an embarrassment to the tribe, she must go and, ever the Alpha male when someone else was pulling the strings, Mr Cowen put the bite on Bev.

Some appeared to think the party did not demand much. All it requested was the betrayal of a father for some temporary convenience. Beverley said, 'A Flynn must stand by a Flynn' and the political and media establishment twittered before the concept of Twitter was born.

As they hissed about that 'bold as brass' Beverley, the younger Flynn was being typecast as the original brazen hussy without remorse. But what child who is half normal is going to reject their father for some passing convenience? Instead, a wise figure would be more inclined to be suspicious of the bona fides of a person who would betray their own blood for some temporary political advantage.

Years ago it must have looked as though it would be so easy for Beverley, for any child with such wondrous parents as Padraig and Mrs Flynn would swiftly realise she is a special creature. But then you have to go out and face the real world and there has been more than a small element of the daughter paying for the sins of the father about the career of Beverley.

It is hard to be the prisoner of past events when you have ambition and talent. But like a latter-day Lady of Shallot, Beverley is locked in a tower separate from the living world of opportunity that exists for those politicians who have a future. Caught between the conflicting impulses of the past and pious new moral FF, she resides on a hamster's treadmill where the name that made her is the incubus that stymies all future preferment.

Beverley continues to fight on but it is a poignant state of affairs. She may be intelligent, bright and ambitious but in a party devoid of talent Beverley is a scarlet woman who is guilty of the worst crime of all. She was caught.

Sadly, in spite of all her vivacity, as she patrols the corridors of Leinster House her career is now as circumscribed as the dusty old men in the portrait gallery that adorns the sibilant corridors. Like those dead patriots who are gazed at with disinterest by the odd passing tourist, her unfortunate eternal status is now that of yet another living ghost loitering around with nowhere else to go and nothing better to do.

Chapter 29 ❧

MARTIN CULLEN AND THE UNFORTUNATE ART OF TRIPPING INTO GARDEN RAKES

In a very real sense nothing became the career of Martin Cullen more than the manner of his departure. After being a front-line Minister for almost a decade he suddenly resigned and was never heard of again. Intriguingly no one from Fianna Fáil, let alone anywhere else, was too sorry, for from the beginning of his Ministerial career, Martin simply kept tripping over garden rakes.

The OPW is one of the more harmless Junior Ministries where you mostly engage in pleasant activities such as the opening of canals or expressing support for the linguistic delights of Ulster Scots. Sadly, in spite of the utter impossibility of getting into trouble at such a harmless gig, like a latter-day Custer, Martin couldn't avoid a series of entirely unnecessary scrapes. Firstly our hero spent a small fortune acquiring a place no one had ever heard of called Farmleigh. On securing this delight, he spent a somewhat bigger fortune turning it into a state-of-the-art guesthouse for visiting dignitaries. This had the appearance of a good idea, were it not for the unfortunate fact that nobody except for the occasional lost North Korean communist leader or Mr Cowen when he is 'working late in Dublin' wants to go there.

It is perhaps typical of Martin that when a furore arose over the similarities between Farmleigh and *The Shining*, Mr Cullen appeared to be more irate over the fuss as distinct from the collapse of the project. And in fairness to Martin, spending twice as much money as was necessary on a project that was utterly without merit meant he was merely doing what every other Minister was doing at the time.

That, of course, was not the end of the troubles for FF's unlucky talisman. One would think, again, it would be difficult to get into trouble over refurbishing Leinster House, but as everything went above cost and behind schedule, the TDS began to complain.

It all provoked Cullen to such an extent he at one stage wailed, 'What do they want me to do, get a hammer and nail bag and put in the floors myself?' In truth, it was the best idea we heard that day for he would at least have been doing something useful.

The problem for Martin was that he had begun to acquire the most dangerous trait any politician can secure. In Eamon Dunphy's soccer classic *Only a Game* there is a poignant passage where he describes how the Millwall crowd turn against one of their long-established stars, who becomes the fall guy for all the failings of the club. From that moment, even when the player did well, he was booed by a crowd who had weighed, measured and wanted him out no matter what he did.

Within FF it was often hard to avoid the impression that unlucky Martin also became the party's designated fall guy. But did he actually collude in his own fate? For it is surely telling that in the aftermath of his swift departure, the kindest defence that could be entered on his behalf came from RTÉ's saturnine political correspondent David McCullagh. On being asked the impossible legacy question, McCullagh paused for some time before offering the charitable assessment that Martin had acquired great expertise in defending the indefensible.

McCullagh's languid comment cut to the core of the Cullen dilemma. A great deal of Martin's 'bad luck' was down to his excessive anxiety to prostrate himself at the feet of Bertie Ahern in an act of atonement for the original sin of having joined the PDS. This very weakness meant he was of great use to a Taoiseach who liked having cat's-paws as Ministers. Sadly he was to learn, as many others before him did, that loyalty beyond the point of decency does not attract respect.

Of course, Cullen also believed he was simply unlucky but failed politicians always believe their misfortune is a creature of the fates as distinct from their own ineptitude.

In fairness to Martin, he did not receive a gentle press. It is, for example, doubtful that any other politician has inspired so many pleas for his removal in the various fantasy reshuffles that political correspondents indulge in. It would be correct to say there were always far worse Ministers, such as Brendan Smith. Martin, in contrast, was a hapless but essentially harmless Minister. The difficulty for Cullen, though, was that whilst it was often hard to understand how the country would be saved if only he would go, it was equally clear his departure would make absolutely no difference either.

Meanwhile for Martin the bad luck just continued. The two most enthusiastic proponents of electronic voting were actually Bertie Ahern and Noel Dempsey but it was poor Martin, however, who ended up playing the role of step-father to the ugly baby when it all went sour.

The difficulty for Martin was that Dempsey had already acquired his reputation (see Jackie Healy-Rae and the virtue of being seen getting up early in the morning) of being a far-seeing innovative Minister whilst Bertie Ahern was still the modest golden calf of the Celtic Tiger.

It may seem to be unfair that what was portrayed as being a groundbreaking innovative idea when under the guidance of Bertie and Dempsey became under Cullen a symbol of the benign stupidity of Ahern's second administration.

The irony was further intensified by the obvious disfavour Cullen felt for the idea.

Martin was supposed to be a Minister in a hurry who had issues and ideas to be resolved. Instead, Cullen found himself looking like an idiot by the likes of FG's Bernard Allen. But it was Cullen who designed the trap for himself courtesy of his anxiety to be seen playing the role of Bertie's unquestioning servant.

Any chance the Minister who kept on walking into doors possessed of regaining his political credibility sank without trace after the Monica Leech episode. In retrospect, given that our Ministers were throwing around the taxpayers' money like confetti, when it came to the great list of Ministerial expenses, Leech was not a major issue. When it broke, Martin certainly managed to convince himself he was some Dreyfus who had been hounded by the merciless ethical lags of the national press. But the nub of the thing was if you will pay political acolytes a small fortune from the public purse it does seem to acquire the appearance of graft. Sometimes in life, as in politics, you make your own bad luck.

The Minister was sufficiently upset about it all to claim almost a decade after the events had occurred that what had happened was the equivalent of being raped every day. It would, at the best of times, have been an unfortunate analogy. But at a time when the country was in a fury over the systematic rape of Irish children the metaphor was crass.

It also cut to the core of Cullen's political failure, for in the end the biggest source of Cullen's 'bad luck' was that he did not have any class. By that we mean that contrary to all expectations certain qualities outside of low cunning or vociferousness are needed for success at the upper end of politics. The latter traits are a good start but top-level politicians also possess the qualities of wit, imagination and empathy and poor Martin, the honest, unlucky plodder, possessed none of these.

There is another reason to suspect the issue of class played a role in Martin's fate. In Katie Hannon's *The Naked Politician* Cullen described how he would roar at top civil servants and throw Departmental files if he did not get his way. Though Martin appeared to believe the civil servants found it all to be great sport, our mandarins—who are not at all used to this treatment—can be swift and stealthy with vengeance.

Of course, there is no evidence to suggest the great league of mandarins decided to strew the rocky path of 'Calamity' Martin's unlucky career with hidden garden rakes.

Mind you, with our gentle mandarins there never is.

Ultimately the real trouble with Martin wasn't the mandarins or bad luck or the readiness of the Taoiseach to use him as a political cat's-paw. Instead, unlucky Martin kept on walking into garden rakes because he really wasn't very good at what he did.

Chapter 30

BEGOD THAT DOG COULD ALMOST TALK

Tales of the great Irish eccentric

The disappearance of the Irish political eccentric is one of the more tragic consequences of the new professional school of politics. In fairness, we cannot fully blame the noxious members of pious new Fianna Fáil for this development since it is hard for the political eccentric to thrive when society as a whole is less eccentric. That, however, happened over the last decade when we were far too busy making money to tolerate nonconformity. And the problem now is that we are far too busy trying not to lose our homes to take a punt on the eccentrics.

Of course, many of our great eccentrics were actually drunkards but that did not make them any less entertaining. Few moments will ever match the riposte of a drunken Minister who, on being stopped driving the wrong way down a one-way street, responded to the query of 'Did you not see the arrows, Minister?' with a wail of 'Jaysus, I didn't even see the Indians.'

Some of the finer practitioners of the art must remain anonymous but one of the more delightful moments from the front-line of eccentrics involves a TD cursed by an atrocious stutter who ended up canvassing on some desolate farm. Our man's difficulties were not enhanced by the presence of an evil-tempered dog, who took up residence an inch behind his right calf and barked threateningly throughout the candidate's set speech. As some rural churl listened silently eventually it all became too much for the TD, who emitted a desolate series of stutters that could be roughly translated as 'Begod that dog could almost talk.' Sadly life did not get any easier as the farmer glared sourly, spat and growled, 'That would make two of you, so.'

The late Brian Lenihan Snr was another figure who had a wonderful insouciance of spirit. This was best epitomised when, on hearing a phone ringing in a bar that was doing a thriving trade well beyond closing time, our man lifted the receiver and said, 'Hello, Minister for Justice speaking.'

Happily, even in the new sober age of Cowen, there are still eccentric souls patrolling the corridors of Leinster House. Within Fine Gael strong arguments have been made in favour of John Deasy but he is the sort of natural-born contrarian whose ongoing political existence is a source of terror for a party that tries to operate as efficiently as possible without a brain.

Convention would suggest the Greens might supply us with a hothouse of oddities and there is a real case for Trevor Sargent, who resigned from the leadership of his party after breaking a pledge to not go into Coalition with the Great Satan of FF. Trevor may also be the first and he is likely to be the only Irish politician to resign for the sin of leading his party into the well-upholstered comfort of the Ministerial Mercedes. The one thing that compromises Trevor's status was his role in sourcing us with some excellent vegetarian recipes for such delights as the Brussels sprout and the parsnip. For this achievement alone Trevor was more useful than the rest of Mr Cowen's Junior Ministers and half the Cabinet.

Others would claim Paul Gogarty is a top contender. The lively Green TD made his initial application via his claim that coalition with FF was like lying 'bollix naked' being 'screwed' and expressed the intriguing hope that whilst 'we have been screwed by FF a few times and we are trying to roll them around to get what we want'.

This was followed by further dramas when, in the middle of a long dissertation by FG's Frances Fitzgerald at a public meeting, the Green deputy began to roll around on the floor.

The incident was the catalyst for a superb subsequent putdown by Labour's Kathleen Lynch, who silenced Gogarty when he was getting uppity one morning with an icy comment of 'Sit down there, roly poly.'

The problem, however, is that if we apply the highest standards of eccentricity, Gogarty does not qualify. After all, when it comes to the first incident, he was making an entirely logical assessment of the scenario, whilst anyone who has listened to Frances for an extended period of time has also experienced similar emotions.

Some simple souls may believe Jackie Healy-Rae is an eccentric. Jackie, however, is actually a cute hoor and therefore belongs to a far higher caste of the political race.

The ginger FG TD James Bannon has often attracted the eccentric tag. Though he has acquired the indelible nickname of 'Bonkers Bannon', courtesy of the kindness of the *Irish Times* satirist Miriam Lord, Mr Bannon simply does not qualify. He may be an odd soul whose contributions are a source of mirth to even his own, but it is important not to confuse the gobshite with the eccentric.

Surprisingly it is the normally disciplined ranks of FF who provide us with some hope on the eccentricity front. One of the finest modern examples of this particular species is Martin Mansergh. Even before he became a TD this last of the eccentric Mohicans was dogged by tales about the happy occasion when some of the crueller souls within FF convinced the good Doctor that a television remote control was actually a mobile phone. The memories of Mr Mansergh's attempts to use the infernal device over a subsequent week are still cherished by a special few.

Of course, FF's resident intellectual really only came to our attention when he escaped the dusty old retirement club of the Seanad and accidentally ended up experiencing the bright sunlight of the Dáil. Thus was born one of the most astonishing rivalries, for if Mansergh was the perfect aristocrat, his running mate Mattie McGrath was definitely a member of the peasant class. So far the relationship has left poor Mansergh looking like a modern version of the Irish RM.

Though one of his more delightful Dáil performances consisted of a dissertation about sodomy during the Dáil Civil Partnership Bill, a subject we suspect Mattie would not be at all comfortable with, the finest example of Mansergh in full flight is supplied by a wondrous cameo from his role as the living curator of Mr Haughey's legacy.

Writing in 1994 of the furore around the wealth of Haughey, which would ultimately take three Tribunals to resolve, Mansergh noted of those who 'cribbed at his acquisition of wealth' that 'anyone in a position to buy farmland or indeed any property before the 1960s were bound to see it markedly appreciate'. Mansergh added that this could 'happen just as easily to a middle class Labour politician' and slammed the 'deep distrust of the success that was achieved largely by [Haughey's] own efforts as opposed to that achieved with the assistance of the comfortable connections that tend to come with inherited wealth and position'. We're still waiting for the revised version.

Ultimately, the real eccentricity of Mansergh has less to do with his mad professor appearance than his status as an eclectic original thinker who is not afraid to hide his erudition. And the sad feature of Irish politics is that within Leinster House you really don't get too many of those to the pound.

In fairness, Mansergh is not alone, for perhaps the finest eccentric is Éamon Ó Cuív, who has determinedly played on his image as the last heir to de Valera. And though the era of the micromanaged FF conference means the days when earthy men of the soil would take to the stage to shout about the principles of (sic) 'Yevvelera' is over, rather like the lovers of the pre-

Vatican II Church, with its comforting Latin masses and *Ne Temere* decrees, those who believe in the de Valera myth are still legion within the party.

The essence of Dev Óg's political centre is beautifully captured by a vignette in a history of the FF party where he tells the 'lovely true story' about a woman from Maam valley in Galway. On the last time de Valera ran for office the woman told a group of FF activists who arrived for her in a car to go away. Dev Óg noted fondly that when they asked why, she said, 'This is the last time I will ever be able to vote for Eamon de Valera and I am going to do it the hard way.'

As Dev Óg approvingly noted, 'the woman walked the six miles that day to the polling booth and the six miles home as a demonstration of her commitment', it looked like an extraordinary example of political self-obsession.

However, like the political version of Rainman, Dev Óg's Delphic conclusions are sometimes accompanied by accidental moments of genius, for at the conclusion of the odd tale he noted that if FF ever lost the 'unique spirit' that drove this woman they would become just another ordinary party.

Like many of our best eccentrics, young Master de Valera was far more correct than those fans of Bertie who were snickering on the sidelines.

| HALFWAY THERE

Sad tales of the Junior Ministers

The Minister chuckled contentedly as he explained why there is no sadder soul than the disappointed Junior Ministerial candidate.

It always starts, you see, with such hope. The Taoiseach is tapped to give our TD the nod on the basis that poor X has been around for a long time. The plea goes in to at least 'consider him, sure the poor man can't do any harm, he's afraid to get out of the way of his own shadow'.

Of course, 'once the plea is made it swiftly emerges our man is in the frame'. This is the most blissful of times for the aspirant Minister for 'he can dream at night of the opportunity of being driven around, of his new status in the rugby club, the golf club, the Chamber of Commerce'.

The Minister took a contented sip of his pint and continued, 'Suddenly the wife is happy for there are the prospects of trips abroad. The luxury of life in the past is nothing compared with the comfort, the pampering, and the elevated sense of self-importance that waits in the future.'

Then the day arrives, the new suit is unveiled, the call is awaited and there is only silence.

The Minister finished his pint and chuckled, 'That indeed is the sad old day, the dream has died, the sun has not shone for me, my aspirations are no more, the wife is cross, the golf club is snickering and the only way to swallow the bitter pill is to wail about the direct snub to my constituency before disappearing back into the abyss.'

In truth, it is sometimes hard to understand why, outside of assuaging the delicate ego of the long-term back-bench TD, we have Junior Ministers. Bertie may have created so many Junior Ministries, Committee Chairpersonships, Vice Chairmanships and Convenor positions, finding a simple FF backbencher became somewhat like one of those old-fashioned *Irish Press* X the ball competitions.

The Taoiseach defended the apogee of the politics of graft on the grounds that it was necessary for politicians to 'learn their trade'. But seeing as his creation of a record 20 Junior Ministries, and then the hasty abolition of four, scarcely caused a ripple in how we were governed, that claim does not really stack up. Some Junior Ministries are, in fairness, more important than others. Our Chief Whips are not as important as their British equivalents but you do get to sit silently at the Cabinet table and watch your betters with awe-filled eyes. It also helps your promotional chances, for when it comes to Mr Cowen, being elevated appears to be closely related to his capacity to actually know your name.

This is epitomised by the recent experiences of Pat Carey, who for ten long years struggled to even secure a Junior Ministry. It did not, of course, help that he shared a constituency with Noel Ahern, who is so endowed with talent the best of us struggle to single a particular one out.

Pat was also cruelly hampered by the belief of Vincent Browne, much to the puzzlement of just about everyone in Leinster House, that the fate of nice but dim Pat was the greatest injustice Western civilisation had experienced since the Dreyfus affair. It would be at the best of times hard enough to be promoted when you are sharing a constituency with the Taoiseach's brother but Carey's new status as Vincent's 'Orphan Annie' really did put the tin hat on things.

And yet from the moment Tom Kitt's terribly big sulk about the non-recognition of his talents saw Pat being accidentally launched into the Cabinet circle as the new Chief Whip, his rise to full Ministerial status has been meteoric. No one might know what on earth it is that he does but Pat is one of the big lads now. Sometimes, indeed in Irish politics generally all the time, simply being there is enough.

In truth, Pat was also lucky because for the most part the job of being a Junior Minister is an apprenticeship to the land of nowhere. However, in spite of the much-reviled neither fish nor fowl nature of the position, there is always a queue and within the current administration the hapless Sean Haughey is the finest example of the importance of at least being seen to be halfway there.

It may be unfair but the suspicion has always dogged Sean that were he not his father's son he was best qualified for a long career as a junior clerk in the passport office. However, back in 2006, after 20 years of national obscurity Sean began to suffer from the notion that it was now surely time for him to get the half car, if only to prove to the world that he was not an utter dimwit.

Sadly, when the vacancy for the great prize arrived, there was a problem.

After her demotion from his original team in 2002, Mary Wallace threw such a strop there was no way that Bertie was going to suffer that earache again. So it was that Wallace secured the bauble and Sean embarked on his own great sulk.

Such was the whining and whimpering about this non-recognition of Sean's greatness he eventually acquired the nickname of 'An Beal Bocht'. Happily whilst no one outside of our man's cat noticed, all the whinging meant that when the next mini-shuffle arrived, our man got his most cherished wish and was put in charge of the nation's school buses. The Mussolini of the school buses has not been heard about again and that essentially suits everyone but at least honour had been salvaged.

Of course, when it comes to the great puzzle over what it is they actually do, 'An Beal Bocht' is not unique. Nothing epitomises their role as the political equivalent of *domestiques* more than the Junior Minister who acquired the nickname of 'Buns'.

This had nothing to do with his physique but came instead from his senior Minister who, when confronted by some outraged delegation of the agricultural type, developed a policy of appeasement where the delegation was sent off with the Junior Minister to the Dáil canteen for 'tea and buns'.

On another occasion a distinguished but cruel civil servant was heard to note of Fine Gael's Bernard Durkan that 'he's a very handy useless sort of a fellow for posing for photographs opening some welfare centre at a place the Minister can't be bothered going to' whilst the sole purpose of a host of other Ministers appeared to consist of going on to late-night chat shows to be abused over policies they did not have a clue about by a permanently enraged Vincent Browne.

In spite of all these humiliations, the Junior Ministerial post is a cherished thing. After all, in all shades of life even if the bone is small, so long as it's yours it's loved. Of course, if you are there for a long time it can become unsatisfying, for you become aware one of the primary purposes of the Junior Ministry is to take the bad look off mediocrity. It says essentially that whilst you are not as thick as some of your back-bench colleagues, you will never sup with the elite. Instead, you are going to be the eternal version of the teaser, that poor misfortunate animal whose role is to excite the mare before the stallion arrives. In short, for ever and a day you will always be halfways in but never fully there.

Ironically, in spite of all the indignations, the worst thing ultimately about the Junior Ministerial position is the hope. You may know you are there simply because the Taoiseach believes you are possessed with the sort of low colonial cunning where you will cause him some trouble unless he buys you off with a shiny tin medal. But there is always the possibility, as appears to be the case with our current hapless Minister for Agriculture Brendan Smith, that you may be promoted simply because the Taoiseach of the day becomes embarrassed by your eternal half-door status.

Of course, after a couple of decades of pottering around opening village fetes and eating sandwiches with pensioners even the most gormless man can crack and seek some sort of relevance. Sadly there is, however, nothing so poignant as the Junior Minister who feels their talents are being overlooked and heads off to the Taoiseach's office in a strop, for theirs truly is the kingdom of 'don't let the door handle hit you on the arse on the way out'.

One really piteous example of this was the fate of poor Tom Kitt, who had being plying an innocuous trade in a series of high profile Junior Ministries without making any sort of a stir in the world. It all inevitably came to a head when, in the aftermath of Bertie's departure, Brian Cowen told Kitt there was no place for him at BIFFO's high table either. Tom then threw the mother and father of a strop and warned the Taoiseach that unless he got a senior Ministry appropriate to his high intellect and status he would resign his commission.

Tom is now a backbencher and, in truth, were he capable of thinking about things deeply he would admit that he has probably had quite the lucky escape.

Ultimately, the saddest tale of all from the Junior Ministerial ranks is the poor soul who told a colleague that on four occasions he had approached Bertie after being overlooked in a reshuffle and had been assured on each occasion that when the Taoiseach next had his opportunity our man's talents would be considered. Our hero's rueful admission that he was starting to mistrust Mr Ahern went a long way towards explaining why he remained at the level he was.

Chapter 32

GET UNDER THE TABLE, EVERYONE, HERE COMES JOE JACOB WITH THE NATIONAL NUCLEAR SAFETY PLAN

There is no better explanation for the age-old question of why Irish politics fails than the career of Joe Jacob. It may seem harsh to load all of the faults of Irish politics on the shoulders of this harmless essentially unknown political creature who has now departed to his eternal and quite highly paid reward. And during his time in office the rare profiles of Joe all mentioned he was well liked within the party. This is, of course, nice but in Irish politics popularity amongst your colleagues is generally a sign of amiable uselessness.

Nothing epitomised the reality of this particular concept more than two moments in the career of Joe. The first famously occurred on the day Bertie forgot poor Joe's name. This did not prevent Bertie from re-appointing the great unknown from Wicklow back to mediocre office. The problem, of course, was that he put Joe in charge of the apparently critical issue of defending Ireland's shores from nuclear accidents.

It all went reasonably well for a time. Within the safe environs of the Dáil our hero displayed a serious but by no means excessive level of cluelessness about his Ministry. But in fairness, the whole area of nuclear power is a complex one, what with all that fission stuff and the various complicated chain reactions.

Still, no one could disagree with Joe's decision to approach nuclear power with a deep level of suspicion. Joe may not have had a great deal of hands-on experience, but it was clear that he at best thought the nuclear thing should barely be tolerated, and it certainly should not be actively encouraged.

So it was with Joe that when it came to issues such as Mox he would pronounce the word with a level of fearful distaste that suggested he was thinking of a slightly different more personal contagion.

And then Joe got unlucky.

The most important quality a successful Junior Minister should have is a talent for invisibility. In times of danger, like the hare and the hounds the Junior Minister is generally best served if he lies still, flattens his ears and does not move.

Sadly Joe caught a bad old break when the eagle eye of Marian Finucane was drawn to his existence. If Joe were wise, the first response of this harmless idiot savant to her request for an interview would have been to find a thousand urgent appointments that would have made his presence on Marian, much to his great regret, utterly impossible.

The Achilles' heel, however, even of these lowliest of creatures, is their subservience to the ego. Joe decided that when it came to Ireland's nuclear safety plan, he was on top of the job. So it was that, entirely of his own free will, the Minister whose Taoiseach didn't even know his proper name decided he would unveil the immensity of his intellect to a world that had up to this point known nothing about this hapless poor booby.

It was on one level a tad unfair. Few of Joe's other colleagues would have fared any better had a further series of lights been shone beneath the deeper waters of Leinster House. But Joe managed to cram an entire *annus horribilis* into a brief half an hour on 'Marian Finucane', as the sonorous tones only emphasised just how much each sentence was loaded with a complete absence of knowledge.

And as it became palpably clear that Joe had abandoned any level of self-awareness, an enchanted Marian was now aware she had reached the glorious state of having a complete fool at her mercy.

Even as Joe left to be congratulated doubtlessly by unctuous officials, out in the real world the great national swell of indignation had begun. In defence of Joe his disaster did provide the nation with a fortnight of mirth. But if we accept that it is perfectly fine that our Ministers are fit for nothing other than offering us a belly laugh, then we should not be too puzzled that our politicians are set up to fail.

Of course, it should be noted that absolutely no damage was done to Joe's career by his appearance on Marian. In other countries if it is proven that the Minister is an idiot, the PM sacks him. But in Irish politics he just forgets the poor man's name.

Still, it could have been worse.
Bertie might have put Joe in charge of something important.
Oh wait, he actually did.

Chapter 33

ALBERT FAINTING IN THE BUSHES IN BUSWELL'S

It is now hard to imagine that when it came to the first 40 years of Fianna Fáil, the great issue of 'Who leads?' was as definitive as the mosaic tablets of stone. From the 1920s to the 1950s de Valera guided FF like some stately Victorian monument before Lemass, the political son of de Valera, took over for the 1960s. Since then, however, there is something quasi-biblical about the extent of the great art of shafting at the top level of FF.

After 1967 the unofficial record tells us of a party where Lynch shafted Haughey, George Colley and Neil Blaney by 'accidentally' backing into the leader's seat. Haughey and Blaney then deliberately tried to shaft honest Jack in 1973 before the Arms Trial shafted them. Eventually, of course, in 1979 Haughey shafted Lynch and Colley, after Lynch had attempted to shaft Haughey by retiring early in the hope that Colley would shaft Haughey. In so far as the historians record these things, Albert, who had helped Haughey to shaft Lynch, then shafted Haughey (and Bertie) after a series of failed attempts by Dessie O'Malley to shaft Haughey.

Of course, when Bertie was shafted he was not running for the leadership and therefore wasn't really shafted anyway. Still, Bertie then shafted Albert (by accident of course) by not handing him the Duggan file during the Brendan Smyth crisis, where Dick Spring also took a brief hand in affairs, before the son of Albert called Cowen shafted Bertie, but only by acclamation, after Bertie shafted Albert a second time, also, of course, by accident.

Sadly no sooner had Cowen 'the unready' secured the throne than he too discovered that he had been shafted by the legacy that the shafted Bertie had left behind him. And lo there was also great woe and lamentation throughout the land, for the people found they too had been collectively shafted by the obsession FF had with shafting each other, and they now plan to wreak a great shafting upon the ranks of FF the next time they receive their opportunity.

Amidst all of this festschrift of shafting surprisingly only one isolated moment stands out. Back in 1997 when Mary McAleese, who apparently is our President, was elected to prate, pray and parade around the Áras we were still fortunate enough to have not yet seen the face of a dead person. On the day, however, that McAleese was chosen we experienced a premonition of what it must be like.

In the aftermath of the decision at a post-selection press conference there was the usual hullabaloo. The media presence was low, for the result was one of those foregone conclusions that party managers work so hard to secure. You can only therefore imagine our surprise at the absence of one figure at the top table. The McAleese woman was there smiling and nodding like Churchill the dog in the insurance ad and Bertie was there, but why had the candidate gone missing? And then like a summer mistral the whispers began to be whipped up. Albert was not there because the choice was not Albert.

Though the skies had darkened a little Reynolds had been the warmest of favourites. It was, after all, hardly propitious for la McAleese that the man who had been squiring her around was the less than beloved Dick Roche. But shockingly it was Albert who would have to play the role of the defeated ghost at the feast of the victorious.

Less than three years before he was an international statesman who had put the bridle on a British PM. Up to an hour before he had still been the hot favourite to lead FF to another humiliating Presidential defeat but in Buswell's no one noticed the stooped figure who looked as though he was at the point of fainting.

In truth, our approach was more informed by concern that there might be a death at the conference than any real curiosity. But there, half swaying beside a large bush in the foyer, was the former Taoiseach Albert Reynolds. It was a shocking sight, for as he undulated his eyes were glassy and the mouth was fixed in a weird rictus grin. Ultimately, though, the starkest feature of Reynolds was the pallor of the skin. Its half-grey half-pale luminous colour was something one would expect to see stretched across the bones of a dead man.

On one level it was difficult to understand why Albert was so shocked, for the great ongoing exorcism of the Haughey era meant he was a candidate who simply could not be elected. The outside world in Europe and America saw Albert in the guise of an honoured peacemaker but the new Tiger was frantic to shed the old skins of the perceived 'Country and Western gombeen' days that Albert so visibly represented.

Even FF knew Albert as a Presidential candidate was simply a Pee Flynn waiting to happen, for the *Irish Times*—so much the paper of record in these unimportant things—would simply not allow an Albert to ruin the Park for everyone else.

But still the ruthless brio with which a party whose central principle is supposed to be loyalty, but which actually is self-interest, despatched Mr Reynolds was fascinating. Albert, it has to be said, had little reason to cry foul, for at the end of the great age of Haughey the exalted ones from the old regime had pleaded with Reynolds to let their man go with dignity. Instead, Reynolds had moved in with the hunger of a dancehall owner heading for the night's cash-box takings. Then, when the possibility emerged that his succession might be threatened by a young ward boss, 'supporters' of Albert had mysteriously appeared to cast poison into the ears of the voters about the location of the pillow where the aspirant Taoiseach lay his gentle head at night.

In the aftermath of these concerns there had been a congenial meeting between Bertie and Albert after which Ahern spent the next decade muttering about all he had ever wanted to do was 'get me Budget' through. Others believe that, like the infamous Bruton–Spring meeting after the 1992 election, Albert called his rival in and coldly laid out the facts of life at the top end of the power game in a manner that told Bertie if he wanted to do 'me Budget' he would have to either back or behead Albert.

This had then been followed by the day of drama—the great St Albert's Day massacre—where, like Agincourt, the flower of the FF Haugheyite aristocracy were called into the new Taoiseach's office and despatched with the same pragmatic efficiency the English long-bow men showed to the French aristocrats.

First was Gerry Collins, who had issued the simpering plea to Albert to not bust up the party. Then Rambo Burke, the grandiloquent corrupt Minister for Justice, Bullying and Buffoonery, departed snarling into that dark night. Dermot Ahern issued a plea for quarter and was simply told he had backed the wrong horse. John 'the Bull' O'Donoghue was equally despatched for similar sins. Mary O'Rourke memorably recalled that such was the disinterest Albert had in her fate she was dismissed whilst the new Taoiseach was eating a sandwich.

Of the old Haugheyite regime only Bertie survived Albert's belief that he would be the master in his own house. Of course, it was to be a different world when Bertie was the master in what had been Albert's house and the surprising aspect of Albert falling into the bushes in Buswell's was that he had ever thought, after all his experiences, that it would be any different.

Of course, like that famous meeting between Bertie and Albert before Reynolds secured the crown, Mr Ahern refused to admit Albert had been politically poisoned. But though all we had was circumstantial evidence, Albert already knew all too well that no one fishes with a longer line than the Drumcondra ward boss.

It will be of little consolation to Reynolds but even the most successful ones see the two days of it in Irish politics. His predecessor might have talked about tending to his roses but, even before the Tribunals raised ancient toxins, every day for Haughey after his departure from power must have seemed like a preparation for death. Albert back then would have had scant time to worry himself about the fundamental truth of politics. But as he stood shivering by the bush in Buswell's, even he finally realised no 'Slasher', no matter how cunning, escapes unscathed from the great FF power game.

SECTION 6

Cute hoors

Chapter 34

THE POLITICS OF BEING GOVERNED ON THE BACK OF AN ENVELOPE

There is a story told that once at an EU Council of Finance Ministers meeting the newly appointed Nicolas Sarkozy asked who that odd burly silent fellow is over there that looks as though he's sleeping the whole time. The official beamed enthusiastically and said, 'That is Mr Cowen, the Finance Minister of the fastest growing economy in Europe, who has just brought in a record Budget surplus.' As Mr Sarkozy shook his head at the futility of first impressions, you can only say they were different times.

Sadly, as we return to a more normal state of affairs, we have discovered that the warped era where a politician could spend his time as a Minister in the political hammock has had other consequences. In particular, the great Celtic Tiger party meant our politicians have lost the critical capacity to make the best of a bad hand. In the past, given the perennial bankruptcy of the state, this quality was a necessity rather than a virtue. But the soft life and the soft praise they enjoyed for so long means our elite can now respond to crises only with petulance rather than art.

The erasure of this capacity means that the government has been affected more than it thought it would be by the loss of Seamus Brennan. The finest display of the art of Seamus occurred when he was being harassed on 'Prime Time' over the curious set of circumstances whereby the great plan for three interconnected LUAS lines that would cost €250 million turned into two non-connected LUAS lines that cost a billion. At that point others would have begun to snarl and bluster. Instead, Seamus looked humbly across at Miriam O'Callaghan and admitted the wonderful plan for LUAS had been 'a bit of a back of the envelope job, really'.

Astonishingly the Minister's moment of honesty totally defused the crisis.

It was as though we were so shocked by a truthful politician we had no public school of discourse to turn to. Instead, Seamus scampered off scot free as the country simply fell about the place laughing at the élan of the admission.

It did help that we were living in that wonderful time where losing the odd billion here or there might have been embarrassing but not terminal. However, even as his colleagues chuckled about how 'that's Seamus for you', they failed to realise the admission was a classic example of the political astuteness of Brennan. Unlike so many of his colleagues, the much-missed Minister was wise enough to realise that sometimes the best thing to do when caught is to play the hapless poor idiot. And that is particularly the case when you actually have behaved like that idiot.

It was, of course, that strange honesty that meant Seamus was looked down on by figures such as Brian Cowen, who is far more enthusiastic about the back of the hand 'it's sorted, take it or leave it' approach to public controversies. Poor BIFFO is, however, learning slowly that whatever about the Boom, the humility of a Brennan is far more appropriate for our current circumstances.

It is likely recession memories went a long way towards informing the style of Brennan. He remembered enough of previous hard times to be in a state of relative shock about his uniquely fortuitous circumstances. Past experience meant Brennan also had a residual suspicion about the transience of the Tiger. This meant that unlike his Tory Boy FF colleagues, Brennan was also wise enough to realise a bit of humility now might serve one well in the future.

And perhaps he knew more about the capacities of his colleagues than he let on. Brennan was, after all, a creature of the age of real meat-eating political animals such as Haughey, O'Malley, MacSharry, Albert, Maire Geoghegan Quinn, Liam Lawlor, Charlie McCreevy, Rambo Burke and Bertie. Now we know some of them may have been corrupt and this, of course, was a terrible thing but they were tough, able politicians. In contrast, Brennan must sometimes have looked at the current crew trotting around like bin men who have won the lottery and wondered just how many of these lads were seven-bob notes.

LUAS was not the only display of the art of Seamus. After the election of 1997 his ongoing absence from a Cabinet containing such giants as Micheál Martin cut him to the core. And when Brennan was overlooked in a subsequent reshuffle, others might have thrown a strop and stormed into the Taoiseach's office.

However, when the Opposition teased Brennan over his retention in the post of Chief Whip and general assistant to Jackie Healy-Rae, and Bertie slyly muttered that 'Seamus is too valuable in his current job to be moved', Brennan's response was a master-class in the politics of making the best of a bad hand. As Brennan rolled his eyes, shrugged his shoulders and held out his hands in a poignant gesture of resignation crossed with supplication, the House could only laugh. They were, however, laughing with Seamus and against Bertie and, unsurprisingly given the refinement of Mr Ahern's political nose, within a year Seamus got his promotion.

In retrospect, Seamus may have been trying to tell us, or maybe even himself and his colleagues, something via the admission that LUAS was put together on the back of an envelope. Of course, we know our grandchildren will one day respond to the echo of our laughter by saying we should have responded differently, but it's hard to swim against the forces of gravity. And LUAS was in no way unique, for during the Boom the entire country was really governed by the politics of the back of the envelope.

But, of course, that was all right because our government were the special ones of Europe. Like the dog driving the car, they didn't quite know how they were doing it but if everyone tells Rover he's doing a great job on the boreen then he is going to take his chances on the motorway.

The problem was that at the end, instead of being servants of the people, our leaders turned the country into their plaything. Like some mad aristocrat who litters his estate with follies, Ireland suddenly became one giant experiment. As our politicians took the fatally unwise decision to trust their own genius, a great list of disasters from decentralisation, which resembled a series of drunken doodles on a beer mat, electronic voting and the HSE were applauded at birth and binned at leisure.

The surprising thing is that all these disasters were actually sustainable, for our cataclysm only began when the banking classes replicated the stupidity of our politicians and nobody shouted stop.

Well, no one except for one man. Sadly, as we stand in a stunned disbelieving state around the smouldering ashes of the bonfire of the Celtic Tiger vanities, Seamus Brennan's wide-eyed admission that we were being governed on the back of that infamous envelope means no one can say we weren't warned.

Chapter 35

THE GREAT ART OF
HIDING IN FULL VIEW

One of the most critical political skills has always been the art of lying successfully. Sadly the unique problem Irish politicians face is that the understandable determination of our cynical electorate to believe absolutely nothing they say means this is no easy task. Indeed, some cynics would argue the best way to deceive the voters would be to speak the truth but that would be far too radical.

In one sense it is a bit harsh to criticise our politicians over their little deceits for society always gets along a whole lot better if our politicians have some expertise in the art of cultivating gentle fictions. These, after all, are only what the Church used to call a white lie and that was the most venial of sins.

Good politicians know that, like film makers or novelists, they are the inventors of myths. They are chameleons who, if they are to succeed, must adopt various exteriors such as the strong man, the populist, the John the Baptist or the caring reformer. And, alas, politicians must also fib, for if the truth of how we are governed were to be revealed most civic-minded people would be quite upset. It would not do to admit all taxation is taken at the point of a gun, or that our system of governance is designed to facilitate the interests of the mandarin class rather than the people, for whilst the impulses of Saturday shopping mean there will never be blood on our streets everyone would be terribly cross.

However, though these difficulties are found in all societies, when it comes to Irish politics we have elevated the crucial art of lying to a new level of baroque greatness. This trait may be informed by our Catholic heritage for, unlike our plain-speaking Presbyterian cousins who do not lie enough for their own good, Ireland's colonial past means we have a naturally elliptical relationship with the truth.

Anyone who has seen a Tribunal witness solemnly promise to tell the truth knows that, whilst our churchmen only recently unveiled the doctrine of mental reservation in order to take the edge off clerical collusion in the rape of mostly working class children, it has always been a popular practice amongst our unconvicted white collar criminals.

Of course, it would be great fun if our politicians were ever surreptitiously administered with a collective truth drug. Were the new improved loyal Fine Gael front bench asked about Enda's capacity to be the Taoiseach, they would wail about how 'the guy is terrible but we got stuck with him after the election and we haven't got the bottle to take him out'. They might even, if an excessive dose of the truth drug were administered, admit that 'only a fool would want to be in charge now, we'd prefer to keep the other lot in and wait until the economy takes off'.

Of course, the views of Fianna Fáil TDs, be they true or not, about the current incumbents' 'social habits' would be far more interesting than the press releases they now serve up attacking the Opposition for their failure to reform FF. However, our spirits would be swiftly lowered again by the answers of 'I haven't a clue. The civil servants run things here' that we would receive if we asked any of our Ministers for their honest views about the goings-on in their Departments.

The truth of things anyway is that people soon tire of the truthful life. If we were like the logical horses in *Gulliver's Travels* we might get used to it but human nature is not easily transformed. And we should remember that when Gulliver returned and tried to spread the philosophy of the Houyhnhnms, his neighbours thought he was mad.

The endemic dislike amongst humanity of too much truth goes a long way towards explaining why FF has been in power for 62 of the last 78 years, for no other Irish party has come close to mastering their facility at the great art of hiding in full view.

Most politicians, you see, manage to look slightly embarrassed when they are deceiving the people. Some would even say it is their most charming trait. However, the essence of the FF tactic was that if you lie without essaying the slightest of blushes, unlike our British neighbours, we are far too polite to confront a politician or banker or barrister and simply say 'You are not telling the truth now, please desist or I shall call a policeman.'

The critical art of hiding in full view was a creation of the Haughey era where necessity meant that the then Taoiseach had to lie about every aspect of his dishonourable life and times. Outside of Haughey, one of the better exponents of this art was Liam Lawlor. Though he had much practice in this regard, before it began Mr Lawlor's finest hours occurred in the Flood Tribunal. One of the few things that could with certainty be said in that wretched place was that when Liam claimed, 'I'm trying to help, his honour' this would be followed by a long-winded farrago about anything, from the fate of Copernicus to the nature of life or the fall of communism, rather than anything that might possibly be of use to the poor addled judge.

Ultimately, though, there was no better man to play the guerrilla tactic of hiding in full view than 'the Bert'. The reason for this was that, like George Washington, the former Taoiseach never told an actual lie. Even during his cross-examination at Mahon, though Ahern was often at bay, at no point was his great enemy Des O'Neill able to engage in a reprise of that fabulous moment when Charlie Haughey's imperial pretensions of five decades crumbled under the simple question 'Is that not a lie, Mr Haughey?'

Instead, like the Italian soccer tactic of *catenaccio*, Ahern buried his inconvenient truths under a monstrous concoction of malapropisms, disconnected facts and a preference for mumbling as distinct to speaking clearly. It was as effective as the old Roman tortoise defence, for after a decade of trying to understand the densely layered circumlocutions it was easier to give him the fool's pardon of 'if he said it was dry you'd bring an umbrella but sure that's Bertie for you!'

Mr Ahern used other tactics as well. He was, for example, a great enthusiast for the practice of defending decisions on the basis of 'legal advice'. This, of course, was informed by the rather simple fact that lawyers are like taxis. Once you tell them where you want to go, the average amoral lawyer will—quite correctly, we add—give you the 'legal advice' you want. Another variant of this false legal theology was the promise to set up a well-resourced independent tribunal that would swiftly (you there, in the Four Courts, stop cheering) establish the facts. Once that claim was made, you could be sure the fix was in.

Of course, even Mr Ahern was not perfect for he suffered from certain little verbal tics such as 'all as I is saying', which immediately indicated that he was in trouble. And after a time we learned that there was nothing accidental about the malapropisms of Bertie, for whilst in domestic politics he cherished his image of being a guileless bumbling idiot those who went abroad noticed that on foreign soil he was a clear, intelligent, concise speaker.

In fairness to Mr Ahern, it should be noted that after the great fall we are experiencing lots more transparency and no one appears to be at all happy about that either. Mind you, we are sure if he could have his way, Mr Cowen would retain the core philosophy of the *ancien régime*, but the hole in the national bucket is so big no amount of cover-ups could hide it.

Sadly when it comes to the fine art of hiding in full view, FF are no longer unique. FG has now developed such a facility they can now say with a straight face that Enda Kenny is the solution to the greatest crisis Ireland has experienced since the civil war. There indeed, my friends, is confidence for you.

And there is a new left-wing contender who may even be better, for even as stern a critic as John O'Donoghue was moved to note of the elusive skills of Eamon Gilmore that he was 'like a gadfly around the tail of an old cow. He circles, one does not hear him, sometimes he might land but ... in the final analysis one will never quite know what he is up to, where he is going or how he will get there.'

Now, who does that remind us of!

Chapter 36

THE COUNTY COUNCILLOR AND THE SENATOR SHALL BE FRIENDS

It was late at night, or to be more accurate it was early in the morning, and David Norris was in the company of the then Fianna Fáil councillor Peter Kelly. Earlier that evening Norris had given a talk in Longford. When the refreshments stage of the evening began, things had been a little 'polite' but as the night wore on FF showed that, as with many other things, whilst they might be opposed to homosexuality in theory, in practice, once they met one, they had no problems at all.

Indeed, by the close, relations were so warm that Kelly offered Norris a lift back to the hotel in his undertaker's hearse. As they drove at a pace that was not much swifter than the walking speed of a pensioner, Norris began to get quite nervous. The problem, he remarked, some three decades later, wasn't that 'Peter was driving with one eye shut or that he would turn regularly and wink at me.' Instead, the main concern was that 'every time Peter winked he would close the eye that was open'.

The councillor is a strange creature indeed and some curiosities survive even in these pragmatic times. It is rare for Vincent Browne to be flabbergasted but on one of the rare occasions this occurred the man who silenced Browne was a mere county councillor rather than one of our distinguished Ministers. It happened when Browne condescendingly asked Michael Healy-Rae (yes, he's the son of the other fellow) who was the most influential woman in Irish politics. All the rest of the panel had thrown in the usual worthless worthy crew of Robinsons but Healy-Rae's response of 'Denise Marie Wojcik' left Browne flustering for five agonising minutes before Healy-Rae put Vincent out of his misery. Healy-Rae had chosen the escort who had been found with Ben Dunne on that strange night that would lead to the respective falls of Haughey, Lowry and Bertie.

It was another example of why you should underestimate the councillor at your peril. Mind you, we should not be too surprised when the odd one stands out, for we certainly have enough of them. They might not have the power to erect even a traffic cone but Ireland currently has five city councils, 29 county councils and 80 town councils. And the 883 county councillors and 774 town councillors is not the end of it either for outside of the 1,657 councillors the grand little country is lucky enough to have the benefit of there is also, of course, the 60 Senators, the 166 TDs plus the 12 MEPs and the President.

That brings the number of our elected representatives up to 1,896 and we are sure if you factor in a couple of regional quangos the total number of dependents upon the charity of the taxpayer is well past the 2,000 mark. It is odd that a country that has tried to destroy the power of the poor local councillor in such a dedicated fashion has so many of them. But what is perhaps even more curious is that we know and hear so little about the activities of the largest grouping of elected representatives.

They do occasionally come to our attention over their expenses, or when they engage in some outrage, such as comparing the local Travelling population with pedigree greyhounds sunning themselves on the porch. Outside of this it does appear to be the case that the main function of the councillor is to entertain us with their stupidity. And in fairness, this is no small task, for a demoralised people need to experience feelings of intellectual and moral superiority on a regular basis and our councillors do a fine job in that regard.

The template for the perception of the county councillor was originally set by the infamous denizens of Ballymagash Town Council. In more modern times the public profile of the councillor was defined by the somewhat unhappy peregrinations of Michael 'stroke' Fahy through the courts system.

In truth, the national stereotype of the councillor is an elderly corpulent man in a flat cap who races greyhounds, dreams in his bachelor bed of shooting Travellers at night and who sorts out the odd bit of planning in the hope that it will finish off the environment for once and for all.

Before every councillor complains, we are sure there are many who do arduous long hours in the community. Sadly, well, for our councillors at least, we prefer to hear about the exploits of fellows like Desperate Dan Kiely from Kerry, who once ended up in trouble with the law after an unfortunate series of events involving Desperate Dan staggering out of a bar, looking for 'blueshirts' to have an, er, political discussion with.

In spite of the exploits of characters like Desperate Dan, there is one thing that our councillors are no fools about. They may practise the politics of

Ballymagash when it comes to national affairs, but when it comes to their re-election our councillors would make Talleyrand look like an ingénue.

The native cunning of the species was personified by one wise soul who, when playing against the stiffest of breezes, devised an audacious tactic for dealing with the unrelenting hostility towards FF. After cautiously approaching the house, if the door was opened by an enraged-looking voter, our hero informed them he was soliciting help for the local tidy towns committee, and backed away gently before the shouting started. Only if he thought there was a possibility of securing a vote did our man openly state his intent. We should not perhaps be all that surprised that he kept his council seat whilst hundreds of others were losing theirs.

Most of us would wonder why he wanted to be re-elected at all, for the task of being a county councillor is not an easy one. The ambitious ones are viewed with utter suspicion by TDs, for the cross-party consensus is that there is nothing worse than having an 'ambitious curate in your own parish'. And if that is not bad enough, the poor councillor is equally detested by the new nobility of the unelected county manager and his directors of services.

Their purpose is uncertain, for the good ones desire only to leave as swiftly as possible, and the rest desire only to stay in a job where they control no budgets, make no real decisions and get all of the blame for anything that goes wrong. The strange quasi-cruel world of the councillor was encapsulated by the curious experience of Richard Humphreys. The Labour councillor, who was a former advisor to Ministers and a constitutional expert of the highest order, accidentally found himself being elected to a South County Dublin council.

Once there, one of his first tasks was to lead a campaign to place netting at the boundary of Foxrock golf course to ensure that stray golf balls wouldn't damage the residents' garden trellises and sweet peas. It's as well George Lee didn't start at the bottom rung of politics. Richard, in contrast, went to some pains to note he was delighted 'to be of service' on the golf balls front.

Of course, the humble councillor still enjoys the occasional triumph. Recently, when one of the species was attempting to secure 'a result for a deserving case'—and in rural Ireland is there any other type of planning issue?—the dreaded county manager curtly informed him there was no chance the request could be granted.

That in itself was manageable but our councillor noted that the manager 'had sat there like a little round bishop' and delivered a lecture about the asinine nature of the request and the terrible waste of time it had represented in his very busy day.

A week later the councillor entered the office metaphorically tipping his cap and informed the manager as 'a matter of courtesy' he would be tabling a motion inquiring into current rates of expenditure on gold credit card spending for all county managers. The planning permission was swiftly passed and a far happier template has been set for all future 'deserving cases'.

There is one being to whom the councillor is the sweetest and most fragrant of brides. Indeed, our Senators have a special phrase for those trusted voters who are known as 'special friends'. Sadly, as in other forms of life, 'special friends' do come at a cost. Nothing epitomised this more than the apocryphal story told of a national figure, who, on an ill-starred attempt to get into the Seanad, was canvassing a councillor whilst clothed in a lovely new coat. The councillor had little interest in our man's vision of the spirit of the nation. Instead, he spent the evening sighing about the lovely nature of the coat, until our naïve idealist departed sans coat and probably without the vote too.

Of course, all this has changed now. But mind you, if you do trot into the Dáil bar on a discreet Wednesday afternoon you will often see large groups of councillors being royally entertained by Senators. And oddly enough, as the rounds fly in, the councillors are never seen putting their hands in their pockets.

Chapter 37 ∾

JACKIE HEALY-RAE
CARRIES A BIG STICK

There is, within Leinster House, no better example of the old rural adage about how a wise man should be out and about early at least once in his life than Jackie Healy-Rae. Jackie, of course, also knows that if you are out and about you must be seen by the neighbours, for once you get a reputation for getting up early in the morning you can sleep till noon for the rest of your life.

It should be said that in spite of his current high profile, Mr Healy-Rae was not an overnight success. Instead, when he first ran for the Dáil, though Jackie's age was shrouded in mystery, his status as a child from the Neil Blaney era suggested our man was headed for the high sixties. The oppression of the new cult of youth meant that was bad enough. But if you were being cruel it could have been argued the owner of a pub that still has that anachronism known as 'the singing lounge' looked and sounded more like a stock character in *The Quiet Man* than the new virile, ruthless, single-chinned candidates Fianna Fáil were looking for.

Our Jackie might have been a 'friend' of Bertie but the whole cloth-capped, turf-burning, eccentric D'Unbelievable appearance was just too out of date. Head office sifted, weighed and decided there was no reason in God's green earth that Healy-Rae would get more than the flea's ear of a couple of thousand votes from the people.

Bertie, of course, told Jackie he was fine and then disappeared as the clever men from central office sent Jackie the fool's pardon of having been 'a great servant of the party' whose only entitlement was, like all great servants, to be used up and spat out. What, of course, added salt to the wound was that Healy-Rae's main opponent for the seat was some nonentity from the FF O'Leary Kerry dynasty. The latest addition was as lively as a duck slumbering by a summertime pond in St Stephen's Green. But such colourless creatures have been winning seats and slipping around unnoticed in the murky depths of Leinster House for eight decades now without being of use or causing damage to anyone.

As we know, for once absolutely nothing went to plan for Bertie, who could only watch as Healy-Rae romped home and arrived up to Dublin followed by a series of colourful tales about his campaigning days. Some might even be true. One of the more typical ones involved the time when the Healy-Rae lorries were busy tarring the road and the archetypal little old lady asked if there was any chance they might drop 'a little biteen of tar' from the road up to the front door of the house.

The ever-courteous Jackie immediately said such a minor task would not be a bother at all. However, the old dear being of Kerry stock was not going to miss out on the main chance now that a half chance had arrived, and quickly asked our man if he could be spreading another small little bit of it around the side of the house too. That was no problem either but our man's patience began to fray when the lady of the house said, 'Oh and whilst you're at it, Jackie, I have a little biteen of a hen house out the back and it would be lovely if …'

To forestall any further raids on his tar supplies, for it was a long rambling homestead, the formidable candidate bellowed, 'Madame, if I get elected you will be up to your arse in tar.' In a real sense he was true to his word, for if the Healy-Rae machine is to be believed Kerry has been up to its collective arse in tar since Jackie was elected. And, of course, Mr Healy-Rae did not do too badly out of it either.

There was, it must be said, a serious purpose behind these tales. One of the most important political arts is the creation of myths, for they capture the attention of the public and define the persona of our politician for good or ill. And it must be said that Jackie garnered more myths than most. We were at different times told that the services of one Junior Minister alone were needed to ensure our man was ferried to the train on time every Thursday and that the main job of the late Seamus Brennan during his time as Whip was to ensure the interests of Jackie were taken care of. Apparently after that the full Ministry was a doddle.

The intellectuals and the stenographers were equally anxious to note that, like the widow, the only thing Jackie has secured for the constituency is the 'little biteen of tar'. Inevitably they, and the Opposition, claimed the grants and harbours would have arrived even if Jackie wasn't there. But the wise country voters know there is no harm in having your own fox in the hen house.

Ultimately the most paradoxical aspect of Jackie Healy-Rae's unique time in politics is his utter failure to live up to the ongoing high-minded concern that his political career would see the Dáil being debased by regular outbreaks of the politics of 'Killinascully'.

Instead, nothing became the parliamentary career of our hero less than the arrival of Jackie, who came through the Dáil gates accompanied by more scantily clad models than an American rap star. This was followed by a thundering debut speech where Healy-Rae colourfully warned the grinning government Deputies that his vote could not be relied on. Then, just as the nation's political sketch-writers happily settled down for five years of *Irish RM* style comedy, where the Prodigal Son who was discarded by Ahern would regularly bait the Taoiseach, Mr Healy-Rae disappeared.

There have been occasional rumours of a vicious turf war between Healy-Rae and a snorting argumentative 'Bull' O'Donoghue but, outside of the early morning when he can be seen consuming a substantial cooked breakfast accompanied by a nutritious bowl of porridge, he has been more invisible than Lord Lucan.

That is not to say that Mr Healy-Rae does nothing. Instead, in a measure of how things really operate in Irish politics, Jackie does all of his important talking in the corridors. The outside world may believe our hero is rampaging his way through the Dáil chamber making colourful speeches, playing the fiddle in the Dáil bar and hugging models wearing 'Kiss me quick I'm from Kerry' caps, but he is as discreet a presence in the Dáil as a bishop's secretary.

In one famous year he spoke once in the chamber and asked a grand total of four parliamentary questions. But of course, whilst such results might upset Fintan O'Toole, the reality of things is that Mr Healy-Rae does not need to send queries to civil servants when he can talk directly to Ministers.

The irony of Jackie Healy-Rae's political career is that the wrong myths have been attached to him, for Mr Healy-Rae is not just the finest example of the importance of getting a reputation for getting up early in the morning. He is also living proof of the very different political theory that the best way to get on in public life is to speak softly and carry a big stick.

There are some who say the ongoing existence of Jackie as an Independent TD debases politics. It could be said that when it comes to that issue, there is a long queue ahead of our Jackie. And at least during his time in politics the torment Mr Healy-Rae has inflicted on a variety of Ministers who are less well known to the public than Jackie's hairstyle has added to the gaiety of the nation. It is more than most have achieved.

Mind you, he must sometimes chuckle at the great irony where, if FF had given their great old warrior the green light, Healy-Rae would probably have garnered a respectable 4,000 votes and elected the man from the dynasty to the Dáil.

Now whatever happened to him?

Oh yes, in the last local elections he lost his Killarney Town Council seat.

Chapter 38

PHIL HOGAN FINALLY LEARNS THE GREAT ART OF CUTE-HOORDOM

The night we saw Fine Gael's Phil Hogan being gazed at in apparent rapture by *Irish Times* Ethicist in Chief Elaine Byrne, it came as quite a shock to us all. In fairness, Phil was on TV3 outlining the basis of Fine Gael's plans to institute the most dramatic reform of the Irish political system since the 1930s. But it was still hard to acclimatise ourselves to the halo of morality that was gathering like an aurora borealis around the man known in Leinster House as Cute Oul' Phil. And that was not the end of the shocks either, for Vincent Browne, the greatest contrarian of all, was also in a similar awestruck mode.

Before you ask, the reason for our surprise over the love of the ethicists was that if there is one prize Phil Hogan dreams of it is to acquire the hallowed status of being a 'cute hoor'. Our ethicists will, of course, say it is a measure of the debased state of Irish politics that one would actually want the laying on of the hands of cute-hoordom. But rather like one of those Amazonian tribes, the ways of Leinster House are different and within its walls the 'cute hoor' is a highly respected creature.

The respect that is given to our 'cute hoors' is increased by the difficulty surrounding the acquisition of such a status. Like ordination, where the descent of the spirit is invisible, becoming a 'cute hoor' is a complex affair. Many, of course, try but as with greatness cute-hoordom is more often than not thrust upon individuals whilst those who seek the prize most frenetically spook their quarry.

Unsurprisingly, the species is somewhat rare in FG, for the blueshirts are generally too posh to be indulging in this cute-hoordom. Unlike their tribal brothers in FF, the big farmers and small-town barristers of the blueshirts prefer to be seen as statesmen-in-waiting. And, in truth, FF are more than happy to agree with their view that minor issues such as circumventing the planning laws or quashing fines for pollution are best left to FF whilst our men prate away about the state of the country on 'Pat Kenny' and 'Prime Time'.

The one exception to all this is Phil, who has been loping around for two decades grinning like the dog that has managed to purloin a pound of sausages from the butcher without being apprehended. Some would use the phrase 'busy doing nothing' to describe Phil's 'cute hoor' activities of nuzzling, conspiring, planning and scheming but one supposes it at least passes the time.

Sadly the great problem for Hogan is that by being so open about the absence of any core belief he is not being a 'cute hoor' at all. Others may know that 'the great game'—or at least what passes for great here—is what it's all about, but they manage to disguise their avaricious streak with some modicum of pretend idealism.

But when it comes to Hogan, once he acquired the 'Cute Oul' Phil' moniker it was like belling the cat. Now all of his schemes are uncovered and he can fool no one, for all of his acts are deemed guilty of being informed by malice aforethought. Even where Phil has a serious point, and he is not an unoriginal politician, it is utterly compromised by his status as the bad girl in town.

There are other reasons to suspect Cute Oul' Phil is not half as cute as he appears to think he is. Generally unless a dead girl or a live boy is found in your bed, or you're Ivor Callely, it is quite difficult for a Junior Minister to be seen, let alone sacked. Phil, however, was in the job for just three months before he resigned over the accidental leaking of some aspects of the Rainbow's first precious Budget from his office by fax. Had Cute Oul' Phil known then what he now knows about what Ministers can get away with, we suspect it might have been a tad more difficult to dislodge our hero. But instead Phil the Innocent walked the plank with scarcely a prod. John Bruton thanked Cute Oul' Phil for his nobility of character and within a week everyone except Phil had forgotten about his great sacrifice. That, we suspect, was a lesson not easily forgotten.

Hogan began the long climb back to the centre of things after Enda fell into the FG leadership with all the élan of an insurance fraudster leaping down a manhole. But though he became his leader's designated enforcer, Cute Oul' Phil learned the hard way that leaders always deny those who abase themselves most totally in their interests.

Enda Kenny may have cost his party the glittering prize after the debacle of the Bertie debate, but the failure of Hogan to disguise the alleged shafting of his running mate in the Carlow Kilkenny constituency provided Enda with the perfect scapegoat.

In the post-electoral debate Enda noted he would have put €10,000 on FG winning two seats in Carlow Kilkenny and then promptly sacked Phil from his role as the party's chief electoral strategist. Afterwards an awestruck political neophyte murmured, ''Twas unbelievable it was the ten grand kick in the hole.'

Still, his appearance on TV3 did suggest that after a modest two decades in the Dáil village Phil may yet be getting the hang of this 'cute hoor' game. Some innocents may believe Phil is really about to drive a bout of political reform that might transform our dusty old political system. Happily there's no need to worry. Even before Cute Oul' Phil persuaded all those Senators whom Enda Kenny is planning to abolish to vote for Enda (one wonders how he did that), should FG and Labour return to power we would have suspected that Seanad reform would prove to be terribly difficult.

Indeed it would be such a complex issue any reformist government would have to set up an All Party Constitutional Committee. Such a Committee would have to hold an elaborate series of hearings, involving much public consultation with a vast range of advocacy and civic groups, no matter how small. They would then, on the basis of the elaborate public consultation process, have to reach an all-party agreement on a document for the abolition of the Seanad.

That would merely be a good start, for obviously the government would have to set up a second Expert Group to consider the consequences of the first Expert Report. A Junior Minister, for such a figure would most accurately reflect the status of the proposal, would have to be chosen to devise a Green Paper.

This, when completed, would be referred back to the All Party Committee, which would refer its response back to the Junior Minister, who would then on the basis of the response devise a White Paper, which would be referred to the All Party Committee.

The Committee would consider, consult and refer their response to the Junior Minister, who would then refer the White Paper to the Law Reform Commission for legal proofing. After that the Junior Minister would then refer any proposed referendum text to the Attorney General, who would then revert to the Junior Minister, who would then present the legally amended text to the Cabinet for discussion.

Of course, Seanad reform would have to take its place in the queue of pressing issues for Cabinet consideration after which, as a gesture of respect to the democratic process, any referendum text would be referred back to the All Party Committee.

On securing All Party Agreement on the final revised draft text, the heads of a Dáil bill would have to be drafted. Of course, the bill would have to initially take its place in the legislative queue and on being drafted there would have to be an extended five-stage debate in the House and we reckon a decade might see us through to the end of the process. As for the list system and gender quotas for women ... well, that would have to wait until we resolve the issue of Seanad reform first.

It would be terrible to think that should Cute Oul' Phil ever actually get into power, Elaine and Vincent will learn the hard way that ethics really is the last refuge of the villain. But should it actually happen, Cute Oul' Phil will finally have lived up to his nickname, for FF learned a long time ago that in Irish politics the swiftest way to become a successful 'cute hoor' is to pretend you are an idealist.

Chapter 39

OUR POLITICIANS WOULD SELL THEIR SOUL FOR A PHOTO-OPPORTUNITY ... IF THEY HAD ONE

Nothing epitomised the power of the camera in Irish politics more than a recent quiet Friday afternoon in Leinster House. Two politicians are sighing about how nothing much happened in the week apart from the addition of an extra €4 billion to the national debt over some small banking thing. Outside a group of disinterested old dears are taking photographs when a dusty-looking Bertie Ahern shambles out the door. Suddenly all is 'changed, changed utterly' as the women coo, the cameras are raised and, even though it is only old ones, it is as though a new Bertie appears. In a miracle of reinvention that mirrors the rebirth of the Phoenix, the expanding tummy—for there can be no doubt that Bertie has let himself 'go' since losing office—is tucked in. There's a blizzard of 'howareye ladies the hardy women working hard' great activity, and many photographs. Thanks to the wonderful camera, everyone and particularly Mr Ahern, has a purpose in life.

Of course, not everyone's attitude to the camera is the same. Some Amazon tribes are thought to be terrified of photographs because of the belief that they rob the soul of the subject. It goes without saying that our politicians have a slightly more promiscuous attitude and it is not, contrary to the cruel commentary of some, because they do not have a soul to lose. Instead, the real truth is that our politician only believes they have a soul if they are in the lens of the camera.

The desire cuts across all classes and ages, for nothing lightens the heart of everyone from the local county councillor to the Taoiseach, well, the former one anyway, more than the sound of a clicking camera shutter and the erotic phrase of 'Smile, everyone'. But why is it that every Irish politician would walk across the bodies of a thousand naked women and, more seriously still, a thousand pints to secure that precious photograph?

The reason, we suspect, is that for our politician the photograph is a cross between celluloid Viagra and childhood memories of night-time cocoa from Nurse. They excite the virility but also soothe the savage insecurity of the soul of the shallow politician.

This unlovely combination means we should not, perhaps, be surprised that the great apogee of the photo-opportunity arrived during the Celtic Tiger. This new development was the life buoy of politicians with little worthwhile to say and few purposes in life outside of preserving their own greatness in amber. Of course, it also helps that whilst the camera never lies, it can certainly help things appear to be a little better than they really are.

Our politicians love the photograph for this precise reason since it does not cross-examine or berate or contradict. Indeed, Enda Kenny once kicked off one supposed press conference by saying 'Photographs please, no questions.' Our astonishment at the statement increased even further when we realised he was serious.

Ultimately the greatest virtue of the photograph is that it creates the illusion of activity. It is a long old day when you are a Minister sitting in the office with nothing to do, outside of avoiding the Dáil and staring hungrily at the packed lunch that's nestled temptingly in your briefcase. Photographs, however, command the dead empty spaces of that section of the paper in which journalists once used to write about politicians.

Such, indeed, is the undying love of our politicians for the camera when corrupt TDs like Ray Burke or Dennis Foley (Fianna Fáil, Kerry North) were creeping into one or other of the Tribunals, once the shutters began to click they would turn and smile for the camera with all the blushing delight of the father of a bride on the wedding day. It is hard to defeat instinct.

However, it can be an uncertain mistress, for we have already referred to that unfortunate summertime occasion where the camera turned on poor Mr Ahern courtesy of that photograph of Bertie lounging around in a slightly off-white tracksuit. The colour and the garment were bad enough but what really captured the public attention was the sight of Mr Ahern's grandfatherly tummy nestling like a plump cuckoo in the baggy folds of the tracksuit.

It still being the age of the Celtic Tiger, the saga of the tummy that Bass and Bertie built dominated the summer. But there was worse to come, for the cameras also ruined his debut with the G8 leaders as a country—most of whose people have a relationship with fashion that is not dissimilar to foxes and the fur trade—fell around laughing at the disaster that was Mr Ahern's canary-yellow linen suit. Mind you, amidst the smirks it has to be admitted that if there was ever a man who was totally unsuited to the 'smart casual' style, it was Mr Ahern.

Bertie's ambivalent relationship with the camera may also have been influenced by health and safety issues. When it came to being photographed beside the Taoiseach, the public were fine but the battle between TDs and, more dangerously still, aspirant TDs to be caught in that precious doughnut beside Mr Ahern occasionally genuinely threatened the life and limb of Bertie. Happily it is not a problem Mr Cowen suffers from.

Mr Ahern may at best have tolerated the cameras but two other figures came to define the love affair of the Irish politician with the photo-opportunity. Significantly 'the Bull' O'Donoghue and Martin Cullen both spent their careers in the step-down Ministry of Arts, Culture and Sport. In spite of the Venetian water taxis, it is not an easy old spot but during that time there was a certain grandeur about their willingness to do anything, no matter how asinine, to get their photos into the papers.

Some of the scenes were as unreal as the artwork of Dalí. The one thing our leaders detest more than artists is manual labour, but yet you would see regular photographs of Martin Cullen hanging off the rails of dustbin lorries. John O'Donoghue was photographed beside an incredible variety of dragons, poets and philosophers whilst other politicians were even photographed on a far more mythical creature, in their lives at least, which is called a train.

Some wondered what purpose these galleries of politicians being photographed with twenty-something models in bras and knickers actually served. One supposes at least the models got paid and that was, of course, a good thing. Sadly these days our politicians are rather less keen to be photographed on Grafton Street beside semi-naked models. Kinder souls will say it is because there are somewhat fewer initiatives to be announced. The more hardened cynics would suggest that they are actually more informed by the fear that, if recognised by a gaggle of irate members of the public smiling insipidly beside a half-disrobed Glenda, they will be stripped of their own clothes and thrown into the pond.

Chapter 40

SO WHY DON'T WE WANT THE LOCK-KEEPER'S SON BACK?

He may not be universally loved now but at least Charlie McCreevy was always different. The unique bravura McCreevy brought to politics is epitomised by a tale by Emmet Stagg about the Finance Minister's response to that much-dreaded moment when a constituent would approach him with a problem to be solved. McCreevy would halt the supplicant in mid-flow, take out a well-thumbed card from his pocket with a phone number and tell the man to 'contact this fellow, he'll sort you out'.

The phone number in question was that of Stagg, who noted with amused astonishment that often after he had resolved the problem 'McCreevy would get a phone call from the constituent thanking him for sorting out that issue. They thought I, in contrast, was just the man in the council.'

McCreevy was rare in that he was one of the few Irish politicians whom the electorate actually liked. Indeed, for a short blissful time such was the reverse of the normal rules of politics that the harder the straight-speaking Minister tried to be disliked, the more the public flocked to him.

It did, of course, help that no Minister ever returned more of the taxpayers' money back to where the people thought it belonged. There were, however, more subtle factors at play. The reason people liked McCreevy wasn't so much because he was a rogue. It was rather that, unlike his Uriah Heap-style forelock-tugging, voter-hating colleagues, he was a straight-talker who avowedly didn't give a hoot about what we thought of him. You can trust a man like that.

That alone would be enough to make him an oddity but there were other critical factors at play. McCreevy's public persona may have been that of a lad but alone amongst his colleagues, he had a certain understanding of and liking for strong women. That, allied to his independent wealth, meant he was that exceptional figure in Irish politics known as a rounded human being.

This rare status was enhanced by those tales of horrified bureaucrats, and even Bertie, being chased out of the Minister for Finance's office by a man determined to do things his own way. It added to the myth of McCreevy, the upwardly mobile lock-keeper's son, who was the independent-thinking, living, vibrant reverse of the politics of 'Yes, Minister'. Sadly, even as a public that never liked the Sir Humphreys of Killiney lapped up the tales of his derring-do, we should have known good things never last for ever. In McCreevy's case the end was nigh once he informed the nation that 'sometimes I astonish myself with my own brilliance'. The statement was not exceptional by McCreevy's tongue-in-cheek standards but on this occasion the Minister appeared to genuinely believe it.

It was unfortunate, but the evidence was that McCreevy had finally gone over to the other side. He had begun to join the Aherns, Dempseys and the rest of that great Cabinet cabal who believed the summit of human perfection had been perfectly timed to arrive at the auspicious moment of their birth.

It did not help that by this stage the evidence of McCreevy's greatness was becoming thin. Of course, for a time it looked as though that transient greatness would never occur. McCreevy's image was formed by the Haughey era when he looked into the hooded eyes of the daemonic figure from Kinsealy and grinned with utter amusement at the very notion that he might be supposed to genuflect before the august pretensions of Haughey.

It condemned him to the political wilderness, for no one singes the beard of their leader quite as often as McCreevy and escapes. However, as the wise ones who were in office sibilantly condemned McCreevy for having more courage than sense, this only added to the myth of McCreevy, for we have far too many sensible politicians in Ireland and not half enough courageous ones.

This was not the only myth surrounding McCreevy. The former Finance Minister may have rejoiced in his ordinary-son-of-the-soil-style persona. But whilst McCreevy may have been the grinning Cheshire cat of Irish politics, there was a hidden serious side to the Mr Champagne image. He was a secret devotee of the Lee Trevino adage that 'the harder I practise, the luckier I get'. We were to learn this the hard way, for the bad news for the country was that when the 'jovial fun-loving' McCreevy left and the 'serious' Mr Cowen arrived, the Department went into 'schools out' mode.

In spite of McCreevy's smiling persona, we occasionally saw the hint of teeth.

After the decentralisation demarche Tom Parlon might have hastily erected 'welcome to Parlon country' posters but McCreevy ruthlessly deflated

Parlon's pretensions that he had been in on the act with a chortle of 'he must have heard about it in a pub because we told him nothing'.

In fairness to Charlie, for most of his career in Finance the self-praise was justifiable. Back in 1997, when the Rainbow ran with a cautious, economically just fiscal manifesto, McCreevy simply promised to give the people their money back with tax cuts rather than all that meandering around with bands.

It was enough to bring Fianna Fáil over the line in 1997 whilst the fulfilling of those promises, surely back then a landmark in Irish politics, gave Bertie the space to engage in the extended glory of a first solo run of 2002. At a time when ethics was becoming a stifling influence on public life McCreevy's irreverence continued to provide politics with a welcome salty touch. McCreevy would holiday where he wished, say what he wanted and if his friends wanted a pleasant spot in Punchestown for the horse-racing, he would oblige and let the devil take the hindmost.

However, when the great change began there were more straws in the wind than McCreevy's proclamations about his own greatness. It may have looked as though McCreevy was once again revealing his rare take on the 'ordinary people' when he famously declaimed that all the common man wants is the GAA, a few pints and a bit of fun with the wife on a Saturday.

Technically he was right but the common man is a far more complex creature. Fatally, and like too many of his colleagues, McCreevy was starting to become supercilious about the people he theoretically served. Distance was setting in and he was getting far too fond of telling the many irritants that plague Finance Ministers, most of whom are other Ministers, to fuck off. The suspicion began to grow that Charlie was laughing at rather than with us.

Surprisingly for all his front, he went easily enough in the end. When McCreevy claimed he knew 25 per cent of Bertie Ahern and the rest of the party knew 1 per cent, the ward boss laughed, for when it came to the political accounts McCreevy was in credit. The problem for Charlie was that when the fiscal engine began to run out of oil, Charlie knew 24 per cent too much.

In the good times Bertie was prepared to go along with a public show of bemused deference to his good friend Charlie. But when Ahern decided he wanted a cat's-paw in Finance, the only feeling left in the once special relationship was that of the door handle hitting McCreevy on the ass on the way out.

Charlie knew a lot more than 25 per cent of Bertie after that occurrence.

Still, our man made one final glorious return to Irish political life. As the first Lisbon referendum began to sink, McCreevy jovially informed an even more delighted press corps that he had not read the Lisbon treaty. The Commissioner may have been right in his assertion that no sane person would engage in such a task. But later that year as a despairing political elite watched the growing pile of 'No' ballots in the Lisbon count, and McCreevy's scornful dismissal of the notion that an EU Commissioner would waste his time reading an EU treaty was constantly replayed, it was clear none of his old colleagues were at all anxious to witness a return of the lost fiscal emperor.

They are surely right too, for the last thing Irish politics needs is an iconoclastic, fearless, self-starting, original thinker.

SECTION 7

Welcome to the club

Chapter 41 ∾

THE SECRET WORLD OF
THE BAR LOBBY

One of the more intriguing subsets within the Fianna Fáil family is the famous Dáil bar lobby. Like the economy, they are experiencing a bit of a decline now, but during that brief gilded time when the Celtic Tiger resembled a Roman *vomitarium*, it was the most popular club in town. Of course, the growing importance of the bar lobby was intimately linked into the heir apparent status of its unofficial leader Brian Cowen, who was apparently using it as a training stint for governance.

In these changed times it may seem to be odd that, for the most part, we thought the bacchanalian status of Mr Cowen as the leader of FF's most hardened carousers was a matter of mirth. And we would endure a harsh growing up process from that adolescence, where we gloried in the tale of the shocked American tourist who was told the fellow in Doheny & Nesbitt's with a pint and a cigarette in his hand singing 'Paddy's Green Shamrock Shore' was 'our Minister for Health, Mr Cowen'.

But as Mr Cowen's star rose for no great reason beyond the absence of any viable alternative, it was inevitable interest would grow in this group of 'special ones'. On one level this was surprising, for normally when politicians reach the summit of their profession, interest is centred on their families, their political allies and even, sometimes, though rarely in Ireland, their ideas.

In Mr Cowen's case, however, it was hard to avoid the impression that the lobby was his real family. In rare interviews the Taoiseach made it clear the Dáil bar was a sacred 'sanctuary' and perhaps we should have been alarmed by the prospect of having a national leader who made the pub his Shangri-la. Mr Cowen certainly bristled about our enquiries into these affairs, but you could hardly blame us for displaying an interest in a group who were his soulmates.

Indeed, there were many who claimed the group were also his sole mates.

It was certainly the case that amongst the media much blood and treasure and, to be frank, the consumption of porter went into identifying the membership of this elite cadre. In truth, though newspaper editors were never told this, trying to identify its members was a waste of time for, rather like an alcohol-soaked version of Buddhism, the bar lobby was a state of mind rather than an organised religion.

They were in a very real way the political equivalent of a flying column, for the faces and membership regularly changed. Not all were drinkers either, for Charlie McCreevy, who gave up alcohol after he was 40 and became a resounding political success, was spiritually attached by virtue of his interests in horse and dog racing.

It would be incorrect to claim the bar lobby did not have core principles but they were most assuredly not the political equivalent of some Fine Gael-style ideological ginger group. Instead, like Bill Shankly, who believed football was far more important than life or death, if the lobby were passionate about any issue it was the right to watch horse racing without being disturbed by constituency issues or legislative work. Indeed, our bar lobby friends were creatures of the *Racing Post* as distinct from the *Financial Times* to such an extent that on their rare incursions into the Dáil chamber, the members would be seen anxiously perusing its pages whilst governments rose and fell.

We could, of course, at this point become very po-faced and say it is a terrible pity 'the lads' never displayed the same level of passion over the many varieties of scandal Irish politics experienced. But in some respects that was an impossible demand, for the most charming feature of the bar lobby is that they were, indeed still are, the human face of Irish and FF politics.

In many respects they were also a *cri de coeur* against modernity, for the members of this select group were less than entranced by the growing professionalism of modern politics. Others such as Bertie, or their sworn enemies amongst the pious new moral wing of FF, may have been enthusiasts for focus groups and research bodies led by academic Saladins with Harvard and Yale degrees. However, the bar lobby advocates believed the issues exercising Irish society could be just as easily discovered via the pub as distinct from the focus group. And you could at least have a drink in the pub.

It would be unfair to claim the bar lobby were lazy or cruel. They were instead consumed by a latitudinarian pessimism that suspected that legislating or debating would do little to change society. They were the 'country' wing of FF who believed the world was the way it was and nothing much they could do could radically change that. In short, if they had a political ethos, it was a form of elegant pessimism marinated in porter.

This article of faith meant their greatest distrust and severest mockery were reserved for ambitious colleagues like Dick Roche. Such unquiet souls were a threat to their view of the Dáil as a safe snug from the cruelties of the real world.

Of course, the amiable contrarians of the bar lobby would have gone unnoticed were it not for Cowen's apparent comfort in their company. It was intriguing, for other aspirant leaders would socialise with poets and philosophers or, more commonly these days, with economists and academics.

On one level this lack of quality control over his preferred choice of boon companions made Cowen all the more fascinating, as we wondered if he was the Irish version of Shakespeare's Henry IV. In a sense he even became more attractive, for if the next leader had a preference for the company of Falstaffs, perhaps he would be closer to the people than those who had gone before.

Ironically, in spite of the understandable anxiety of this flying column of political refugees from modernity to maintain their privacy, the moment that most clearly revealed the soul of the bar lobby occurred in public. In a despairing attempt to take the bad look off the number of sitting days, the government commenced a series of pointless debates on Fridays. Since there were no votes or questions, attendance was always low, for most TDs prefer to be at home harvesting their constituencies rather than listening to state of the nation addresses.

Some government TDs did have to be in attendance, for the Opposition possessed the power to call a quorum, whereby the Dáil is suspended unless a sufficient number of TDs are in the chamber—and yes, it's quite difficult to see the point really.

But this is Leinster House, it has its own odd rules and some abstruse theory indicates it is embarrassing for the government if they are unable to muster up enough TDs to keep a Dáil debate going. On one Friday afternoon such had been the exit of government TDs there was the potential for real embarrassment. As the Chief Whip Mary Hanafin sprinted back from Grafton Street, where she had been engaging in some misfortunately timed retail therapy, the numbers were so tight Bertie Ahern had to be dragged in. As Mr Ahern entered the chamber his face was like thunder, for one of Bertie's core hatreds was being in the Dáil for more than a minute past noon on Wednesday. Surprisingly the Taoiseach's face darkened even further when he saw who was in situ. The one group of TDs who were actively delighted by the Friday debates were the bar lobby, for the necessity to be in attendance gave them the priceless benefit of spending an extra day away from their constituents. Happily, when the quorum had been called, some six of them had been in close proximity to the chamber in a meeting room known as the Dáil bar. As one of the members looked up glassily at Bertie and informed him, in the uniquely cheery manner of a man who has had a long lunch, that there was no 'need to worry, Taoiseach, you can count on us', one supposes that was half the problem.

The great flaw of the bar lobby is not so much that they were bad but rather that they were lazy. Like the rest of our feckless nation, they were affable creatures who were careless not so much with the lives of their constituents but with the country they were supposed to protect. It was, of course, fun for several decades but we are certainly suffering the hangover now.

Chapter 42 ⌇

| WELCOME TO THE CLUB

Why are so few Irish politicians great?

It is easy to forget these days that there was once a time when on long peaceful afternoons in the Dáil bar politicians would sigh about the absence of challenges to pique their interest. Sometimes they would even wonder just how different 'the 1950s might have been if there was a Brian Cowen around to shake things up a bit'.

If there has been one plus to come out of our current trauma, it is that we have a pretty good idea about how effective Mr Cowen would have been in the 1950s.

The slightly less good news is that the greatest psychological disruption we have experienced since the Famine accelerates when we look for leadership and we get ghosts.

In fairness, like the famous graffiti in the pre-historic city of Ur that bewailed the bad behaviour of the youth, one of the staple complaints of any generation is that they are unique in suffering under the misrule of the worst generation of politicians.

This, however, was not always the case in Ireland, for whatever about anything else, we once were famous for the quality of our politicians. In our schooldays we were brought up on tales of Grattan, Tone, Emmet, O'Connell, Thomas, Davis, Parnell, Davitt, Griffith, Pearse, Connolly and Collins. And though the supply of heroes did appear to dry up after Independence, there were still dramatic and colourful figures. Fianna Fáil had de Valera, Lemass and the talismanic Donagh O'Malley. Though his strutting and his poses were, for many, closer to the mock heroic than the real thing, Mr Haughey certainly wasn't cast from the normal mould whilst some would even make a case for the reckless but daring Albert.

Labour provided their own school of impressive politicians such as the tough wily Dick Spring, whilst, though their reputations are well poisoned now, at one stage the public had a genuine faith in PDS such as Dessie O'Malley and Mary Harney. We are also sure that, whilst none spring to mind, Fine Gael also had some heroic figures.

Now, sadly, just when we need them most, we are experiencing a drought of talent last seen in the 1950s and even that beggared era had the Romantic nihilism of Noel Browne. But when it comes to this generation, our politicians are only fluent in coming up with excuses for the absence of greatness.

One of the most common defences our politicians use is that they are the 'victims' of our clientelist system but it is difficult to see how being knowledgeable about the woes of the people they represent should be a hindrance to political capacity. Economists sort out the economy, priests look after religion and it is the job of politicians to represent the people who elect them. The only qualification we would add is that they should attempt to cultivate our better selves but even this gentle rule appears to be too much. One answer to our greatness dilemma may lie in the famous old saying about marriage being about love and divorce being about money. Rather like the blushing bride, the neophyte politician enters the doors of Leinster House in a state of agape over the beauty of the people who have elected him to this privileged position. But the state of married bliss between politicians and people rarely lasts long. Instead, generally within the year, they are sleeping separate beds, for our idealist has been transformed into a hardened cynic who devotes hours to his expenses and delegates the constituents to his secretary. Leinster House is, alas, full of these manacled slaves. They still smile, they still interact with the voters but deep within their heart they are filled with a cold hatred for their enslavement to the whims of their ruthless masters.

A lot of it comes down to the Bertie Ahern school of apprenticeship. The new young politician will want to shake things up but they rapidly learn the hard way they would spend a long time peeling potatoes in the kitchen before they would be invited to join the other chefs on the hot plate.

And even when they do secure Cabinet office the difficulties of achieving greatness could best be summarised by the beatitudes of Bertie Ahern. It might be perceived to be unfair to blame one man for the absence of political heroism but the nature of the king defines the vices and virtues of the age and FF's sun king left a political desert behind when he departed.

The problem lies with Mr Ahern's defining philosophy over his 11 years in power, which was to tell the people you'll give them what they want, give it to them, tell them you have given it to them and then give them a bit more.

This meant, of course, that no vested interest could be opposed. Instead, it was a case of blessed be the Princes of Social Partnership for under their capacious wings there shall be peace and no division in our land. Blessed also was the politician who was clear about nothing for he shall be loved above all others, secure the three in a row and his place in history.

Bertie Ahern is not the first politician to confuse the needs of his country with the cravings of his own ego. It was, however, his very effectiveness at this particular game that wrought such elemental damage upon his country and his party. One of the cruellest examples of the consequences of the dead hand of Bertie is provided by the fate of John O'Donoghue. In 1997 the Bull entered the Department of Justice like an elemental force of nature. Then the Minister faced his first challenge via the infamous 'blue flu' affair when, instead of going on strike over pay and conditions, the police force went on the sick. It was a challenge to the state that should have been beaten back if necessary by putting the army onto the streets.

Instead, the principles of Bertie were applied, the Bull buckled, the Gardaí were sorted and all was well again. Well, except for the poor Bull who from that point, in his secret soul at least, became nothing more than a timeserver.

As with all sun kings, his party was about to learn the hard way that nothing was to detract from the needs of the leader. This of itself need not be a problem but Mr Ahern's unique school of man management sowed the dragon's teeth of our current collapse of governance.

Bertie never took the axe to the heads of his turbulent priests but instead he disorientated them to such an extent that they became as pliable and lost as Winston Smith in Orwell's *1984*. The problem was that being governed by a Taoiseach who would not tell them what it was he wanted, but who cut the legs from them when they failed to do that which he secretly desired, corroded the character of his Ministers.

The insidious duplicity of the courtly politics of Bertie meant that when the opportunity for greatness arrived, the Irish political system resembled one of those Italian armies who flee before the battle even begins. Our fat generals may have been weighed down with medals but they were made of tin. The uniforms were impressive but they could not organise an orderly retreat let alone a decisive counter-attack.

Sadly we should not be surprised that some, like Mary Coughlan, were visibly terrified by the new order. The problem, you see, is that Bertie Ahern's Cabinet acquired the characteristics of slaves. They could obey a master but these vainglorious fops were utterly out of their depth when they were put in charge of anything. They were, in short, like their current Taoiseach, fit only to follow rather than lead.

Chapter 43 ∾

THE GREAT TRIUMPH OF
THE IRISH DYNASTY

It is a measure of the endemic deference within the Irish state that we regularly refer to the 'glorious' dynasties of Irish politics in a manner that suggests they are our local version of the Austrian Hapsburgs. Sadly in these changed times, as with the general anxiety to inform the public that all Senior Counsel are distinguished, it increasingly looks as though the concept of the 'glorious' Irish dynasty is somewhat overstated.

Bertie Ahern was certainly less than impressed by the delights of the political dynasty. As with everything else, the ward boss was not precisely clear about his disposition but it was heavily implied that when it came to the concept of inherited political power, Mr Ahern was a bit of a municipal socialist.

Nothing clarified this position more than the relish with which his acolytes described the taking out of 'the old women' of the patrician Colley dynasty. The detestation was undoubtedly influenced by the belief that, rather like the Mafia, where those who are not of pure Italian blood can never become the boss, anyone who was not part of the Fianna Fáil royal lines was at best seen as a useful outsider.

Mr Ahern was not the only successful outsider in the FF *famiglia*, for it was a trait he curiously shared with his political hero Charlie Haughey. Ironically, given its Republican designation, this was enough to make both figures unique, for there is no more dynastic party within Europe than FF. Within their ranks it is not enough that sons and grandsons inherit seats, for uncles, cousins and even the odd daughter all protect the family political shop.

Dynastic politics has always had certain down-sides. It was said of the final king in one Spanish dynasty that the royal genes were so depleted the unfortunate creature could dine only on the gizzards of chickens. It will not come as a surprise that from this point the Spanish Empire began to go into decline. Fortunately, none of our political dynasties have reached that point, though some are getting close.

Of course, the creation of a political system of Venetian doges, where power is acquired by birthright rather than any genuine talent, has not happened by accident. It was instead facilitated by the absence of ideology in Irish politics, for where you are not battling for the soul of socialism or for the rights of the humble millionaire capitalist then it is always more likely you will see the rise of a school of politicians who have, at best, the characteristics of clever tradesmen. This might be good enough for some, but whilst tradesmen may enjoy some skill in implementing other men's visions, if they are asked to design their own building they are as lost as a boy in a convention of algebra professors.

The tradesman principle may go a long way to explaining the reason why outwardly sane people actually do that 'it' called politics. It had been thought this was some virus or a great mystery on the lines of the Holy Trinity. In fact the answer to the great mystery of why they might do 'it' is that these dynastic scions know of no other life.

As with so many other things JB Keane was ahead of this game, for his fictional TD Tull McAdoo famously willed the priesthood to one son, the farm to another and his Dáil seat to his most stupid child. Judging by the characteristics of many of our TDs, Tull was a wise man.

In fairness, the dynastic impulse is not confined to politics, for the closed shop is endemic in the law, medicine and all the other vested interests now gnawing frantically at the whitened bones of the Celtic Tiger. But politics is unique in the sense that if it is to prosper it needs new blood to reinvigorate the tribe. Instead, what we have is the progeny of the sort of dynasties that one TD colourfully noted were 'butchers, undertakers and drunkards and then they became politicians'.

It was perhaps an unfortunate coincidence that the great apogee of the dynasties coincided with the collapse of the Celtic Tiger. Never before had representatives of three 'glorious' FF royal lines held the three great offices of state. However, as Cowen, Lenihan and Coughlan smiled nervously at the world it was easy to forget during that glorious moment that Bertie Ahern had been less than fulsome about the qualities of the special triumvirate.

As Taoiseach, he had confined Mary Coughlan to the relatively obscure backwaters of Agriculture whilst if Mr Ahern had a single core value it appeared to snuff out the political career of Brian Lenihan as quickly as possible. And his initial suspicions about Mr Cowen's 'work ethic' were only stymied by the need for a useful cat's-paw to secure the triumph of Operation Three in a Row.

Mr Cowen, however, was possessed of different views and appeared to think an academic lawyer and a non-practising social worker were the best-qualified souls to save the economy. Unsurprisingly, with man management skills like that, we are indeed where we are today.

Amazingly the triumph of the dynasties was not confined to the triumvirate of neophytes either, for Barry Andrews from the non-illustrious Andrews dynasty was also tagged on as a partial afterthought for he was only dealing with children.

We've seen how well that went.

The power of the dynasties is not set to change in a hurry either, for the selection of Dara Calleary as the coming man indicates how Mr Cowen's comfort zone does not exist beyond the comforting, familiar FF blue bloods.

In truth, dynastic politics is not confined to FF for within Fine Gael Enda Kenny is the child of a TD and he is not at all unique. Indeed, for a time it appeared to be impossible for FG to pick a leader unless he came from a selection of golden dynastic calves. Thus it was that Liam Cosgrave Jnr succeeded Liam Cosgrave the First in the way that one inherits the family grocery store. Garret FitzGerald meanwhile painted himself as being some radical outsider, but Garret the Good was the child of Desmond FitzGerald, a former FG Minister.

And the phenomenon retains a certain half life even to this day, for the most recent FG leadership contest was between a dull 57-year-old dynastic politician who finds it difficult to connect with the people and a dull 55-year-old dynastic politician who finds it difficult to connect with the people. Spot the difference, everyone!

Enda Lite and Bruton the Lesser are not the only dynastic creatures within the party. Charlie Flanagan, Deirdre Clune and Simon Coveney are all from royal lines, whilst on the back benches there are habitués of dynasties that, rather like parts of nineteenth-century darkest Africa, have still to be discovered by the outside world.

Sadly, though it appears to be as outwardly harmless as the chinless wonders it produces, dynastic politics is not a victimless crime. The sorry history of our Spanish kings tells us one needs a good scattering of mongrel blood to freshen up the line. Instead, we are getting sons and daughters infected by the excessively wise cynicism of parents who learned too much and stayed in the game too long.

The problem isn't just that they are too wise for idealism and too embedded to be radical, but that we have also created an enclosed political elite that is as separate from the people as the poor lost final Emperor of China.

Chapter 44 ∾

WALKING AROUND
SALUTING THE PEOPLE

A portrait of the perfect Fianna Fáil
backbencher

There are more of them than Cabinet Ministers and their votes are just as important. However, one of the more astonishing features of the Fianna Fáil backbencher is just how little we know about them. Or rather, what is even more surprising is how wrong the outside views of the quintessence of the good back-bench TD actually are.

The conventional beatitude of the good backbencher says he should be a straight-talking, moralistic original thinker who is openly ambitious. However, even politicians such as Brian Lenihan have learned the hard way that if you want to get on in the Dáil club, you have to be very careful about how you play the game. FF's cleverest barrister might have thought when he came into the Dáil that intellect was the road to preferment. But whether it is Clongowes Woods, Malory Towers or Leinster House nobody, and particularly those who are in a position of power, likes the smartest boy in the class for the simple reason that he may soon be nibbling at their ass.

Mr Lenihan might have terrified Junior Ministers with lectures about the jurisprudential theories of seventeenth-century Dutch philosophers. However, a country ruled by the top civil service mandarins (and the Cabinet too, of course!) treats any intellectual running around the back benches with the gravest of suspicion.

It goes without saying that the overly ambitious are not trusted either. The classic example of this consists of a certain TD who shall remain nameless because of the libel laws. Our man's bad reputation was acquired courtesy of his propensity during those precious moments where a humble backbencher was in conversation with a Minister to delicately slide his portly form in between the two with a sinuous grace that would have impressed the writers of the *Kama Sutra*. As the vast, beetle-black back blocked out the other backbencher's access to the sunlight of Ministerial attention, hatred is too soft a word for the emotion this gentleman inspired. Sadly his courtship of the Ministerial classes did him few favours, for there was no shortage of TDs who were more than willing to let their views about this dastardly activity be known to the very Ministers he was trying to seduce.

Within the culture of 'the lads', intensity is another despised quality. Perhaps the most dramatic example of how such a dangerous concept can destroy careers occurred during one of those unfortunately titled FF think-ins where, on seeing Bertie make his usual sun king style entrance, one yet to be promoted TD with the highest of views of his abilities hissed, 'There he is, there's the c**t that's stifling my career.'

He may well have been correct in his analysis but unfortunately our man was drunk and talking loudly and Mr Ahern has excellent hearing. We did attempt to calm things down by insisting, much against any existing evidence, that the Taoiseach thought he was a great lad, and that when sober the TD thought Bertie was the finest of fellows. Sadly the TD's state meant he repeated an unchanged analysis of the political landscape, in an ever more certain and louder fashion, until the Taoiseach doubled back towards our anguished politician who would not be promoted for a further five years. The half smile on Ahern's face as he was greeted by joyous ejaculations of 'Taoiseach, it's wonderful to see you! Have you lost weight?' was the most human response to a scenario we have seen Bertie indulge in.

Of course, everyone in politics is an independent republic, but 'the lads' and the odd isolated country girl on the FF back benches are infused by principles of collective self-interest that would impress even Mao.

The core value of this philosophy is a Sinn Féin-style ideology of 'the lads together against the world'. Such 'lads' may listen to complaining constituents with reserved polite nodding fear but, in spite of all the lip service, our politicians do not think they are servants of the people. Instead, their self-image is of the endangered members of yet another vested interest, who must protect the club at all costs, and who regard the cursed voters with the same warmth as a Revenue audit.

This philosophy is also extended to the dangerous pursuit of political combat with the enemy. The ambitious politician may wish to throw the occasional jibe at Enda, just to keep his eyelids from closing during the morning ennui of Taoiseach's questions. However, outside of laughing at Fine Gael's James Bannon, 'the lads' are utterly resolute in their refusal to engage with the Opposition, on the wise World War I principle that if everyone starts shooting then someone is bound to be hurt.

It might contradict the theories of Machiavelli but ultimately if you are to be a successful backbencher the most important talent is the ability to be loved rather than feared. City sophisticates may chortle and laugh at the sort of country TD who, on eating his first ever Indian meal, wails in between the billowing smoke leaving his ears that 'Jaysus, I'll never have one of those Italian meals again.' But within the comforting love of the family our man is simply known to be 'a character' who must be looked after lest he harm himself let alone anyone else.

Outside of a total absence of knowledge of the cuisines of the world there are other critical characteristics and traits the new TD must acquire if he is to secure the coveted position of a good, non-ambitious, 20-year timeserver, who poses a threat to no one bar the electorate. Happily the methodology for success is actually quite simple, for the first thing you must do is join a little club like the infamous bar lobby and spend the day engaged in such critical networking activities as sipping fine porter. Nobody, you see, except FG, likes a legislator.

The good news is there's no need to bother about the constituents either for your Dáil Secretary, who earns a quarter of what you do, will have all that in train. You should still try to engage in the odd useful task such as the fetching of the aspirant leader's porter or ferrying racing dockets to the bookie's shop. Some useful talent for late-night entertainment, such as the capacity to juggle a pair of shoes after 15 pints of stout, is also a prerequisite for success.

We admit, when it comes to this great quintessence of man that is the successful FF backbencher, all this is a tad theoretical. We do have a real-life example of the essence of this political animal courtesy of the recent travails of the wise but little-known FF TD Peter Kelly.

In spite of Peter's determined efforts to avoid the national media, our man recently found himself engaged in a high profile radio interview over the complexities of NAMA. In the aftermath of an event that frankly did not go well, Kelly was rung by a distressed constituent who told him, 'Peter, you should stay away from radio interviews about complicated things. That's not what you are good at.'

The TD, sadly, made the critical error of asking our man what he actually was good at. Eventually, after an agonised pause, he was told, 'Well, you're very good at walking around the main street saluting the people.'

Of course, urban sophisticates will sneer at such a 'talent'. But, in truth, a man could be at worse things in his life. Walking around the place saluting the people might not resolve too many of our woes. However, it will do no harm either and when you look at the destruction all the clever ones have wrought on poor Ireland perhaps a Dáil of Peter Kellys is not the worst thing that could happen to the nation. At least they'd salute you anyway.

SECTION 8

A thousand tales of the Ministerial ego

Chapter 45

A THOUSAND TALES OF
THE MINISTERIAL EGO

I t is rare that the Fianna Fáil party acquires the traits and characteristics of an AA meeting. Yet as the humble FF back-bench TD MJ Nolan, of whom absolutely nothing has been heard since he was a member of the gang of four who started the process that toppled Haughey 20 years ago, began his tale of woe the assembled FF TDs were soon experiencing a unique confessional moment.

MJ has been in and out of Leinster House for two decades, displaying all the forensic rigour of a piece of wallpaper falling off a slightly dampened wall. But, like his other colleagues, one of the few powers of any real value that a TD has is the right to tug deferentially at a Minister's jacket and request the granting of some small favour for a constituent.

This need not be and rarely is a corrupt act. It is more likely to be something unorthodox like reversing some act of stupidity by one of our thousands of inept bureaucratic nonentities. But it is of critical importance to the back-bench politician, for it creates the impression in the golf club that he is a person of some prestige and standing.

In this case poor MJ, who is far too polite for his own good, had been for months trying to get a Minister to sort out some constituency matter before eventually he had been granted an audience. Sadly, when our hero was imperiously beckoned into the office, nothing went according to plan. Nolan stood politely and waited, for the Minister was obviously having an animated phone conversation about a matter of some importance.

The Minister, however, wagged an imperious finger and told Nolan to state his case. Just as MJ began, a series of wails about shirts made it devastatingly clear to Nolan that he was playing second fiddle to the pressing matter of the collection of the Minister's dry cleaning.

It is indeed at times like this that the iron does enter the soul, for it is hard when you have 10,000 votes in your back pocket to be relegated to a status far behind that of the laundry lady.

The experience of MJ was by no means exceptional, for one of the few top-level politicians who, even as Taoiseach, at least pretended to have time for the humble deppities was Bertie Ahern. In contrast, the attitude of his other senior colleagues is more accurately captured by the famous 'Arabian Nights' series of fairy tales where a heroine preserves her life by inventing a new story for a thousand nights.

There might not be a thousand stories of the Ministerial ego but our politicians would probably run the heroine fairly closely. Indeed, such are the notions amongst some, the wonder of it is that they don't, like the priesthood, have a ceremony similar to ordination. There again whilst our Ministers might be able for the incense and the Latin, they would not be capable of prostrating themselves on the altar in a gesture of supplication.

In fairness, the well-cultivated Ministerial ego is not a new creation. One of the most classic tales of this vice comes from the former Fine Gael TD Gerry Reynolds. As a new TD, one day as Haughey, Ray Burke and Gerry Collins passed him by in the corridor, Reynolds issued a cheerily irreverent 'Howareye, lads' to the distinguished trio.

Ten seconds later the rather surprised deputy was confronted by a furious Ray Burke. Rambo's career might have ended in rather controversial fashion courtesy of his unfortunate propensity to engage in acts of corruption but our man knew his etiquette. So it was that Reynolds found himself being berated by a Rambo as the incandescent Minister told the new TD that 'Sonny, around here the correct term is Taoiseach and Minister.'

We will note in passing that this was a Minister from the Republican party that theoretically takes its ethos from the ideology of Tone, Emmet, Pearse and Connolly.

The current Enterprise Minister also recalls his first encounter, when as a lissom trembling backbencher he sought a small favour from Pee Flynn. On the day in question the vainglorious Pee was in full *muinteoir scoile* mode and bellowed, 'Who are you and what do *you* want?' The Minister then contradicted his own feigned ignorance with a dismissive snap of 'Why would I give you anything? Ye have too much in Cork as it is.'

A sanguine O'Keeffe did note that 'and then in fairness he came back to earth and dealt with the issue. With Flynn, you see, you had to go through the motions, be snubbed, frowned upon and looked down on and when you were brought down to size, then he could deal with you.'

It might appear strange to want power just so you can insult your fellow human beings but that certainly does appear to be the way in Leinster House. We have become a little more refined since Haughey, but at least half of the

Cabinet still retain a remarkably similar attitude to their own colleagues, let alone the ordinary punters, to the views of the Irish episcopacy towards their flock before Vatican II.

Our Ministers do, at the start and in some cases for a brief period after their appointment, resemble normal citizens. But in almost all cases the newly appointed Minister undergoes a mysterious metamorphosis that is not at all dissimilar to the evolution of a caterpillar into a butterfly. Sadly the one exception in their case is that precisely the opposite process takes place at the very moment they enter office with holy shining faces.

In a way they cannot be blamed for after they are appointed, the first task of any Minister—way ahead of any outlining of policies, for most Ministers do not have a clue about the Departments they are appointed to—is the acquisition of the Ministerial retinue.

This is the busiest and most stressful period of the Minister's tenure, for a press officer must be acquired to bruit to the nation's indifferent press about the triumphs of the Minister, in the Department whose functions he doesn't have a clue about. Of course, a policy advisor must also be acquired to take the edge off our man's utter state of ignorance. Generally this individual must come from the vastly increased ranks of the Minister's friends, though if our hero is in a particularly patriotic mood he may recruit one of the party's press officers, thus serving both God and Mammon.

It goes without saying that the 'policy' advisor will be as clueless about the Department as the Minister, but this is not a serious issue for, as ever, the mandarins will run the shop.

Then there is the acquisition of the constituency staff. The round dozen of those and the two Garda drivers means that in a fortnight the whole retinue of Ministers and Junior Ministers will generate more jobs than the Minister for Enterprise manages in a year. Of course, they are all non-productive posts but this genuinely is a case of never mind the quality, look at the quantity.

You might think our mandarins would be concerned about this waste of taxpayers' money. But in fact within the Irish system of governance the role and status of the Minister is to be the cat's-paw of his avaricious mandarin bosses and the best way to facilitate this is to ensure our man is a happy busy fool.

Happiness is the easy bit for, rather like a much-loved house cat, the first job of the new retinue is to shine the Minister's backside every day and compare it with the face of Princess Diana. In fairness, it is not hard where everyone from fellow politicians, businessmen and, yes, even journalists are a supplicant to develop an ego that, like any ferocious beast, devours everything that crosses its path.

One of the better examples of this creature is a certain Dermot Ahern, who started his Ministerial career as a gopher for Bertie Ahern. Oddly enough, though, when it came to the frolics of Ray Burke, Dermot displayed the forensic instincts of a bloodhound that has had his nose dipped in turpentine, and our man's career and sense of importance under Bertie prospered at an equal rate.

Such indeed was the extent of our man's *amour propre*, Dermot even began to correct those journalists who did not use his rightful Ministerial title. Sadly occasions of sin still exist where the delicate ego of the Minister can be accidentally bruised. One such poignant moment occurred at a FF think-in after the notoriously prickly Ahern smiled with delight as a female journalist noted of a strategically placed photograph of our hero surf boarding that he looked very well.

Alas, the bonhomie lasted for less than a second as the wretched hack asked, 'When was it taken, I'd say about a decade ago, was it?' As the Minister's face rapidly transformed itself into a more than passable imitation of a bulldog licking a nettle, it was unfortunate to see that sometimes, even when it comes to *la dolce vita* of the Irish Ministers, some rain still falls.

Chapter 46 ∾

THE STRANGE IMPORTANCE OF ETHICS IN A MOST UNETHICAL TIGER

It is surprising to think that outside of the building and celebrity industries the top growth area in our amoral Tiger economy was ethics. However, whilst the vast abandoned housing mausoleums that are dotted across the countryside are the most visible legacy of the Tiger, none of the 10,000 square foot houses is as hollow as the dusty, unfinished, unread reports created by the great Irish ethics industry.

The link between our ethicists and the Tiger culture of celebrity is less immediately obvious but both traded on gossip and celebrity for, in spite of their pomp, Tribunals were little more than soap operas whose foundations were the sort of spiteful whispers that died a gentle death when the stars left.

Of course, their establishment did provide us with yet another insight into the genius of Bertie. The Opposition may have hoped our Tribunals were a serpent that would bite the Fianna Fáil heel. However, anyone who believed these Potemkin star chambers were some great Moby Dick that would sweep away an entire culture had been gulled, for all of our inquiries were defined by the key characteristic of legal sterility. In short, no matter what corruption they uncovered, the Tribunals could not fine or imprison their witnesses. Instead, rather like a Fintan O'Toole column, the most they could do is wag their finger for an awfully long series of decades. Once again clever Bertie had, with his Irish solution to a FF problem, made sure the fix was in before the game had even started.

Though he may not have planned it this way, the Taoiseach managed to hogtie our Tribunal in one other critical way. Ahern's failure to limit the areas our Tribunals could investigate was the legal equivalent of letting a cocaine addict loose in a crack factory. Sadly once the barristers savoured their first hit, they ran riot for, like any other addict, one module was never enough.

Everyone is now cross about the cost and the handful of dust we have received for our billion euro. However, it is not as though Paddy was never warned, for the apogee of the American great age of ethics was reached when the Starr Inquiry spent four years and $30 million trawling through the affairs of the Clintons. Yet all Kenneth Starr discovered was that Mr Clinton liked to receive oral sex from women who were not his wife and, when caught, he understandably lied about it.

Compared with us, they got out of it cheap.

As America now looks back at its iconoclastic fury with puzzled distaste, the most surprising feature of our age of Tribunals was our initial enthusiasm for the process. The DIRT Inquiry was the most praised event in Irish media life but the response of our genially corrupt electorate, once we got a say on the matter, was to turf its celebrated Chairman, Jim Mitchell, out of the Dáil. We should not have been too surprised either, for one of the more delightful discoveries of DIRT was that an awful lot of respectable people such as teachers and doctors do not like to pay their taxes.

However, when it came to our Tribunals, Pat stood on the rocky foreshore, closed his eyes and leaped straight in. Initially it even looked as though the thing might work, for when the Planning Tribunal issued its first preliminary report, nobody raised a query over the fact that it had taken five years to get there. Instead, such was the excitement over the awesome discovery that Rambo Burke was corrupt, had any cute hoor Dublin councillor been wise enough to propose that the statue of Daniel O'Connell be taken down and replaced by dear Justice Flood, it would have been carried unanimously.

So what went wrong with a Tribunal system that started so well that we soon had half a dozen of them? The Flood Tribunal, after all, captured our hearts to such an extent the 'people's Tribunal' became the legal equivalent of Princess Diana. Sadly, like Diana, the private truth was less edifying than the public profile. The mood music was set early as its first star witness collapsed in a theatrical heap and wailed, 'in the dock is it I am, Oh mother of God, the dock'. We may have fallen in love with James Gogarty as he laid waste to a succession of pompous barristers by telling them they were overpaid wasters who gave him 'a pain in my face'. However, in spite of superb one-liners such as 'Will we get a receipt … will we fuck', Gogarty was a garrulous old fraud whose role in the Tribunal was informed by the desire for vengeance over some obscure pension dispute rather than the public interest.

The next favourite, Frank Dunlop, was a serial perjurer who once famously claimed he had 'balls of steel'. In fact, when the heat came on Frank had a centre of marshmallow, for when caught, he swiftly cooked up a road to Damascus style moment on the appropriately named Spy Wednesday of 2000. Frank, however, was simply too much of a creep to carry this act off and by the close of business we were being treated to the singular sight of Tribunal counsel savaging their own stool pigeon.

As the fantasist Tom Gilmartin added his own unique presence to the heady flux ultimately the most loved figure of them all was the little judge. Sadly, though he was a great man for the witty *bon mot* about how his Tribunal was wandering around 'like an Arab lost in the Sahara' (not that he ever did anything about it), Flood was no crusading iconoclast.

Of course, it should be noted, the poor lawyers within were dealing with no ordinary men. Nothing epitomised the nature of those who were there more than a vignette involving the testimony of Liam Lawlor. As the Tribunal headed off on a small excursion into Liam's property dealings in the Czech Republic—and though we had already spent time looking into the details of a proposal by Liam to use bulls' blood to manufacture human blood products, we were as puzzled as anyone by this turn of events—Lawlor engaged in a vivid description of his arrival in that country after the fall of the communist regime.

In truth, it all left us feeling quite sorry for the plucky little Czechs. After decades of Nazi and communist oppression, the Prague Spring and the quashing of the velvet revolution, they were entitled to a break. Instead, when democracy arrives, the first representatives of this noble tradition to come through the door are Liam and the lads looking for dealing.

Ultimately, just as Falstaff once mused about the excessive importance given to honour, perhaps we should ask what precisely has this ethics thing done for us? The McCracken and Moriarty reports have been described as triumphs yet neither discovered a single act of corruption by Mr Haughey. And, outside of Mr Haughey, the list of Tribunal casualties is a thin one. Journalism did for Michael Lowry whilst the other victims consist of the odious PR puffball Frank Dunlop, Liam Lawlor, George Redmond, a couple of mice-like county councillors and a toad called Rambo. Of course, Des O'Neill won his tortuous battle for the head of Bertie but he took out a man whose powers had been hollowed away by the erosions of a decade in power.

The problem with Tribunals was not just the scale of the price tag. Instead, the real damage they inflicted was that politics became a contest of morality where politicians vied to prove their ethical superiority. Sadly the decade-long rampage of our 'resign now and prove your innocence later' Savonarolas thinned the political bloodstream to the point where virtues like independent-mindedness are impossible. Instead, we have created a new political caste of pious nonentities whose only achievement consists of being so politically ineffectual no one would bother corrupting them.

In fairness, our Tribunals were of service to the state in one surprising respect, for they shone far more light on the true nature of the legal profession. In a world where Senior Counsel, as they prefer to be called, never tire of telling the rest of us just how ordinary we are, the Mahon Tribunal was a rare social experiment where we were allowed to see how much better the country would be if the M'Luds were allowed to run the place.

We certainly got our answer as our legal Big Brother became a national joke. The Mahon Tribunal was supposed to be about the cleansing of Augean stables. Instead, like some modern version of the East India Company, it became a monopolistic cash cow for a fortuitous elite.

Unsurprisingly, long before its close, even our barrister friends were anxiously calling for the abolition of this gravy train before public attention turned towards how well the really big beasts were doing. Sadly amidst all of this despair there was one other piece of bad news. Like any other plague, ethics had initially been confined to the one site but now the virus began to extend its brief to all aspects of Pat's life.

Chapter 47 ∾

POOR PADDY IS STANDING IN THE RAIN

So that's the triumph of ethics

The one thing that can be said in favour of the recession is that it ended the great age of ethics, for we are far too busy simply trying to survive these days to be worrying about Tribunals. Sadly the plain people of Ireland are still suffering from the outworking of the last sting of our dying liberal wasps. The man sitting in a pub reading the *Racing Post* as the smoke from his cigarette curled lazily towards the ceiling may have been doing no harm, but if he believed that it was enough to be left alone by the forces of the state, he was wrong.

Instead, under the great age of quangos, simply doing no harm is not enough to save you from being denounced by the state. The British common law system may have a doctrine called the right to be left alone by your neighbour, but in Ireland the priest-ridden country of the 'Valley of the Squinting Windows' has been replaced by the new oppression of the sociology-ridden quangos of the squinting liberals.

The great attack by the state on the poor old smokers was all the more surprising because in general Fianna Fáil is wise enough to avoid the great dangers that accompany leadership. But in fairness to Micheál Martin, when it came to the solitary political triumph of his career he had a clearer understanding of the real nature of the Irish than his opponents. The dismissive response to the possibility that this non-smoking horror might work was filled with confidence in our status as a rebellious nation of lawbreakers. That, however, was predicated upon the great revolt against the rod licence, when rural Ireland rebelled over the possibility we might actually pay to retain fish stocks in our rivers as distinct from maintaining the grand old tradition of poisoning and netting them all.

The actual truth, as our recent history after Independence shows, is that like all colonial peoples we are actually a docile race who will accept almost any form of maltreatment. We, after all, calmly surrendered to basic indignities like the abolition of any expression of sexual desire in the Free State except for delicately cloaked clerical paedophile tendencies. And on a more elevated level, a nation that trades on its reputation as a centre of literature accepted the censorship of all free thought that was driven by a few petty clerks and mad priests.

We should not, therefore, be surprised the surrender to the smoking ban was so meek, for our governors knew us better than we knew ourselves. The bad news for us was that our government also realised after the smoking ban that they could do whatever they wanted and from that point on, as we are finding to our cost, they generally did.

It didn't help that the Opposition behaved disgracefully and rowed in behind the ban lest they be left hanging on the hind tit of the great moral crusade. But oddly enough, in spite of the fret, no one answered Moore McDowell's elegant point that seeing as the smoking ban would not abolish morbidity there was little point to it.

Instead, Micheál Martin's Mothers' League of health professionals were hungrily dreaming of the many fine jobs as anti-smoking Czars that our sociology graduates, who would not even in an age of full employment have been capable of getting gainful employment, would secure.

Alas for us, the new ban encouraged the government to terrorise an otherwise blameless people. Suddenly Ministers rattling around with nothing between their ears that might provoke them to do something useful had a purpose as they competed to find new things to ban.

The finest example of this was the war on the great social evil of the happy hour. Ironically the chief victims of this were pensioners who would drink two pints of Beamish on a Friday afternoon. One would have thought they were not a threat to society but, in truth, the miseries of the poor old fellas were forgotten as the war was swiftly extended.

The whole concept of the perfect body even infected the realm of politics as figures like Enda attempted to persuade us they should be Taoiseach simply because they could climb up African mountains. Seeing as the humble ape possesses similar talents, it was difficult to decipher what precise message Enda was sending.

Sadly a subsequent celebration of the Fine Gael leader's athleticism certainly sent a few mixed messages when a large poster of Enda, looking as though he had just won a wet t-shirt competition, was pasted to the wall by a

FG leader who was utterly oblivious to the real meaning of the wolf whistles coming from a nearby gay bar.

As our ethical Czars went to war against the racist tendencies of politicians that were so invisible none of us even knew they existed, the great apogee of the new inquisitiveness occurred courtesy of the creation of the Equality Authority.

This was set up to go to war with all sort of nefarious things such as boys and men and they took to the job with such a venomous will they even went on the hunt against the poor golfing bores of Portmarnock. Of course, that was the great Waterloo of the oppression of the ethicists but the critical factor behind the curbing of their wings had nothing to do with the return of sanity to the public discourse. It was instead informed by the fact that the money had run out.

It certainly didn't do our reputation in Europe much good either, as Ireland swiftly became the European example of the domino theory of ethics. As governments across Europe gaped in awe, our acceptance of the smoking ban sent out a sombre message for free-thinking ordinary citizens of every other country. After all, if the mad Irish could be tamed with such ease then the more civilised Mediterranean states would fall. So it was that the poor peoples of France, Italy and, most astonishingly of all, Scotland were skittled like nine-pins and it became clear Ireland's two main 'gifts' to Europe now consist of Christianity and the smoking ban.

Is it any wonder they hate us so?

Back in Ireland, the sole clear message that the Valley of the Squinting Windows' smoking vigilantes sent us was that when it comes to the oppression of the citizen, the only thing that changes is the apparel. Once repression was signalled by the swish of the cleric's soutane but now it comes garbed in a suit, with a generic speaker-phone and a huge taxpayer-funded salary.

It is perhaps typical that one question no one ever asks is: What precisely did the Great War on pub smoking achieve?

One supposes that those bureaucrats who only want the sort of job that means they will have nothing useful to do were happy. As for poor old Pat, all he knows about the great age of ethics is that he has ended up smoking in the rain whilst his pint goes sour on the counter.

Chapter 48 ❧

THE BAR LOBBY IS DEAD, LONG LIVE PIOUS NEW MORAL FIANNA FÁIL

Back in an age where jokes were still not illegal, PJ Mara famously joked about how the new breed of non-drinking, non-smoking, and non-carousing Fianna Fáil advisors were Ireland's first 'Taliban'. As was so often the case, Mara was being more prescient than we thought he was. But FF's affable old Mephistopheles was also signalling the arrival of his own sell-by date.

The relationship between FF and morality had, up to 2002, been a simple one. We understood that sometimes out of necessity FF, in Opposition, would adopt morality as a flag of convenience. But even back then they would wink and nod so as to assure us nervous ones that their heart wasn't really in it.

The passing of that day is best symbolised by the surprise innocent souls in Leinster House feel over the fact that Thomas Byrne, the new FF TD for Meath, never smiles. The reason is simple, for Thomas is part of that gathering force in Irish politics known as pious new moral FF. And whilst the numbers of paid up members of the new Taliban are not yet legion, men like Pious Pat Carey, Noel Dempsey, Dermot Ahern, Peter Power and Micheál Martin are well advanced in the critical task of deleting the poor old roués of the bar lobby from the pages of history.

Seeing as we have spent decades lecturing the dusty old FF dog about their bad habits, one supposes we should be pleased about this new evolutionary advance.

The problem, of course, with the rise of pious new moral FF is that life in Ireland is never simple. It is not that Pat has ever been specifically against morality. However, we did get quite a bucketload of it from the Church and, after the iron rule of Archbishop McQuaid and a series of scarlet-faced divines, we have always preferred it in theory rather than practice.

Occasionally, after years of excess, we would detox ourselves with a grand brief Fine Gael led administration but, like the bad lad who sometimes goes out with a nice girl for a change, we always swiftly tired of the camphor-and-carbolic-style regime of the FG nurse. It was hard on FG but life was simply more enjoyable in a world ruled by those affable FF rogues. We did suspect they were a little corrupt—well, to be truthful, we knew they were—but we elected them to ensure that our own lax standards would be protected, for what harm does a little bit of corruption do? It allowed the old widow (and coincidentally the billionaire builder!) to get a bit of planning, the pub to stay open beyond all decency, the lads to draw the dole and work and if the thing ever escalated out of control, well, then we and FG knew our place in the world.

Sadly all our certainties have now been destroyed by the new breed of FF TDs who have taken to lecturing ourselves and the Opposition about our sins. That in itself would be bad enough but, even if they had been indulging in the old-style FF politics of hiding in full view, all that snarling at the Opposition (and us!) for our collective failure to save FF from themselves would have been a step too far. What was even worse was that these guys weren't even winking, for they actually believed this tripe.

We do understand the main factor in the collapse of support for FF has been their role in the reduction of the Irish economy to a state where Albania now looks like a model of fiscal rectitude. However, the rise of piety within FF has played its role, for it is hard to cope when, like that poignant denouement of *Animal Farm*, we look at FF and see a posse of Eithne FitzGeralds.

Once again the Ministers were to blame, for all this morality thing began inevitably with Noel Dempsey and the plastic bags. It was entertaining to see something so minor being turned into a moral crusade, but we should have known this was only the start. This, of course, was followed by Micheál Martin and the smoking ban and the wars against happy hour in pubs. With leadership like that, it wasn't the TDs' fault that morality finally wormed its way into the back benches of the party.

In fairness, the evolution of the FF Taliban would probably have occurred anyway, for another unfortunate cultural shift played an even more serious role in the rise of the pious new moral politician. You see the pious new moral FF really only became a problem when politics became a respectable career. Suddenly, an entirely disreputable class of person began to enter the profession, as an array of barristers, priests and schoolteachers replaced FF's happy old drunkards.

The rise of the pious new moral politician was aided and abetted by the evolution of a new hydra, as the excesses of the age of Bertie created a monstrous new regiment of quangos. The problem was our new cadre of advocacy officers had nothing better to be doing with their time than calling for the abolition of various previously harmless pastimes. Oddly enough, these were primarily working class and rural pursuits such as drinking, smoking, gambling and hare coursing.

Much of the impulse had more to do with the economy than any concern about the people's moral and physical well-being, for when the Celtic Tiger was in full swing we needed healthy workers and consumers to keep the conceit running at full tilt. Ironically now that we are in bits the only thing that's left for poor old Pat to do is the drinking, the gambling and the smoking. Indeed, these three are now the sole remaining healthy aspects of the consumer economy.

The bad news for the people was that the rise of the pious new moral politician and the creation of a new autocracy of quangos evolved into a toxic combination. The success of the country filled our politicians with a dangerous sense of moral superiority. How they had actually secured all of these triumphs continued to be a bit of a mystery to them but they were certain of this one thing: it was they, not accidental world events, that were responsible.

The problem this, of course, led to was that our heroic politicians now had to hunt for new worlds to conquer. And our quangos were more than willing to give them the tools and a list of things to do.

So it was that after decades of avoiding the great fundamental error of their opponents, FF abandoned their old policies of pandering to the people and decided to devote their energies to the none too easy task of improving them. After all, the public are a mirror image of its governing class and, to be honest, the ever-fatter, alcohol-sodden Irish were letting their glorious leaders down.

It is unfortunate that a mere eight decades after overthrowing the British we grew a new set of oppressors. However, in fairness to the electorate, as FF replaced all their old dealers with national schoolteachers the party's support began to collapse. There was, after all, no joy in seeing your average TD creeping around like a latter-day Uriah Heap who, even as he smiles, cannot disguise his detestation of you.

It was all enough to make you nostalgic for the time when FF was run by cattle dealers and dancehall owners. Ray MacSharry and Albert might not have spent a lot of time in church but they knew how to run a country. In contrast, if you take the current lot out of their comfort zone of banning things and ask them to do something useful, they're lost without their moral compass.

In the end nothing could protect us, or indeed even these poor souls, from the inexorable truth that the affable rogues of FF had been infected by syphilis of the soul. They were that rare creature who becomes embittered by success.

Happily we do suspect the reign of the Taliban will be a short one. It is not just that the people are tired of morality. The problem is that, like their clerical predecessors who fluttered about dirty books when children were being murdered by colleagues in cassocks, our Taliban missed the big issues.

Whilst they were raising quite the furore about junk food, the country was being collapsed by junk bonds. And whilst our cold creatures of the Taliban prided themselves on the mastery of the cold steel of morality, when the great crash occurred they collapsed in as much of a heap as their priestly ancestors.

Chapter 49

MEET THE MAN
EMBITTERED BY SUCCESS

I f he were useful, or even efficient, we might just forgive him, for slaves can learn to love a benevolent tyrant. And in fairness to Mr Dempsey, his ten degrees of separation from the people is not perhaps entirely his fault. They may criticise Dempsey over the new Taliban-style drink-driving regime he has imposed on the rural bachelors of Ireland, who are apparently constitutionally entitled to consume a gallon of porter before driving 'harmlessly' home on the new motorway at 40 miles to the hour.

But when you consider it appropriate to use the Ministerial jet to deliver a dusty speech to a summer school of bores, it is easy to forget how ordinary people live. And besides, the fret and concern of a rural farmer is minor enough when compared with the importance of creating some sort of faux Ministerial legacy.

Some charitable souls believe the mystery of Dempsey is that, in yet another one of those ironies where we become what we most hate, Noel has been captured by the great cabal of bureaucrats. In a classic example of the art of hiding in full view the man without an idea may pose as a great public intellectual, but Meath's man of straw has been devoured by the great machine.

It is certainly clear that like most bureaucrats, one of the few smug pleasures Noel appears to enjoy is imposing restrictions on the lives of harassed individuals. It is as though he is the modern reincarnation of the sort of parish priest who eased his own frustrations by driving summertime couples out of heated ditches with a blackthorn stick.

It is, of course, possible Mr Dempsey was even genuinely idealistic once, but we do not care anymore. Instead, all we see is the sour face and the hectoring words and that is enough to switch us off for, along with Mary

Harney and Dermot Ahern, he is the most public exemplar of the acid corroding the soul of this government.

During the rare occasions when this trio dignify the Dáil with their presence, as Mr Cowen sits in his solitary isolated little bubble, the troika begin a bitter little discourse. They rarely speak up and never deign to look in the direction of their inferiors in the press gallery or Opposition. But as they chatter together like three impotent queens in The George, the curl of the lips and the sneers that flit past their spoilt faces are instilled with a contempt that is almost chilling.

Such, indeed, is the level of *hauteur* we are sometimes filled with embarrassment for the inconvenience the exigencies of democracy impose upon their grandiose schemes.

In truth, we suspect our three blind political doges believe if there were a respectable way to do away with the inconveniences of democracy, it would take very little to convince them that a Fianna Fáil dictatorship of the proletariat (with one seat for the mendicant PD too, please!) would be the most appropriate road to take.

When it comes to Dempsey, the most defining characteristic of this grandee has been his acute distaste for the actual operation of Irish democracy. This process began courtesy of Mr Dempsey's abolition of the dual mandate where TDs could also be councillors. In retrospect it is almost embarrassing now to realise the great defence of this proposal was that TDs would no longer have to dirty their hands with parochial matters. This would, in the world according to Noel, create a Dáil of legislators who would debate great affairs of state. Seeing as Mr Dempsey's own Dáil contributions rarely amount to much more than a few dry polemical sneers, it was a big ask to expect that our poor deppities would rise to such wondrous heights.

This was not the only side-swipe Mr Dempsey took at excesses of populism in the democratic process. He was also, not that this is bruited all that much these days, the genesis behind the great electronic voting debacle. Martin Cullen may have taken the hit for that but it was Dempsey who let this particular genie out of the bottle.

Of course, once again Mr Dempsey gilded this spiteful decision to replace the one day of theatre and drama Irish politics experiences with a computer printout in the elevated language of efficiency. It is hard, however, not to believe that Mr Dempsey's enthusiasm for 'reform' was actually informed by a Puritanical dislike of all forms of theatre. He, in short, believes the people should be enumerated rather than entertained.

The Minister's grandiosity means it is easy to forget Mr Dempsey is no philosopher king. He is in fact nothing more than an overly ambitious jumped up secondary schoolteacher from Trim. Of course, after 13 years of being surrounded by deferential hacks it is perhaps understandable he believes himself to be the reincarnation of Louis xiv. However, the third-level fees disaster was far more typical of the Dempsey style of governance. Anyone with sense would have staked out the battlefield and realised such an act of social inclusion would not find favour with the politics of Mary Harney. But, of course, like a one-man version of the Light Brigade—or a man desperately in search of some positive media coverage—Dempsey proposed and reversed within a month. And in moving too swiftly our man buried the prospect of any genuine reform within our universities for another five years.

This had scant impact on a man who simply continued to sail on in a soft cloud of oblivious self-regard that nothing can dent. He is in the perfect place now, for the Minister's final berth in Transport suits his particular qualities.

Sadly the reason for this is that, in a remarkably similar fashion to his larger doppelganger Ms Harney, the Transport Minister has outsourced so many functions there is no Ministry left for him to govern. Like the Emperor with no clothes, he is the Minister for Transport who is not in charge of roads, trains, planes or automobiles.

The most impressive example of Mr Dempsey's absolute determination to keep it that way occurred after we experienced our worst weather crisis in 30 years.

The Minister for Transport flew off on his holidays to Malta.

In fairness, when he finally returned to a very cross country, the Minister was crystal clear about the pointlessness of having him around for such a crisis. Such, however, is the ignorance of the people that even when Dempsey said he could not think 'of one other item that could have been done if I was in the country over the last four or five days', the furore did not abate.

Dempsey was not unique, for Mr Gormley made it eloquently clear he was not in charge of the council response, nobody quite knew what to do with the army and, as is always the case in a crisis, Mr Cowen was nowhere to be found. Still, you might think the political system would be a bit embarrassed when Ray D'Arcy and Matt Cooper provide the public with far more useful information about how to deal with a crisis than the entire apparatus of government.

Unsurprisingly, they weren't.

In spite of all the old guff about 'blue skies' nothing epitomised the nature of the final sands of Dempsey's career more than his response when Alan Shatter courageously published the Tracey Fay report into the death of a child under HSE care. Dempsey spent the next day in the Dáil bitterly condemning Shatter's act of transparency.

So why has Dempsey turned into such a strange political creature who is so obviously miserable in his job? The problem with Noel is not that he is uncertain about his own brilliance or the worth of the job he is doing. He is instead that rare creature that has been embittered by success. He is not, of course, alone for we have in the main a Cabinet of misanthropes whose defining characteristic is stupidity crossed with a prim, dour Puritanism.

Noel, however, is, even amongst their ranks, the high king of the politics of self-pity. It is this belief that informs the curious spectacle where the happiness of others raises a dull ache in his soul. You see, like the scowling Cromwell passing the laughter of theatregoers, Noel believes a people that can never live up to his imperial standards are sinners who must be punished and whipped into shape.

And, by Jaysus, but Noel the overpromoted schoolteacher from Trim is the man to do that.

SECTION 9

Unloved outsiders

YOU WANT TO BE A TD? WELL, HERE'S HOW TO BE THE PERFECT RUNNING MATE AND SUCCEED

If you are young, ambitious and feel that you have something to contribute to Irish politics, the most important characteristic you must cultivate as an aspirant TD is the appearance of utter stupidity. The reason for this is that most new candidates, if they want to get on, have to kick a member of their own party out of the Dáil. If, as is the case with the majority of Leinster House TDs, you are taking on some dynastic creature whose family have had their foot on the throat of the constituency for eight decades, then it really does become complicated.

It doesn't help either that the biggest issue any aspiring new TD must face is that sitting TDs devote an inordinate amount of their time to the critical task of finding the perfect running mate. One of the finest maestros of this art was the former Fianna Fáil TD Noel Davern. Even his skills were tested when, during the height of Bertie's popularity, the long-term TD for Tipperary was faced with the horror of two by-elections.

The great threat of the by-election is that party headquarters will, like the political equivalent of a Revenue audit, take a close look at the affairs of a constituency and find a bright new viable candidate who will not only win the by-election but also knock the current incumbent 'off his fucking perch'.

It would have been some achievement, given the state of the love affair with Bertie at the time, for FF to lose even one election. Instead, they lost two. On both occasions Davern protested the best men for the job were chosen. However, our suspicions about the quality of the two wandering straw-boys FF put up were subsequently confirmed for, oddly enough when Davern retired, FF won two seats with the most unlikely team of Mattie 'the boy who cried wolf' McGrath and Martin 'the Irish RM' Mansergh in a constituency that prior to that had returned just one FF TD in over 20 years.

The tale of Noel Davern's running mates is an object lesson in how difficult it is to even get on the pitch unless the sitting deputy can be convinced you are an utter fool. Political parties may be little villages of their own, but everyone in politics is a sole trader, and in a capitalist world competition is a vice.

Sometimes there are accidents where a young idealist does slip through the net. Up to the last election Micheál Martin had the perfect running mate, who was elderly and uninterested in anything more complex than the fixing of his constituents' gutters. Sadly through some execrable accident of fate this fine useless soul was replaced by the young FF councillor Michael McGrath. The problem for poor Martin is that McGrath is everything Micheál was two decades ago. He may be no different or no better but he is new and poor Micheál is not so new and now Micheál is in serious trouble.

Of course, outside of the young and the idealistic those who pose the greatest of threats are the women. Happily these can be dealt with quite easily for if they are married the most effective variant of the kiss of Judas consists of subtle sighs about how it will be very hard for her to be looking after the children. And if they are single you can smile blissfully and say your 'flighty' new running mate will have a grand time in Dublin what with the shopping and the nightlife.

Outside of cultivating a persona of utter haplessness, the aspirant TD must avoid the errors made by the still unknown Fine Gael councillor James Daly. The reason our councillor is still unknown is because James launched a ferocious attack on the failures of the Flanagan and Enright dynasties at the Laois Offaly election convention of 2006. It was expected to be a tight race and in a not entirely inaccurate speech Daly portrayed himself as being a new broom sweeping out the empty vessels who had failed FG. The bad news, however, was that this was a terrible crime against the great political philosophy of 'loyalty', where, if the party leader says that the sun revolves around the earth, then the membership nod their heads sagely and agree.

By the time Daly concluded, such was the extent of his sin some of his own voters had even turned against him. It was, for Daly, an unwelcome but valuable lesson about how, rather like those male lions, if you want to be successful in Irish politics you must go around with your ears flattened until you can launch a sneak attack on the king of the pride.

Of course, some running mates do get elected by accident but the process of abasement and duplicity that must occur is only for those who possess the strongest of constitutions. Once elected to the local council, you must listen to the little people's interminable complaints about their lot and effusively praise the sitting TD who is, glory be to God, fierce busy up there in Dublin mixing with the media, out late until 2 and 3 in the morning before he gets back to the four-star hotel. And if you can manage a dozen years of this, then possibly the great chance may arrive.

The astonishing thing is that such a technique crosses all urban and rural divides. And it is only fair to note that unlike other vices that are mostly confined to FF, the destruction of young talent is an all-party operation. Labour are in a state of profound shock about Mr Pink but Perfect Gilmore's new policy whereby any candidate sure of winning the seat must incorporate a running mate. Within FG meanwhile, after the failed coup of the aristocrats the worst punishment that is to be suffered by the rebel losers is the imposition of a credible constituency colleague.

There is, alas, one terrible consequence to all of this. If you do happen to be elected, there is no escape from the image you have created for, like those Russian dolls, there is always a miniature version of yourself waiting to gobble you up. This means that should you try to re-invent yourself, soon the nodding and the whispering, generally led by the recently defeated sitting TD, will begin about your man up there in Dublin getting notions of himself.

You are, in short, the living embodiment of Flann O'Brien's gothic tale about the taxidermist who murders his rival, puts the dead man's skin over his face, cannot get it off and ends up being executed for the murder of himself.

There is, of course, one more victim in all of this, for the intrinsic distrust the voters feel about the prospect of sending intelligent representatives up to Dublin is not without consequence. You see, if we constantly create a house of representatives cast in their own mediocre images, why then should we be surprised nothing ever changes in Irish politics? Just as you are what you eat, we are what we elect.

Chapter 51 ๛

AN UNPOPULAR DEFENCE
OF THE SENATORS

It's late afternoon on Wednesday and amidst the cloistered light that shines through dusty windows into the three-quarters empty chamber 'the lads' and a couple of scattered women are about to start another week's work. Outside, the laughter of the young secretaries can be heard but it is muted, for some Senators complain if it is too noisy.

It might, of course, in these new efficient times seem to be a bit late in the week to be easing oneself into the job. The self-styled Upper House, however, is a civilised place where the old aristocratic values of politics as a part-time sporting hobby still prevail.

As one looks around they certainly are a curious grouping. But perhaps the most unnerving feature of the House is the excited manner in which they look at the press gallery when someone arrives. The gaze is best summarised as being infused by the uncertain excitement of the abandoned habitués of the Battersea home for dogs. As with the dogs, there is a great commotion, but amidst this political equivalent of the wagging of tails there is something irrevocably poignant about the way our lost political pets—like David Norris—are nervously hopeful that they will be petted rather than annihilated.

The excitement makes for some contrast with the Dáil where, in between their critical Ministerial tasks of texting and snarling at the Opposition, the government casts occasional glares of scarcely concealed contempt at everyone else. Sadly there is a reason why, like the fall of Eden, the pastoral innocence of our Senators has been contaminated by a certain fear. Our harmless, dusty old Senators have, you see, become the targets of a certain iconoclastic fury, for an institution that was once chiefly famous for the enthusiasm of its debates over the virtues of banning books is now in danger of being banned itself.

However, is it really the case that our Senators should be booted into the dustbin of history? The Seanad may be responsible for the launch of the political careers of James Bannon and Mary Robinson, and it's hard to know which act was worse, but does it really deserve its reputation as Ireland's last rotten borough?

Let us look and contemplate before making our final decision. In a chamber that is now half full, Rónán Mullen is looking around with the plump self-regard of a monsignor being gazed at by an adoring gathering of nuns at a diocesan get-together. Beside him sits Ivana Bacik, the slightly blowsy pet radical of the Labour party, who has run for every office in the land outside of the mayoralty of Dublin and we haven't ruled out that possibility just yet.

Behind them the bad lads of the Seanad are sitting together chuckling with all the insolent gossipy delight of three gurriers in string vests standing outside a bookie's office. Joe O'Toole may be a left-wing social democrat whilst Shane Ross is the darling of the anarchic wing of the right and as for David Norris … well, David is the darling of himself. However, within the chamber of the Seanad these three very different souls are united by a shared irreverent wisdom and a pleasure in undermining the sanctimonious pomposity of government Ministers, bankers and civil service mandarins.

The afternoon sunlight pours through the gently settling dust motes, coating the thinking man's public intellectual, Eoghan Harris, with an ethereal aura. As Fianna Fáil's Pat Moylan—and yes, he is yet another pet of the Cowen clan who has advanced far beyond his natural abilities to the Cathaoirleach's post—directs proceedings with all of the certainty of an Italian traffic policeman, there is an even more unconventional grouping gathered on the government benches.

Here, for example, can be found eccentrics such as Terry Leyden, who is a political survivor from the Haughey era. Terry, who was out of national politics for a decade before returning to the Seanad, cannot believe he is back, and to be honest neither can we. So far Senator Terry's most dramatic interventions have consisted of the near burning down of Leinster House by a scented candle in his office and a recent spat over an accusation that Fintan O'Toole has been inciting treasonable mobs.

There is also no shortage of dusty FF oul' fellas such as Jim Walsh, Camillus 'one punch' Glynn and Labhrás Ó Murchú who, rather like the pensioners who attend court cases, would be quite lost for something to do if their Seanad bolthole were not there.

The Fine Gael benches, being full of aspirant TDs, are for the most part a significantly drier lot. Frances Fitzgerald and Fidelma Healy Eames are emoting on behalf of the people whilst beside them the last lost leader of the

PDS, known as Mr 'What's His Name?', who is also believed to trade under the pseudonym of Ciarán Cannon, stares despairingly at the ceiling.

As we are consoled by the realisation that even our uncertain world can provide a safe haven for such harmless souls as Mr 'What's His Name?', we do, however, miss the agonised glances of Déirdre de Búrca at Dan Boyle. Dan's great achievement has been to introduce twittering to Irish politics, though those of us who have contemplated Michael Woods for any extended period of time thought it was already here. But for every Dan, there is the consolation of Donie Cassidy, the Senator with the most nervously commented upon hairdo in Irish politics, for it has not changed either in style or colour for two decades. Mr Cassidy, who has recently been involved in an unfortunate furore over doing his duty by going on an Oireachtas golfing junket to Turkey, is a happy soul these days. Our man was once accidentally elected to the Dáil at the expense of Mary 'Madame la guillotine' O'Rourke. It is said of Senator Donie that the happiest day in his life occurred when he lost his Dáil seat and was allowed to return to the Seanad.

As we survey this political equivalent of some dying Welsh mining village it's hard not to be infused by a genuine sense of nostalgia. Half of them look as though they might be better suited for some gentlemen's club in St Stephen's Green. But the rest would make up quite the formidable Cabinet, for the country would certainly be none the worse if the iconoclastic acerbic qualities of Joe O'Toole and Shane Ross were blended with the political cunning of a Martin Brady. Then there is also the practical intelligence of FF's Geraldine Feeney and the latent capacities of Eugene 'the assassin' Regan who managed even from these dim backwaters to inflict more damage on Bertie Ahern and Willie O'Dea than his own party leader.

Looking at them, it strikes us that there is no need for FG's great constitutional referenda, for what we have in front of us is a selection of politicians any list system would aspire to produce.

Sadly we are locked into one of those awful Irish dances of death, where all decent public opinion now believes virtue demands the abolition of our poor Senators. Nothing epitomised this appalling spectacle more than the sight of Enda casting a vacant mind in their direction as he hunted desperately for a cheap target. In truth, if he was genuine about improving the effectiveness of the political system, Enda might have been better off simply axing a few of his own backbenchers and replacing them with our Senators.

Of course, the case for retention was not at all improved by the many misadventures of Ivor the expenses engine. But ultimately, the great problem for our Senators is that, in the great age of Cowenite brutalism, we now live in a state where, like IKEA, virtue is defined by the cheapness of a thing rather than its value. We would, however, posit one small final question. Such is the wretched nature of Irish governance that if an institution does not do any harm, we are ahead of the game. Our Senators may not be of much use but at least they did not bankrupt the state.

Perhaps, before we defenestrate our gentlemen amateurs, we should look at the track record of the TDs in the other side of the building lest we, in fact, abolish the wrong House.

Chapter 52 ⌒

ADIEU TO THE GREAT
SULTANS OF SPIN

T he nature of the relationship between politicians and the media is epitomised by a small vignette in which a rural TD, who had laboured for a long anonymous period of time, was appointed to a Junior Ministerial position essentially out of pity. Shortly afterwards the new Minister was rooted to the spot in terror when he was, in the company of Bertie, ambushed by a posse of cameramen. Happily when he wailed, 'Jaysus, what will I do?' Bertie, who was then still a darling of the fawning media, saw the neophyte Minister's discomfort, leaned over and offered the sage advice of 'Just smile at the ****s.'

You simply can't beat experience.

In fairness to Mr Ahern, he is not the only Taoiseach to have used that particular phrase that dare not name its name about his media friends. On another occasion an even more embattled Taoiseach stared out the window of his office at a drizzle of depressed hacks and mused miserably about how 'there's probably a battalion of those ****s out there'. The mood did not improve when a civil servant, who was too clever for his own good, looked out the window and said, 'Ah no, Taoiseach, there's eight hundred men in a battalion and there's not eight hundred of the ****s there this morning.'

It says a lot about the relationship between politicians and the media that the former use the entire gamut of scatological abuse when it comes to their private description of those who define their public image. A smarter group of people would say this is not the way to go, for one of the oddities of politics is that whilst the one thing most politicians obsess over more than anything is the media, they manage us terribly badly.

This was not always the case, for during the great age of spin we were controlled all too well by figures such as Fergus Finlay and PJ Mara. They were very different characters, for Finlay embodied the traits of some reforming

Calvinist pastor but Mara, in contrast, as he padded gently through the corridors, resembled some Venetian courtier crossed with a latter-day member of the ratpack.

His defining moment occurred during the Bertie era when, at the first campaign launch in 2002, he casually noted, 'It's showtime, folks.' Afterwards there was much high-minded tutting about the need for politics to have higher moral values than showbusiness. PJ, however, was at worst guilty of the crime of honesty, for the ultimate ethos of the showtime remark is the relativist belief that nothing in life is that important. It is all about the great game, having a bit of fun and 'sending the punters home sweating'. And in the era of Bertie, politics was about little more than that.

Finlay's rather more agonised approach was best captured by the marvellous scene in Sean Duignan's *One Spin on the Merry-Go-Round* where Finlay confronts Albert's press officer over the Beef Tribunal report. All one can say of Duignan's description of being 'confronted by this Old Testament whirlwind of wrath, biblical beard quivering like Moses about to strike down the idolaters of the Golden Calf. Repent, repent' is that they don't make them like that anymore.

In his own way Sean Duignan also provides us with the great template of how spin-doctoring should work. If you cannot seduce us, then your last surviving chance is to appeal to our none too well-developed capacity to pity a troubled soul being tossed around contemptuously by the vagaries of fate and a leader intent on self-immolation. This, you see, is a scenario we are all too familiar with and, like Chaplin's tramp, Duignan carried off the necessary marriage of pathos and dignity with aplomb.

It helped that men such as Duignan and Mara were all too well versed in a world that went far beyond the confined cloisters of Leinster House. This allowed them to be sanguine about the apparent dramas of a place that sometimes appears to have all the sense of proportion of Enid Blyton's *Malory Towers*.

It is easy to forget these days that the art of spin-doctoring is essentially simple. Like all great soccer players, the spin-doctor must be able to spot the apparently simple pass that no one else can see that will change a match. One of the finest examples of this was provided by the Fianna Fáil press team of 1995–7. They discovered that the path to power could be smoothed immeasurably by marinating the media with copious amounts of alcohol leavened by much flattery about our wit and brilliance and by either cajoling or threatening the party's leading lights to be at least outwardly pleasant to the media.

This was, of course, no mean feat for, though many of us did not know it at the time, if FF have one core value, it is that all journalists, even the many embedded ones, are '****s'. In truth, so long as the drink was flowing we would not have minded too much anyway. Such, instead, is the innate modesty of the Irish journalist, being called ****s suits our self-image a lot better than the apparent belief of the spin-doctors of Fine Gael and Labour that they are living in the Irish equivalent of 'The West Wing'.

When it comes to the current decline of the art of spin, the two biggest afflictions to affect Irish spin-doctors were the aforementioned 'West Wing' and Alastair Campbell.

The problem is that, as with literature, nothing original ever occurs in politics. So it was that Irish spin-doctors began to model their techniques on the patterns set by these very different prototypes. Sadly FG and Labour have yet to realise that, unlike 'The West Wing', not every ending is a happy one. It is also not, trust me, easy to enthusiastically collude in the view that Enda Kenny is the next Jed Bartlet and we cynical media types should do the decent thing and join 'Enda's team'.

Of course, their long-term status as the natural party of government meant FF developed a particular enthusiasm for the Alastair Campbell school of berating the media for their inadequacies. The finest doyenne of this particular concept was Bertie Ahern's government press officer Mandy Johnston. When it came to Mandy, it was hard to know whether the long silences or the occasional werewolf-style onslaughts against the sinful hack were more terrifying.

On balance, though, the comment of one stunned hack after a particularly severe bollocking that 'she's like Glenn Close boiling the bunny, crossed with Roseanne Barr in *The Life and Loves of a She-Devil*' suggests it was the latter.

However, the politician is really in trouble when the spin-doctor gets into the bunker beside them. The Irish media are an affable pack of dusty old wolves but even the British eventually discovered nothing ever got done any faster in Ireland by shouting at people. It didn't help, of course, that the more they shouted at us, the more we began to realise the reason FF were berating us so often was because they were attempting, without much success, to disguise their own uselessness.

As the sorry plight of Mr Cowen so aptly illustrates, there is only so much one spin-doctor can do. No matter how skilled the jockey is, if the horse should really be trying his luck in the donkey derby then there is no point in running him in the Grand National.

Sadly as with politicians, it generally ends badly for even the most skilled of spin-doctoring practitioners. Fergus Finlay may, during his time with Dick Spring, have carried the biggest stick in Leinster House, but in his second incarnation with Pat Rabbitte it was swiftly evident that Finlay's career was over when he started being nice to all of us.

We do not mean by this that Finlay was some savage misanthrope, but in his first incarnation a very different Finlay had patrolled the corridors of Leinster House. And it is a particular tribute to his effectiveness that those skilled political assassins of FF thought he was a cross between Richelieu and Rasputin.

Finlay's great strength was the intensity of his detestation of everything that could in any way threaten the interests of his political master. And when he started to chat to the hacks and have the odd smoke with us, it was clear something was not right. The problem, of course, was the new urbane, cigar-smoking Finlay had allowed his soul to be contaminated by humanity and a sense of perspective.

And if you plan to be a successful political spin-doctor, such attributes are never going to cut the mustard here.

Chapter 53

THE GOOD POLITICAL SERVANT SHOULDN'T BE SEEN OR HEARD

I ronically the most intriguing example of the good political servant is Brian Cowen. He may, in theory at least, be the leader of Fianna Fáil and the country. However, our unfortunate Taoiseach is so steeped in the ethos of being the party's good servant that he has now almost become a Pearse-like figure.

Under his unique modern take on the triumph of failure, our poor Taoiseach has turned himself into a great, immobile, political punch-bag who is prepared to take all the hits for his party's irresponsible mis-governance of the state.

Sadly when the great agony is over he will learn that, like all other servants, the gratitude of politicians is a thin enough sort of gruel.

Still, if is any consolation, Brian, you will not be alone for it always ends badly. Even PJ Mara, who glided through the turbulent Haughey era with all the grace of a ballerina dancing on a surf board, and saw Bertie just about home, departed disappointed by the flawed state of the cold new world of Cowen.

But perhaps Mara wasn't too surprised, for he is a literate man who would remember the fate of Sir Thomas More, who famously noted as he went to the scaffold that he was 'the king's good servant but God's first'. It wasn't enough for Henry VIII and when it comes to our own politicians, whilst beheadings are out of fashion, they would probably share the view of Henry on loyalty.

There are, however, a lot of innocents out there. Having, outside of Garret's handlers, largely eschewed the virtues of spin for the first eight decades, Irish politics has acquired a lot of servants. And since the wages have increased as exponentially as the numbers of spin-doctors, maybe they're not so innocent after all.

Even Mr Cowen, who so fervently conjures up the image of a 'take me as I am warts and all' man, now has Green advisors, advisors on finance and so many clothes advisors these days the poor man can't even choose his own tie.

But whilst the public view of the spin-doctor may be that of some Machiavellian Prince with a white cat purring in their lap as they cultivate awestruck hacks over gourmet dinners and fine wines at the gentlemen's club, the reality is a lot less delightful.

The problem with working for priests or politicians is that both are essentially vocational professions. To the budding idealist that might sound good, but they should remember that capitalism will only thieve your time. The priest and the politician, however, will want your very soul and a lot more of your time.

In a sense we should not be surprised that politicians treat those who serve them so cruelly for, like the priests of old, they believe they have been touched by the hem of divinity. This, of course, has the happy consequence of ensuring they are not bound by the common laws of manners or etiquette.

Nothing epitomises this particular state of affairs more than the cruel fate of Frank Flannery. As Fine Gael writhed in the dust and disillusion of election 2002, Flannery, who had shared the good times of the FitzGerald era some two decades earlier, made himself available for service.

Flannery was a cunning and effective operator in the private sector but in the strange political sphere he became the willing cat's-paw of Enda. When the hard yards had to be made, and someone had to be shafted without leaving the new leader's fingerprints on the handle of the shank, Flannery took the hit.

One might have thought that as the wise old owl guided Enda through the almost impossible task of rebuilding a party that was the political equivalent of Anglo Irish Bank, the near success of the task would have formed indivisible bonds of loyalty. Then a great furore arose over the suggestion by Flannery that Kenny was planning to engage in a political alliance of convenience with Sinn Féin. Enda and the whole SF thing is ... well, it's problematic. In the aftermath of election 2007 it is believed Enda tried to lure SF into supporting an alternative Rainbow via the none too convincing vehicle of Trevor Sargent. And in a classic example of the utter incompetence of FG in the vital art of political intrigue, Enda tried to disguise his intentions by carrying on the negotiations *as Gaeilge*.

Unsurprisingly, the claims of further moves towards SF provoked a series of conniptions within FG, for this was one of the many periods when Enda's hold over his unruly party was somewhat less than certain.

So in this time of trial did Enda stand loyally by the good servant who had travelled on the long and hard road with him?

Of course, there wasn't a chance of it.

Instead, poor Flannery was stripped of his stripes as Enda proudly claimed he had been utterly clueless about these dastardly machinations.

We'd nearly believe him.

In fairness, FG's actions and the fate of Flannery are by no means unusual. The recent Gordon Brown controversy, where quite the hullabaloo developed over accusations that Brown had bullied aides and officials by using coarse language, provides us with the most accurate template of life as an Irish spin-doctor.

But in its aftermath one top-level advisor found it hard to understand what the fuss was all about. The man in question may have been one of the Cardinal Richelieus in the court of Bertie but yet he noted quite philosophically that on each and every morning he went into work 'I would be lucky walking down the corridor if I wasn't told to "fuck off" four times before nine in the morning.' And those were just his supportive colleagues.

Of course, the most important thing the good servant can do when the axe falls is to accept their fate in a philosophical manner. This was the case with Flannery, who accepted his none too elegant decapitation gratefully. The good servant, you see, always knows that should it suit the interests of his political masters on the next occasion when there is a crisis, the guilty will forgive the innocent and invite them back into the fold.

Now as to why they might want to return ... well, that is an utter mystery to any sane person.

Chapter 54

GEORGE LEE'S SAD TALES OF HOW THE POLITICIAN AND THE CELEBRITY CAN NEVER BE FRIENDS

It was symptomatic of the way the thing ended that after George's great escape the only kind words came from the Fianna Fáil backbenchers. Charlie O'Connor revealed how, once the electioneering and the photographs with Enda were over, poor George was so lonely Charlie offered a 'lost-looking Lee a space in his office' after seeing poor George wandering 'for weeks on end in the coffee dock. Nobody seemed to be showing him around.'

Unlike Charlie, some of George's other FF friends spoke with a rather more forked tongue. One noted he had been astonished to see 'an advertisement for a local function where George was described as being the star attraction'. The strangely innocent TD said he had 'never in my life seen a political function where the political guest speaker was being used to sell tickets. If we charged people to meet a FF Minister we would be before the ethics commission.' They added that 'It was like Fine Gael were pimping out George, who must have found such dubious behaviour to be quite unsettling.'

As another TD recalled that they had seen Lee 'being paraded around Newcastle West by Fine Gael like a prize turkey', it emerged that George had been suffering other concerns. One TD who appeared to be none too concerned about George chuckled about how Lee 'told me on several occasions that things were so bad he was actually waiting for the cheque at the end of the month for the first time in years'. They added, 'George was becoming one of the new working poor. Remember before when he travelled down to conferences he was getting a fat cheque? Now he was doing it for free and being expected to buy a hundred quids' worth of raffle tickets from some bumpkin.'

In truth, even before the 'pimping out' began, we always suspected it would end badly for George the Good. The trouble, you see, was that Lee was the political equivalent of one of those overwrought pedigree horses. And yet on his first day in the Dáil FG put George sitting beside the tender embrace of the resolutely agricultural numbskull TD James Bannon.

But perhaps it was always written in the stars that FG and George would end up in the same bad place as Romeo and Juliet. The first problem with this particular love affair was that if patriotism is the last refuge of the scoundrel, then surely the celebrity candidate is the last refuge of the ideologically bankrupt.

The strange thing about George is that now he's gone, we almost see more of him in Leinster House than we did when he was there. One supposes, though, that rather like Colm O'Gorman, who was a celebrity PD Senator for an even briefer period than George was a celebrity TD, the former FG TD finds the free parking to be quite useful.

And it is always entertaining to see the FG TDs who celebrated George's election scuttle off like earwigs dislodged from under a stone when George trots in the door beaming uncertainly.

One could hardly blame them, for seeing George in Leinster House after the fall is like witnessing an unquiet ghost cursed to remain for ever at the spot of the crime, until some awful wrong is righted.

Outside of James Bannon, the other spectre of George's first day goes a long way towards explaining what was to come. The photographs of George and Enda surrounded by cheering FG TDs appears to bear witness to a happy tale. However, it was only a prologue and epilogues always end differently.

On that bright morning George was happy because he was by then a celebrity and, like politicians, all celebrities really want is to be adored and, more critically still, noticed. But after the first day it all stopped, for once George was elected, he was a mere back-bench TD. Then, well, it really was only a matter of counting down the hours until George got out before they all drove him mad.

It was, you see, bad enough that George was a neglected celebrity. But he was also an oddly logical soul and Leinster House is not a comfortable berth for logicians.

Once there, George initially rebelled against the inability of government politicians to give a straight answer to a simple question. He was horrified by the erosion of the spirit by the waste of time that is debate in Leinster House. And the logical side of George could not understand the unpatriotic inability of the government to engage in any exchange of ideas and the uninterest of his political colleagues in trying to engage FF in such a concept.

George thought this was insane.

But it was, in fact, life as usual in Leinster House.

Before he started to wander around like a latter-day Ancient Mariner, Lee may have been looking forward to abstruse discussions with Kieran O'Donnell and Richard Bruton. But having done the heavy lifting for three years, FG's Batman and Robin were not prepared to move over in the bed for some RTÉ carpetbagger.

Like a tribe of cannibals who can't understand why the UN is making such a fuss about putting a couple of missionaries in the pot, FG never quite deciphered the problem with George. A party of permanent timeservers could not understand how this new posh fellow did not comprehend that you had to serve an apprenticeship of ten years before your leader will notice your very existence.

The greatest problem with George was that, like all outsiders, he did not know about politics. Oh, he was an expert and he knew the bare bones of the thing. But he did not have that sort of intimate knowledge that can guide you safely through the realities of the club.

Now that the milk has been spilt all Enda can do is mourn the disappearance of three glorious weeks with George where the happy shirt-sleeved duo could have set off on a leader's tour that would have wafted Enda into the Taoiseach's office and George into a fine Junior Ministerial post in Fisheries. Dear me, but the canals of the nation would have been transformed as George 'learned his trade'.

It might not have felt like it at the time, but when George got out, he was bang on time. Now that it is all over, however, one of the more puzzling elements of FG's Lee affair is that it was yet another example of how most attempts to arrange a match between politics and celebrity have an unhappy ending. This is all the more surprising since both seem to have similar mindsets. One side does appear to be more obsessed with celebrity and the pointless soap operas of their own lives but, in truth, celebrities like Kerry Katona can be fairly shallow too.

Still, the good news for those of us who like our politics sweetened by the occasional drawing room farce is that the FG love-in with celebrity politicians has not been eased by their sojourn by the banks of their less than lovely Lee.

Instead, the party are planning to recruit further celebrities such as Eamon Dunphy and Eddie Hobbs, who was last heard of flogging property in Lithuania. We suspect that if FG thought gentle George was bad, they will catch a pair of tartars in fast Eddie the fiscal celebrity and Mr Dunphy. Mind you, they might still gain a couple of seats, for quite a few FF voters would be tempted to switch to Dunphy or Hobbs for the simple joy of seeing how Enda would cope with these gentlemen.

Before FG continue their love affair with celebrities they might be wise to bear one small thing in mind. Bertie Ahern may have spent the entirety of his premiership swimming in a sea of minor celebrities but when it came to politics, the man who launched a thousand pubs abandoned the celebrities. There again, perhaps no other politician was better qualified to realise the celebrity and the politician are not the perfect match most think they might be.

Chapter 55

JUST LOVING OUR WACKY PRESIDENTIAL RACES

W e should not be too surprised the political elite do not share the delight our political bystanders take in our Wacky Presidential Races. Our politicians may make such a fuss over the sanctity of the Presidency, it is surprising anyone who fails to genuflect in the presence of Mary McAleese doesn't suffer a similar fate to critics of the King of Thailand. But inevitably, as with all activities that don't carry with them the promise of Ministerial advancement, they really see the Presidency as a necessary nuisance.

It is handy for proving that women are valued equals. The real truth, though, is that once elected, unless they do something absolutely horrific, like speaking their mind, the incumbent is unnoticed for seven, or if you're lucky 14, years as they wander around with the purpose of an Arab lost in the Sahara.

The cruel truth is that a Junior Minister for the inspection of the nation's sock drawers is more important than the President. However, no matter how hard the establishment works to avoid a contest, the awful moment does always come around when the vacancy has to be filled.

On a happier note the Wacky Presidential Races do uphold some great old traditions. Within Labour Michael D always declares an interest before the inevitable betrayal by the party hierarchy occurs. As the main parties race around looking for celebrities or sporting heroes, some Independents even dare to dream. However, outside of the terrible mistake that allowed Dana to run, you can be sure that in a classic example of Irish democracy in action, they are always forcefully nudged off the pitch by one of the blessed de Valera's fiendishly tricky constitutional concoctions.

Our politicians, you see, may be utterly uninterested in the Presidency but, like an ape half-gnawing a slightly blackened banana, they will shriek if someone tries to take the perk. The dislike of the Presidency is influenced by the fact that, in spite of the harmlessness of the office, it has finished off an alarmingly high number of top-level political careers. This includes the most successful Labour leader in Irish history, for whilst the election of Mary Robinson may have made Dick Spring, the poignant debacle of Adi Roche finally convinced Spring that the great game was no longer worth the penny candle.

In fairness, Dick Spring was not the only political casualty of our great Presidential farces, for the earlier triumph of Robinson had cost Alan Dukes his leadership of Fine Gael. Some would, of course, say that losing the leadership of FG could be more accurately categorised as representing a stroke of good fortune, but whatever about his current view Mr Dukes didn't quite see it that way at the time.

FG's Presidential travails were mild when compared with those of Fianna Fáil, where in a classic example of how often it is a case of the smaller the war, the more dangerous the crisis, the pieties of Mary Robinson cost the government its best-loved Minister, almost collapsed the government in the process and lit the fuse that would blow the faux imperial pretentions of Charlie Haughey to smithereens.

And we wonder why our politicians try so hard to avoid an election.

In spite of the wisdom informing their dislike, happily there was no way to avoid a contest in 1997, for Mary Robinson had dropped the Presidency faster than you'd sack an elderly housekeeper for not spotting bluebottles on a window sill once the chance of a fine big job in the UN arrived.

And replacing Mary was supposed to be a critical contest, as for once the election offered a new Taoiseach a critical opportunity to consolidate his premiership. In contrast, a defeat would re-invigorate an Opposition who were convinced Ahern's less than stable Coalition would not last the distance.

Sadly, rather like the Eurovision Song Contest, the twin concepts of high seriousness and a Presidential election are mutually exclusive for the 1997 campaign swiftly morphed into the Spice Girls election. FF had Posh Spice Mary McAleese, FG had Vicar's Wife Spice Mary Banotti and Labour had Ditzy Spice Adi Roche whilst Dana was Holy Spice. In a foretaste of things to come the posh one was distinctly frosty about the Spice Girls analogy for Mary combined the personality of a head girl from Malory Towers with a persona that made Mrs Thatcher resemble a peace activist.

In fairness to la McAleese, she certainly could not be accused of having an easy ride courtesy of the toxic time bomb drama. Ultimately it was poor Adi Roche who became the Edith Piaf of the show. Some in Labour, though not many, fought their hardest to save Adi from herself. However, the surrealism of the entire tragedy was epitomised by an episode on the Adi bus where a

Bulgarian and a Dutch journalist almost came to blows.

Why either of them was on the bus is, to be honest, entirely unclear for there wasn't much added value for either side. When the Dutch journalist was the first man up to interview poor Adi, the bewildered Labour press team could only look on disconsolately as the Bulgarian suddenly engaged in a terrible rant about how 'always it is the Dutch and the Swedish journalists who get the first interview. What has Adi Roche against Bulgaria?'

Poor Adi had nothing against anyone but from the moment she announced she could 'feel it in my waters' that she could win, everything went pear-shaped. The problem was not just that, though they will never say it in public, the voters like to have a bit of posh up in the Park. Ultimately, the real truth was that Adi was caught on the wrong side of history. The voters wanted rid of Dick Spring and Roche was the terrified squawking dove they used to beat the Labour leader on the head with.

Happily a political establishment that was terrified we might suffer from a further outbreak of democratic frivolity caught a break in 2004. Within Labour the terrible danger that Michael D might break out and force a contest was stymied by their own national council. Instead, for a time they played footsie with Eamon Ryan but once a real possibility emerged that Ryan might be elected and embarrass the Labour leader that was the end of that.

It helped, of course, that the ever-thrifty Greens realised they couldn't afford the petrol money for a tour bus. And Mr Ryan, who unlike Michael D was a tad young to become an old relic rattling around the Park, appeared to be quite relieved too.

FG, meanwhile, couldn't find anyone to run for them and proudly declared they would not be fielding a candidate. The Opposition thought they were engaging in clever politics, but in fact their Sinn Féin/IRA abstentionist-style attitude to the Park served to only reveal the intellectual bankruptcy that would hand-trip Enda in the final days of election 2007.

So it was that la McAleese was re-elected for seven years of living on a modest stipend of 300,000 annually for lecturing us about the virtues of frugal living. The bad news for the establishment, if not for the rest of us, is that when she finishes the 14 years in 2011 we can't just turf the princess of the Park back in for seven more lucrative years of prating and lecturing.

We would if we could, but the constitution won't let us. It would be too much to expect that we would have a reprise of the Spice Girls but we could have the makings of a damn fine Presidential equivalent of 'The X Factor'. There is the prospect of Emily O'Reilly, our wounded Ombudsperson, though her chances are hampered by the apparent parity of terror she inspires in every party. The Labour equivalent of an electoral taxi cab, Ivana is limbering up whilst even the gays are being represented by David Norris. For FG, an unlikely duo of John Bruton and Mairead McGuinness is being touted, in spite of the fact that it is Enda who is best qualified for the critical Presidential tasks of nodding, gallivanting and hugging.

Sadly Gerry Adams is somewhat hampered by the whole child abuse thing and though FF (and Bertie) might once have dreamed of a Phoenix Park testimonial where the public would 'do it for the Bert', things, alas, are so bad even Albert might get the nod on the grounds that he represents the party's best chance.

As we wait hopefully for chaos, it is important to remember one critical political point. In spite of the furore that will inevitably accompany this latest episode of the Wacky Races, absolutely nothing of importance will occur.

Chapter 56 ∾

THE UNLOVED JOHN McGUINNESS, RADICAL FIANNA FÁIL OUTSIDER

A quasi-clerical air surrounds the ascetic figure who stalks the corridors, trailing in his wake a chill of slightly lonely menace. Though he does not wear a soutane, the black suit, steely glasses and white shirt collar create the impression of a priest disguised in civilian clothes. Within a Fianna Fáil party, who if they bear any resemblance to priests prefer the Friar Tuck look, he is that oddity known as a man who is separate from his peers.

If Albert Camus, in his novel *The Outsider*, set the template for modern existentialism then, for FF, John McGuinness is that soldier. Though he is a solitary figure, he is not hated, well, not by the rank and file at least. But unlike nice fellows like Bobby Aylward, he does inspire a level of puzzled incomprehension for the one thing the FF 'lads' agree on is that once you accept the lobotomy process, life as a backbencher is not a hard old station.

Like all old lags, they're affable, cute, cynical old souls who believe once you have the few old pints, slap the Taoiseach on the back at the Ard Fheis and paw a Minister sometimes to get a special grant, the job essentially is done. As a life, there ain't much dignity to it but there are harder ways such as teaching to make a living and, truth to tell, there ain't much dignity in teaching these days either.

In an incestuous world such as this outsiders never thrive. They may sometimes blossom in the Seanad, but outside in the real killing grounds of Dáil politics, its status as a trade dominated by dynastic oligarchies is not conducive to the radical.

This core value means the most venomous whispered conversations that occur between TDs of all parties concern those who are ambitious in an ideological sense. Nobody worries about those who are personally ambitious, for they are generally wise enough to hide their light under a bushel (in truth, mostly it doesn't take much work) and ensure that their dreams of promotion are not damaged by being the source of any difficulties.

Those, however, who express an interest in genuine reform are seen as gauche fools. The general view of that sort of stuff is that it's best left to the sort of academics and intellectuals who end up writing boring columns in the *Irish Times*, for once it's confined to those territories reform can harm no one. However, once you release that Cerberus into the real living world of 'democratic' politics, there's no telling what harm you can cause.

In fairness, it hasn't happened that often for there have been so few genuine political radicals in Irish politics. Some may claim that figures such as Garret or Lemass were, but that is only by the wretched standards of our political class. In other more civilised states FitzGerald and Lemass would have been called centrist social democrats.

Those radicals who manage to hang around are generally absorbed by the system. It was, for example, famously said of Michael D Higgins that he would go mad if he became a Minister. Instead, Labour's pet socialist embraced the ermine of power with the sort of enthusiasm the previously Protestant French King Henry IV displayed when he switched religions because Paris was 'worth a mass'.

This theory may explain why McGuinness is so genuinely detested by the party mandarins. When it comes to the governing doges of FF, difficult backbenchers are normally viewed with a genial contempt grounded in the certainty that there will always be some cheap way to buy them off. However, the visceral dislike McGuinness inspires amongst Mr Cowen's closest allies is epitomised by his nickname of 'The Dark Prince'.

In private conclaves they create dramatic portraits of McGuinness as some Nosferatu who stalks the corridors of power waiting to sink his teeth into and corrupt yet another vestal FF back-bench virgin. And yet moments later they contradict themselves by speaking of an isolated figure whose only other friend is 'the terrible twin Tánaiste Noel O'Flynn'. Amidst all the chuckles about the status of 'Taoiseach McGuinness and Tánaiste O'Flynn' as the party's two designated misanthropic bellyachers, the bar lobbyists are always anxious to claim McGuinness had his shot at changing things.

The Outsider's critics contentedly note, however, that when he was a Junior Minister 'he could get on with nobody' and achieved nothing. Mind you, one should hardly be surprised a Minister planning to reform the system would get in trouble with the self-same system, whilst it is surely time to move on beyond the politics of 'getting on' with the people who have got us into the state we are in.

And on thinking about it, who did he fail to get on with but a Tánaiste who throughout her entire career has been inert to reform and who senior businessmen described as suffering from 'a cringe factor' when she represented the country abroad.

Given the depredations that the incompetence of our self-regarding top mandarins have imposed upon the country, we should perhaps be less than inclined to be excessively critical of Mr McGuinness for failing to maintain the diplomatic niceties with the grand panjandrums of our failed client state of the ECB.

Of course, those who detest The Dark Prince do have a case. McGuinness first came to our attention during the infamous Hugh O'Flaherty controversy where political expediency forced the resignation of one of the few distinguished Supreme Court judges. McGuinness initially kicked up over the attempts to cover up this affair before the gentlest of arm twisting persuaded him to embrace the age-old politics of Slattery's Mounted Foot.

Further entertainment was provided by the ill-fated demise of an attempt by McGuinness to establish the FF equivalent of the back-bench committee of 1922, where frantic TDs claimed they were so stupid they had signed application forms to join the committee without knowing what they were.

McGuinness's famous critique of the plump, unfeathered hens of the public sector was also slightly undercut by the mock heroic scale of our hero's Ministerial retinue, which was swiftly released to the media by 'mysterious sources'.

The furore over his 'Late Late' frontal stab of Mary Coughlan lasted a day whilst sickness and the fates put a shuddering halt to McGuinness's increasingly energetic attempts to persuade Brian Lenihan to 'get on the leadership pitch' and take out chief sitting bull Cowen.

In truth, even if Lenihan had triumphed, McGuinness would have been disappointed for the Finance Minister is too much of a connoisseur of the old ways of doing things to want any turbulent priests in his Cabinet. It is perhaps the measure of his declining status that the great fear that he could evolve into a stalking horse has dwindled. McGuinness is as responsible as his enemies for his current isolation for, whilst outsiders are sometimes right and often needed during his long, deeply resented era on the back benches, he has not staked out any coherent alternative philosophy of the state that might attract supporters or drive a vision of a new Republic. Until he does, his long-running status as FF's existential outsider will increasingly resemble a bad case of adolescent self-indulgence masquerading as idealism. It might even leave the Camus from Kilkenny open to the devastating charge that far from being an outsider, he is actually a mere contrarian.

SECTION 10

Political archetypes

Chapter 57

TIME FOR ENDA TO SET FINE GAEL'S WATER CARRIER ON THE HSE

He is one of the least well-known TDs amongst the galaxy of self-proclaimed political talent that admires itself each day on the Fine Gael front benches. On one level this is understandable for Fergus O'Dowd is not gifted with any great talent for rhetoric or grandstanding. He does not shine on the ramshackle catwalk of the Order of Business or the 40 current affairs programmes that batten on the irrelevancies of the Leinster House soap opera.

Yet one secretive group fears O'Dowd far more than a Kenny or a Rabbitte or even a Leo. He is the terror of the fat cat bureaucrats within our well-appointed public sector workers, who normally glide through the world without ever experiencing a hand being placed upon their crisply ironed collars.

O'Dowd is that most solitary of political creatures known as the Digger, who does his best work in private. Others may indulge in the rhetorical stepovers but O'Dowd is more of a Didier Deschamps style water carrier who burrows through the bureaucratic undergrowth ferreting out as many examples of feckless incompetence as he can secure.

Rather like trench warfare in World War I, it is a hidden dirty sort of a war. Our bureaucrats may in theory be supportive of the concept of Freedom of Information but in the privacy of their well-appointed, air-conditioned offices they regard it with lizard-eyed contempt. And unsurprisingly, in no place do the steel shutters come down more swiftly than amongst the mendacious lying rascals of the HSE, who have enjoyed the non-intervention of a Minister who is the greatest enthusiast for the concept of silence, cunning and exile Ireland has seen since the era of Ray Burke.

In speaking about this hidden war with those elements of the HSE, whose concept of accountability appears to be informed by the same ethos as the old royal theory of divine rule, O'Dowd's voice is instilled with contempt. Of course, anyone who has had the misfortune to deal with the HSE understands O'Dowd's lonely passion. And his dedication is all the more impressive because there is little credit to be got from these secret little battles.

It should be noted that O'Dowd does not go for the easy stuff either. Most politicians, if they consider the whole concept of Freedom of Information at all, tend to think of trying to find out what some Minister's expenses are. However, whilst discovering who got the trip to Dubai or Glenties (well, we do live in more straitened times!) secures the headlines, O'Dowd has fought a silent battle on behalf of the disempowered residents of nursing homes.

It was a story few in the media were interested in, but a quiet evisceration of the lives of the elderly has been going on for years in the name of private profit. Some of the stories from our nursing homes, such as the tale of the shaky Padre Pio statue that was a danger to residents, were comical but others were brutal. Amidst all the cruel tales of bedsores, of nails protruding out of walls, dehydration and of patients being treated with an utter absence of respect, there was one consistent factor. It was the utter indifference of the HSE.

They had no reason to be worried, misgoverned, as they were, by a Minister who has over the last five years appeared to be engaged in an apparent policy of ensuring she knows as little as is humanly possible about the health service she is theoretically in charge of.

It is a measure of how we are ruled that we now have a health service boss who is extremely reluctant to have to actually answer a question about the service provided to the people she is supposed to protect. But Ms Harney apparently sees her role to be one of some imaginary monarch whose relationship to the people resembles that of Prince Philip and those remote Polynesian islanders who worship him as a deity.

Of course, O'Dowd is not a total ingénue for, as FG's alternate 'lovely girl' Mairead McGuinness discovered to her cost in 2007, he is equally assiduous in protecting his own territory. We discovered that too for whilst following the leader of FG through Dundalk we suddenly spotted a stratospherically large election billboard proclaiming O'Dowd's status as the *Sunday Independent* Front Bencher of the Year for 2006. A byline or even a few quid would have been nice but sometimes anonymous recognition is as good as it gets for the humble journalist.

But if we put ego aside, the defining image of that day was Enda Kenny's meeting with Mairead McGuinness and O'Dowd. In front of the cameras it was all air-kisses and so lovely to see you all. But there was something curiously strained about the appearance of McGuinness.

It was all the more surprising because there could be no doubt Mairead was the favoured candidate. She had swept to victory in the European elections and in doing so had played a key role in securing Enda Kenny's uncertain leadership of FG. It had not harmed her status within the inner circle of the party that the victory also provided Cute Oul' Phil Hogan with a reputation for Machiavellian qualities he doesn't really possess.

The implicit offer in a constituency that was critical to the FG drive for power was that if you elected the lovely maid of Meath, there would be a Ministry in tow.

Oh and it would be nice if they elected Fergus too.

But on that afternoon, in spite of all the smiles and the white cotton summer dress, McGuinness could not hide the strain. FG's fragrant candidate had sailed through a truly delightful cat-fight with Avril Doyle after her nomination for the EU election, but if she thought Avril was tough this was an entirely different ball game.

In the aftermath of the election there were stories about clashes between election workers, but in fairness to McGuinness she did not make too much of a fuss. There was, after all, the substantial compensation of an EU MEP's seat to fall back upon, and who knows but possibly even a tilt at being Ireland's first FG President.

But whilst she would be lovely up there in the Park in the white dress, with maybe the fragrant scent of a few freshly baked scones wafting across the lawn, Mairead wasn't, however, going to take the Digger's seat. Instead, Mairead turned out to be George Lee before George Lee happened.

After the next election, should he win, when it comes to Cabinet preferment Enda will be surrounded by a lot of tall poppies ... and that's just the habitués of the Labour party and the Greens. However, when it comes to putting together his Cabinet of all the talents, and a few who mightn't have much talent but who will be in the right geographical location, he should consider the latent possibilities of the Digger from Dundalk. You see, if Kenny is at all serious about public reform, no one knows the reality of the public sector better than the Digger from Dundalk. Of course, it would help if he got the lovely Mairead in this time. But even if it doesn't happen, a Taoiseach who must lead an administration driven by Puritanical rather than Playboy of the Western World principles should at least consider putting O'Dowd in charge of the reform of the HSE.

That would chill the souls of more than a few bureaucrats.

Chapter 58 ∽

THE SINGING INDEPENDENT PREPARES TO TAKE OUT THE HAUGHEY DYNASTY

It would be interesting to know just what the ghost of Charlie would make of the prospect of the Haughey name being extinguished from Irish politics by a banjo-playing Che Guevara wannabe. Mind you, the great old populist rogue of Kinsealy might not be at all surprised. In so far as the Independent TD Finian McGrath has a political philosophy that is any more complex than an unfocused love for Fidel Castro, it is that he is for the people. But Mr Haughey also knew that as it is the people who decide who our TDs will be, then being for the people is a very wise ideology. And happily the people are also for Finian, for he is a lovely man who was very good on that 'Celebrity You're a Star'.

The rise of Finian does, however, show just how changed the old political game is.

And Finian is a changed soul too from the gap-toothed political ingénue who entered Leinster House. Back then one of the most poignant examples of the innocence of Finian occurred after Bertie Ahern had let it be known he was becoming increasingly irritated by the low turnout of Fianna Fáil TDs at the Taoiseach's Dáil musings about the state of the nation.

Sadly the loquacious deputy informed some mendacious journalist that the missing FF TDs were generally 20 yards away watching the horse racing in the Dáil bar. The journalist, who was nursing a grudge against Finian, asked McGrath if he would mind being quoted. The notorious publicity hound eagerly agreed, the exposé appeared and pride of place was given to the status of McGrath as being the 'tout' who had 'outed' the lads. Three days later

Finian experienced the shock of his life as an elderly but enraged member of the lobby pinned him up against the wall and none too delicately explained to McGrath that what happens in the Dáil bar stays there.

In spite, however, of his increased cunning there is something enchanting about the ongoing joy McGrath feels about his status. The majority of modern TDS wander around Leinster House carrying an air of condemned men. But with Finian, every time he enters the Dáil his face lights up at the pleasure of being there.

He is, after the departure of Bertie, one of the last great aficionados of the walkabout, where politicians wander around in mazy circles desperately seeking to meet ordinary people who will give out to them. Such encounters make for a pleasant contrast with the pious new modern politician who treats all encounters with real people with the enthusiasm of a dog heading into the vet's to be neutered. But whilst the new modern politician prefers to blog on the internet, Finian, in contrast, treats the walkabout with the same delighted joy with which a woman approaches a hot spa in an upmarket hotel. After each walkabout, once half a dozen old grannies have been greeted, Finian returns flushed with a special secret glow of worth.

After a decade in the Dáil, he is now one of the wise guys of Leinster House. It has probably done his confidence no harm that he has secured a series of ever more important political scalps. In his first election the maverick successor to Sean Dublin Bay Loftus took out the Labour Opposition Finance spokesperson. Derek McDowell may have been so languid he appeared to spend most of his political career in the horizontal position, but he was smart and pleasant and quite a few Labour TDS have survived for decades in Dublin with fewer qualities.

McGrath's next strike was even more impressive, for whilst McDowell was something of a political pretty boy, Ivor Callely was the complete opposite. After his various adventures involving paint jobs to the house, accidents to yachts, mysterious women and kimonos and the unfortunate expenses controversy, Ivor is now something of a spent force.

In 2007, however, he was a political thug in a pink shirt who had once openly dreamed of being President of Ireland. It may be hard to believe but in past elections Ivor had topped the poll. Now, agonisingly, the usual series of transfers from Fine Gael, Labour, Sinn Féin, Independent oddballs and just about everything else carried Finian across the line.

This was surprising enough but now, astonishingly, Finian might take out the last desolate scion of the Haughey line. Sean Haughey may be possessed of all the charisma of an articled clerk but he is the son of the most cunning, the most controversial, the most dramatic FF Taoiseach of them all. However, if the FF vote collapses and the feuding FF candidates are too far away from the quota on the first count, the three in a row is on.

So what changed it all?

It is perhaps ironic but in some way appropriate for a politician who is a creature of the Celtic Tiger that a celebrity TV show swept Finian into the consciousness of the public. Up to that point he was the accidental TD, but once Finian managed to sing a few bars of 'Bad Boy Leroy Brown' on RTÉ he was a national figure. Mr Castro would have been impressed.

It was not, however, a certain triumph, for poor Dan Boyle threw a strop about being called the fat one in the group and nothing has gone right since. But we should not be too surprised that Finian called it right for he, thankfully, is not as gauche as he looks and sounds.

Instead, he has hopped the right way on a number of occasions now. When the people were against Lisbon, he was against it. Then, of course, when they decided an act of national suicide was not really the wisest route to take, Finian was with them. And the man who learned quicker than most that leading from behind is always the wisest political road to take swiftly left the dolly-mixture Coalition of FF, the Greens, the PDS and those few rag and bobtail Independents when the going was good.

However, he has been wise enough to retain good relations with the FF crew, for in the next election you never know where transfers will be needed.

Sadly the worst may yet be about to come. Finian was grand when he was a harmless singing and dancing Independent. But many of us, and especially Sean Haughey, are now having nightmares about the possibility the day may come when some crucial vote arrives and suddenly, like that famous image of Garret FitzGerald kneeling in front of Jim Kenny, Mr Cowen will go down on one knee in front of Finian and beg him to spare us from the abyss.

It is bad enough that the fate of the country has been devolved to the curious talents of Mr Cowen and his addled crew. But how are we and the world's bond markets to react if, through execrable misfortune, on some cruel day the future of the state is laid gently in the trembling palms of Finian McGrath?

Faced with a spectre such as this, even those famous words about the need to 'be afraid, be very afraid' appear to be in some way inadequate.

Mind you, at the end of it all you couldn't dislike him.

That, after all, is the secret of his success.

Chapter 59

MICHAEL RING'S SAVAGE TALE OF THE WIDOW'S GEESE

One of Fianna Fáil's most clever tricks during the 'people before politics' era was the skill with which they outsourced outrage from the political arena. Over the seven, or in our case 12, years of plenty, which will now apparently be followed by 12 years of famine, you could get good outrage if you went looking. But it could be found only in peripheral sink estates such as columns by Justine McCarthy or Fintan O'Toole and that nearly did more harm than good.

Within the real centres of power, however, we became so desensitised to any notion of civic virtue it became the territory of licensed jesters and Fine Gael backbenchers. Indeed, such was the success of the Bertie school of moral *laissez-faire*, even as Ahern, Sean FitzPatrick and Brian Cowen laid waste to the place, the commonly held view was that we were suffering from too much of the politics of outrage.

Sadly these days as we stare glumly at our Castle Rackrent of a ruined country, the opposite appears to have been the case. But this hasn't stopped the more imperious wing of our self-appointed betters from engaging in aristocratic critiques about the pointlessness of the bad politics of anger. Our elites will admit it is all a terrible mess, but we are supposed to shut our traps, take our licks and move on from the scene of the crime without wasting police time by attempting to apprehend the perpetrators.

In short, we are expected to greet the iniquities FF and the great cabal of vested interests have visited upon the state with the equanimity of MJ Farrell's Protestant spinsters, who sat in the drawing room with their knitting needles as the new IRA conquerors burnt their old Ascendancy house down around their ears.

So far our political masters have been quite pleased with us. In Greece and France, when governments make the 'hard decisions' to take the knife to the living standards of the poor in order to protect the terms and conditions of wealthy insiders, the 'sans culottes' riot. In contrast, the best we can come up with is Mr Joe Duffy and Mr Eamon Dunphy and whilst these empty vessels make quite a bit of noise, no government is ever going to fall on their sword because of the radio.

There was a period of time when outrage spread to the ranks of the four angry men, but in spite of the best attempts of David McWilliams, Pat Leahy, Shane Ross and Matt Cooper, no book club, no matter how formidable, can ever be a company of Jacobins.

It should never have been the case anyway that our literary men should lead the revolution. Generally when societies collapse, it is the political system that out of self-interest alone leads the response. However, even within that arena our cunning spider of a former Taoiseach has managed to drown the capacity of his political opponents to generate a genuine politics of outrage.

In truth, even during the worst of times, the timid shopkeepers of FG were a tad short of the Rasputin gene. Our Bertie's kindly decision to ensure Ireland would have the most highly paid politicians in the world means we now have a political class that are utterly unable to rise any iconoclastic furies.

The wealth on offer did not just mean that politics became a profession as distinct from a vocation. In previous eras the relative paucity of the terms and conditions meant that the overdraft alone provided politicians with a spur to be ambitious. However, when everyone is dipping their beak, it is hard not to be drawn into the hidden Dáil culture of 'the lads all together'.

Of course, the Opposition are still habitually outraged. Over the last decade hundreds of grannies on shopping trolleys in hospitals or mothers of a dozen children or victims of the HSE or poorly paid civil servants have been disinterred from the maw of the people and paraded across the floor of Leinster House in the manner of a fashion show on inequity. But there really was always something of the politics of the Widow Twanky about such goings-on. Talking to mums in Tesco is the champagne politics of emotions and focus group research. The hard yards lie in planning and policy, and when it comes to dragging Granny across the floor of the Dáil, a certain absence of systematic thought surrounds this sort of grandstanding.

It did not help either that Enda was always better designed for the politics of winking and nodding than devising a revolution in how we are governed. And for all the fine talk, Pat Rabbitte's liking for supping pints with the legal aristocrats of Doheny & Nesbitt's did not exactly coat the fine, plump Labour leader with a radical hue.

Some might have thought the arrival of Sinn Féin might provide us with a new moral discourse but they were busy covering up bank robberies, fuel smuggling, tarring and featherings, kneecappings, beatings, murders and the sexual abuse of children.

There was always Joe Higgins, but at the end of the day there was also a bit of the champagne footballer around Joe, for Higgins was a creature of Leinster House, the *Irish Times*, bored Dáil sketch-writers and RTÉ. In many ways the presence of Higgins even suited Mr Ahern for, like the concept of licensed dissent in those fascist regimes who want to hold on to some pretence of retaining a people's voice, Joe offered the Taoiseach the illusion of dissent.

In fairness, our politicians are not entirely to blame for the failure to develop any tradition of dissent, for we have kept them so busy chasing constituency issues even those few who were fit for thought had no time to engage in such an oddity. However, we are suffering from a terrible drought of politicians who might possess any ability to voice the internalised shock and anger of the people.

There are, of course, some who bravely attempt to dabble in the black art but politicians such as FG's James Bannon, who is outraged for breakfast, dinner and tea, soon becomes a figure of ridicule. When it comes to FF, meanwhile, all we have is the likes of Mattie 'the boy who cried wolf' McGrath. Nothing, however, epitomises the sort of false politics of outrage as it is practised in Leinster House more than a famous public meeting involving politicians and the HSE in Tipperary. This posed Mattie with a serious dilemma, for as all his constituency colleagues filed in with their worthy list of questions and carefully constructed case studies, it would be difficult for our Mattie to stand out.

Happily there was no need to fear for our man.

Five minutes into the meeting Mattie stood up and informed the mandarins he was outraged at the scandalous behaviour of the HSE.

Our man was, in fact, so outraged by it all that he was walking out of a meeting that had barely begun. In truth, those who were most outraged were his colleagues, for as Mattie fled the meeting with the alacrity of a bride running from the church, they knew all the painstakingly prepared questions were turning to dust.

And sure enough in the next week's local paper the banner headline strewn across its front page told the readers that the outraged local TD Mattie McGrath had walked out of a HSE meeting in disgust.

Outrage is not, of course, merely confined to the FF benches but there is a big difference between FG's great practitioner of the art of outrage and the Matties of FF. There is something more genuine about Ring for he puts so much of his very soul into the outrage. This was encapsulated on a quiet afternoon where Ring's critique of a social welfare inspection of some misfortunate widow left the chandeliers quivering. The attack went on for some time but the best was left for the end. There was a brief welcome silence as the incandescent TD fixed the unfortunate Minister with tear-filled eyes before he detailed the final outrage in a manner not dissimilar, we suspect, to Edmund Burke's impeachment of Warren Hastings.

As the Minister struggled to suppress his emotions, Ring concluded by wailing, 'and do you know what they did at the end to this poor widow woman? She had six little geese. And do you know what the social welfare inspector did? He counted and valued the six little geese and took them off her pension.'

All you could say was that it was a moment that brought Oscar Wilde's observation about the death of Little Nell to mind.

Chapter 60 ～

| THE CONTRARIAN

I t is a pity there are so few contrarians in Leinster House because they are at least entertaining. Of course, the reason why this occurs is because, like 'the fool' in *King Lear*, they have a licence to say the unacceptable. Generally in Irish politics that is called the truth.

Ultimately, in the new age of 'professional' politicians, the real factor behind the lack of contrarians is that, like all genuine vocations, it exacts a price. It is a pretty visible one too for within the great culture of 'the lads' the cost of being a free-thinker is that the top two rows of the House, where the Ministers and the Junior Ministers and their Opposition equivalents sit, are permanently denied to you.

The levels of dedication and the utter lack of interest in the fruits of office that are required means it is not normally a job for a young man. Surprisingly, given their current fractious state, the Fianna Fáil Mafia have produced very few contrarians. Some would say that individuals such as Noel O'Flynn or Mattie McGrath are in that league but those fellows are opportunists and that is a very different kettle of prejudices altogether.

Mind you, seeing as FF have almost been continuously in government for three decades, we shouldn't be too surprised by the lack of iconoclastic outsiders, for there are generally a lot more jobs going in that scenario. Within Fine Gael, up to recent times, their most high profile contrarian was Brendan McGahon, who was often dismissed as nothing more than a bit of a happy idiot. But whilst Brendan was a bit too fond of our old friend Mr Chemical Castration and the chain gangs for the comfort of the liberal classes, he was also a man of some courage. In Dundalk during the hunger strikes, for example, he stood alone against the rampant tide of Provo-ism and refused to hang out the black flag for Bobby Sands.

On one level it might appear to be difficult to see a connection between the handsome young Mr John Deasy and McGahon. It is easy to forget now but back in 2002, when he emerged upon the scene like a young James Dean, it was genuinely believed that John Deasy was the future of FG. It wasn't just that for the women he was the FG equivalent of Mr Darcy, for in a party of fops and wimps, had he ever taken to chomping cigars, the taciturn man from Waterford could have been FG's Clint Eastwood.

Uniquely, within FG at least, he was a politician with presence. The majority of TDs are shambolic fellows who carry the mark of a career spent deferring to the opinions of leaders, Ministers, colleagues, journalists, councillors, town councillors and interest groups. Unfortunately the long-term consequence of this is the creation of a poor, half-alive sort of creature who slinks around in a permanently unreformed state of nodding cynical indolence where the other guy is always right.

Unlike his colleagues and their air of self-satisfied faint-heartedness, which is as indelible as ash on a forehead on Holy Thursday, Deasy was the political equivalent of the noble savage. Ironically it was a different set of ashes that did for Deasy, but all this was a long way away, when he experienced the politician's curse of being appointed to the front bench on his first day in school. Back then, before the iron entered his soul so swiftly, his experience in the US Congress enhanced the exoticism of this fawn for it was rare to see an unapologetic Republican in a House that, even though it practises right-wing economics, prefers the soft hush-puppy language of Democratic pork-barrel politics.

Such was his perceived importance that Michael McDowell provided Deasy with an accidental compliment by way of his absolute determination to take him out. The Minister's opportunity arrived courtesy of a Private Member's Bill proposing the abolition of alcohol from state functions. McDowell drew himself up to new rhetorical heights and denounced Deasy's juvenile politics of 'horlicks and cocoa for everyone'. Oddly enough, the tactic backfired, for Deasy's insouciant response to his rout merely added to the legend. It was even suggested by some that the ferocity of McDowell's assault was informed by the fact that he saw trace elements of himself in the young rebel. Back then it was a far greater compliment than it would be today.

However, after little more than a year it all started to go terribly wrong as Deasy began to fall out of love with the soul of FG under nice Enda. This first became evident when Deasy began to fall into what the Cute Oul' Phils of the party hierarchy would call 'bad company'. And as it was noted by people who have little more useful to be doing with their time than noting these things that Deasy was 'close' to the Noonan faction, there were a number of factors that explained the turbulent state of the soul of Deasy.

It wasn't just that he was appalled by the pointless courtly games indulged in by the Cute Oul' Phil wing of the party. From the start it was clear Deasy was a disciple of the philosopher Hobbes's 'red in tooth and claw' philosophy of politics. And sadly Dame Enda was simply too much of a creature of the milk and water politics of 'it's nice to be nice' to ever secure the long-term respect of Deasy.

It was at this stage that what Deasy urgently needed was the equivalent of the Beatitudes of Bertie. The young FG Lancelot had to be told that greatness in politics was normally most likely to be secured by those who were prepared to play the long innings. In fairness, the delicate young prince was never publicly disloyal to Enda. But perception is all in this game and too many people, and most importantly of all Enda, realised Deasy was casting contemptuous eyes at the party's designated saviour.

The ending was swift, for the self-righteous morality of the smoking ban and the cautious lifeless conformity of the FG support of it was like acid touching an ulcer. Enda was looking for an excuse—Deasy gave him that excuse by smouldering in the holy sanctuary of the Dáil bar. Enda took it and the FG Icarus became the highest profile casualty of the sanctimonious politics of Micheál Martin.

Ironically though he is now FG's unquestioned contrarian, the brief life and times of the Ministerial aspirations of young Mr Deasy may provide us with a classic morality tale about the dangers of being too much in thrall to the septic charisma of contrarians.

The reality of politics is that there comes a time when straight talking and being right stops being brave and becomes self-indulgent. By the close, though he had entertained us royally with his caustic reflections on a variety of FG leaders, there was something poignant about the state of Austin Deasy.

In his pomp the original stalking horse of Irish politics had stirred up the quicksand beneath the ponderous feet of John Bruton. The same Deasy had also challenged Garret the Good and Alan Dukes with just cause. However, in his final term the great concern of Austin Deasy was the declining number of songbirds.

To our eyes the fate of the linnet and the lark was as valid as any of the other issues that are coursed across the floor of the chamber. But we also suspected part of Deasy Snr's belated interest in chaffinches was a calculated act of disrespect to the self-importance of a Dáil that he had finally fallen out of love with.

The problem for John Deasy is that he has become as peripheral at the beginning of his career as his father was at its close. On one level there is nothing wrong with a son wanting to emulate a father, but it sometimes feels as though Deasy was too anxious to be disillusioned and got there too quickly.

Like his father, Deasy resembles the defeated Whig aristocrat who, on being disappointed in court, retreats to his country estates. He, of course, claims to be fully absorbed by his work in the constituency where he has built a powerful base. But he is in real danger of becoming that which he rails against most fervently, for the iconoclastic James Dean of his generation is now poised to become some Brendan McGahan style national institution that is destined to serve out his time as a Dáil lifer. Now how on earth did that happen?

Chapter 61

BEWARE, BEWARE THE QUIET MEN OF LEINSTER HOUSE

Sometimes in Leinster House the unambitious are the most dangerous ones of all. They may be quiet souls who do not wish to even be Junior Ministers, but the half dozen lucky souls who are simply happy to be there are also the most critical political creatures of all. They are the votes that decide if the self-proclaimed intelligentsia on the front bench will actually govern the country or be thrust into the arid desert of another five years of directionless rhetoric.

One of the finest examples of the self-proclaimed quiet men is the Dublin South West Fianna Fáil TD Charlie O'Connor. His is not an easy existence, for when it comes to the ruthless politicos of Sinn Féin, his constituency is a critical staging point in any Southern-based recovery. They covet that lost breakthrough seat of Sean Crowe and that is not the end of O'Connor's troubles for, like a small neutral country in the early twentieth century, poor Charlie is surrounded by ambitious powers. Should there be a change of government, Pat Rabbitte and Brian Hayes retain aspirations for the top table and should either bring in a running mate, that should be a certainty.

And O'Connor's own running mate, the eccentric but highly intelligent Junior Minister Conor Lenihan, is another who dreams of receiving a seal from the perfumed hands of the President at the Áras.

Indeed, if everything goes the way we think it will in the next election, Conor might even fancy a tilt at the leadership in the role of chief representative of the bright new generation … not that actually becoming the next leader of FF will be worth a whole pile of beans.

In fairness to O'Connor, he has not been deterred by his apparently doomed position.

Instead, our man has decided to portray himself as an ordinary fellow in tune with the ordinary people who, critically, are the voters.

Charlie's abilities in the sadly under-practised art of political humility were exemplified at a constituency meeting over cuts in Special Needs Assistants. As the Opposition TDs smirked contentedly, the hostile audience were only short of rushing the stage when Conor Lenihan attempted to defend the government's cutbacks. Sensing the mood, Lenihan swiftly made his excuses and left Charlie to face the anger of the people. And then the extraordinary miracle occurred. An enchanted Opposition politician subsequently sighed, 'so there is Charlie on his own, and he starts off by saying he's sorry the Minister has left because he has somewhere else more important to go, but even though Conor is the one with all the answers, Charlie will do his best even though Charlie doesn't have any answers himself'.

The Opposition TD continued, 'Then, just as they're getting ready to rip out the seats, Charlie starts telling them about how he knew all about the importance of education for he had spent the afternoon with his own grand-daughter walking with the ducks by St Stephen's Green. Jaysus, but doesn't he start going on about the granddaughter and how lovely she is and their chats about school and you'd want to see them at the end, all the old ones, with the tears rolling down their eyes, giving him a standing round of applause and telling him he's a lovely man. Then they go crucify us and we're not even responsible. It would nearly make you want to give up.'

This was not a one-off either, for at another constituency event O'Connor conjured tears out of the stoniest of territories by telling the audience of how earlier that evening when he was putting his granddaughter to bed she looked up and said, 'Granddad, why do you work so hard?'

It is important to note there is nothing fake about O'Connor's innocent narcissism for the audience would spot that straight away. Instead, the private O'Connor is the same as the public Charlie. In short, O'Connor is an enchanted enthusiast for politics, who is a dedicated servant of the people for the entirely understandable reason that he would be utterly incapable of ever being their leader.

O'Connor is not the only quiet man to prevail against the odds. Nothing epitomised this more than the tale of one rural constituency where the lead candidate was, to put it mildly, a controversial figure with a penchant for attempting to start street fights with 'the fucking blueshirts'. It was bad enough that this individual was a bit of an acquired taste but as the second candidate, who was a quite harmless prim sort of a chap, didn't appear to be making any sort of a stir at all, the Dublin sophisticates decided it was time to jazz up the campaign.

The man from HQ was soon reduced to a state of quiet despair as the candidate blinked owlishly at a series of desperate pleas to liven up the campaign via a radical stance on some controversy or even a few stickers. In a despairing effort at securing some sort of result it was suggested a rally with maybe a few balloons might brighten it all up a bit. Our man's hopes were utterly doused by the response of 'Well, now de grandfather he be having a rally in 1954 and he be nearly losing the seat so I'll be having no big rally thank you very much.'

When the great shock occurred and the quiet man triumphed, on being asked about the 'miracle', with the usual wisdom that always comes after the event one local figure said, 'Yerra sure he spends his Sundays up the mountain boreens talking to old dears about the good old days under de Valera. Sure how could we compete with that?'

There are, of course, quiet women too. When it comes to Labour, for example, it is diligent politicians like Joanna Tuffy who carve out seats on their own at the coalface rather than the Ivana 'I'll run for that' Baciks who will play the critical role in sweeping Mr Gilmore into wherever he will end up.

Sadly within FF at least, the quiet men and women are becoming an increasing source of concern for their self-appointed betters. Should the next election turn into a reprise of 2002, when the voters chopped the head off Fine Gael and spared all the nice quiet fellows down in the boreens talking about Collins, it will be the Ministers who face the axe.

Conor, watch out. Charlie 'Mr Tallaght' O'Connor is coming to get you.

SECTION 11

Hope

Chapter 62 ∾

THE RETURN OF THE GREAT IRISH BEGRUDGER

For those of you who are thankfully too young to understand the barren nature of the Irish Begrudger, there is no better guide than the famous exchange between a parish priest and Con the Blacksmith in Breandán Ó hEithir's *Begrudger's Guide to Irish Politics*. The parish priest was in fine fettle for Ireland had just won her independence and there was nothing but blue skies ahead of us. In contrast, Con was muttering darkly about how the departure of the old gentry would ruin his trade. Sadly our priest's attempt to improve his mood via the promise of 'Sure we'll have our own gentry' was deflated by the snarl of 'We will in our arse have our own gentry.'

As it turns out Con was wrong, but when the Tiger began his analysis of the nation's fortuitous state, it would not have been much different. It would, of course, have been nice if he had been incorrect but poor Ireland always seems to manage to live down to the worst prophecies of the Begrudger.

Ironically one of the most curious features of the recession is that at the beginning Pat was almost relieved, for even during the best of it he was not at ease with himself. Part of it was that centuries of oppression by Britain, and a variety of Fianna Fáil governments, meant that, unlike our American friends who believe happiness is a right, Pat's instinct is to treat it as a trap waiting to beguile you into a false sense of security.

Of course, as the Boom entered its peak, Pat managed to bury his natural Begrudger's gene. However, Pat still wondered, for he knew he wasn't doing anything different from when he was poor, but the world was telling him he was enormously rich.

When he was sober, however, and that wasn't often, Pat didn't feel very wealthy. Instead, he was borrowing like bejaysus to keep up with his enormously wealthy neighbours, who as we now know were doing precisely the same to keep up with Pat. Still, the bank said there was nothing wrong with releasing fifty thousand worth of future equity in your house to fund today's lifestyle choices. As is so often the case, those at the bottom of a pyramid scheme do not know where the game is at until it is all too late.

So when the day of reckoning arrived, Pat acquiesced relatively quiescently for there is only so much snorting, drinking, swinging, houses and decking installations you can go through before the joy goes out of things. Pat may once have liked Miska the Polish maid, but when he had made a move, she had laughed at his pot belly and his girly tits, and then a day later asked for a rise in front of his wife.

By the close, even all that positive stuff about Ireland being the greatest country in the world was all too much. It simply laid too much pressure on Pat to be that which he actually knew he was not, for he always knew in his heart that greatness is something the Germans, Americans, Japanese and Chinese possess as of right. Pat, in contrast, knows he is merely a charming scavenger.

Pat, however, does have one small problem, for the reckoning has gone on for a lot longer than a day. He had, after all, been told there would be a soft landing. Instead, he has been falling off a cliff for four years, but in spite of several atrocious bounces against jagged rocks he is still falling.

That time when 'the country girls' kissed Breakfast Roll Men goodbye as they embarked on separate yet intertwined destinies of peace, prosperity and hope now resemble the sort of Indian summer you enjoy before empires go to war and ordinary people are busted up in the process.

Still, as the children and possibly even the grandchildren of our 'country girls' and all you greedy nurses and overpaid care assistants pay the bills accumulated by our billionaire builders, on the plus side there is one potential source of consolation.

It's called Enda Kenny. What's the wheezing, grating sound you hear? Yes, it is the laughter of the Irish Begrudger.

Now, as he sits in the home he cannot pay for, sipping on the sylvan delights of Dutch Gold, can there still be hope for poor Pat that the country he lives in is more than some barren *Béal Bocht* style rainwashed outcrop that is doomed to nestle for ever at the edge of the world's armpit?

But if this is the case, who are the politicians who can defy the Irish Begrudger and rescue us from the abyss?

Chapter 63 ❧

AT LAST A NATION ONCE AGAIN FOR IRELAND'S OLD BALDIES

Ruairi Quinn knew he was in trouble once the voter casually told the then leader of Labour that the one thing Ireland would never see was a baldy Taoiseach. It might have been different if the voter had said it in an aggressive or cynical fashion. Instead, the unsolicited one-man focus group was kindly alerting Quinn to the realities of the politics of Bertie Ahern.

From that moment, if he didn't know before, Quinn realised that in the brash new world of Bertie, the bald, the serious and the even slightly corpulent ones were out of kilter with an age that was iconoclastic and irredeemably youthful. You couldn't really blame us either for the old baldies were surrounded by the weight of the past, and in particular the dreary grey steeples of the recession-poisoned Ireland of the 1980s.

For Quinn or Rabbitte it was a strange irony, for their status as creatures of the gentle revolution of the 1960s meant they rather than Fianna Fáil had always been the progressive ones. However, by the time of the millennium they might as well have been from de Valera's Ireland. Of course, they still survived in a type of half life but they were ghosts from a weird age. On Saturday evenings you might even see them fighting passionate battles on 'Reeling Back the Years' on RTÉ as young voters wondered did people really live like that once?

Our old soldiers still plodded on dutifully, but the only destination they were headed towards was a series of unknown political tombs. Within the safe territories of the Dáil they continued to shout, cavil and ask their questions but it was poignantly clear Bertie was the new boss.

Then the recession burst through the door in a manner not dissimilar to

Jack Nicholson in *The Shining* and at the first snarl of 'Honey, I'm home' our faithless little Celtic Tiger piggies ran squealing for the old familiars. It happened in less than a heartbeat but suddenly that age when Bertie was the great undefeated champion of Irish politics was gone. Instead, these days everyone now has the *céad míle fáilte* and the hand out for Michael Noonan and sure isn't it great to see you back on the front bench, Michael. Yet in 2002 even Ruairi Quinn had felt the desperation seeping down the phone line when Noonan had warned the Labour leader that if they didn't do business, neither of them would lead their parties by Christmas. Noonan was right, and Quinn suspected he was correct too, but a drowning man is in no position to grab the hand of the man threshing even further below lest you both sink together.

Ironically that is what happened anyway but the good news is that all the hard times have been forgotten, by us at least, for now that we think the ones defeated by Bertie are our best chance, like a faithless lover we are casting coy looks and making suggestive coos in their direction. And though, like old Shep going up the mountains, they are a bit stiffer in the joints, suddenly they have been reinvigorated by the warm breath of possible future power ghosting across their formidable necks.

Though we are now experiencing tough times, for our old veterans, the blow of the recession may be cushioned by the non-arrival of any good times for them during the Tiger age. The tyranny of FF may have been a gentle one but the Tiger was still a cold place for those mad enough to not love 'our' Bertie.

Michael Noonan was perhaps the initial and worst victim, for whilst he was a clever, literate man, having first necklaced him unfairly with the ghost of Brigid McCole, FF defined him in aspic as the Baldy Noonan of Irish politics. The Fine Gael leader's fear-drenched approach to the almost impossible task of taking Ahern out did not help, but the despatch of Trotsky with an ice pick was an almost gentle fate when compared with the experiences of Noonan once FF spotted the attendant dangers to being an old man in a young man's country.

As at one point the FF press office even produced an eggcup starring Noonan's agonised face with the logo 'Go to work on a Baldy'—it might have been expected Ruairi Quinn would be a more formidable prospect. In different times the first Finance Minister since Haughey to secure a budget surplus might have been a respected figure. But this was the age of Seanie FitzPatrick, and Quinn was bottled up by FF in a *cordon sanitaire* of outrage, where he acquired the rather unfair reputation of being nothing more than a 'Mr Angry from Sandymount' type.

In truth, there was no reason for FF to bother with the caricatures, for the voters sensed people like Quinn were not fun and we were in the mood to party until the early pubs opened and then go some more. Quinn, in contrast, carried around that knowledgeable matronly chill that always comes with those who have experienced the harsh wintry air of recession. They know that after the fun there will always be a hangover.

The most surprising victim of all this was Pat Rabbitte. Quinn's successor came equipped with the dubious CV of being a superb orator and able parliamentarian. But in the age of Saipan and celebrity pub openings Rabbitte became the political equivalent of an elderly man waving a stick at laughing children.

It was a cruel divide but in the Celtic Tiger era Rabbitte, Quinn, Noonan and John Bruton too were Puritans whilst Bertie's 'lads' were Cavaliers. It was Grandpas and Grumpy Old Men versus 'the lads'. And worse still, some of the Grumpy Old Men were even believed to be ideologues.

We, however, were too sophisticated for ideology or even policy. Ireland was instead an enthusiastic participant in the politics of celebrity, where it was better for a Taoiseach to be photographed beside Emma from 'Coronation Street' or Robbie Keane than some philosopher. Ruairi and Pat could splutter all they liked but that Victorian era of the politics of policy documents was over, for we were Tiger's baby. Of course, we are now racing back to hold the hands of these increasingly balding nurses with such a degree of enthusiasm the wonder of it is that Garret, Albert or Ray McSharry haven't been asked to make a comeback. And it would not be a surprise if appeals start rising for the great Brut to be drafted back into the fray.

It is a bit unfortunate the decision was only made after the 'something worse' had already happened but our political equivalents of Napoleon's old guard have been nice enough to not point out the consequences of our faithlessness to us.

Indeed, in a strange sense the extent of their exile has transformed the Grumpy Old Men too. They have lost that arrogance and the excessive sense of *droit de seigneur* that characterised some of their earlier careers. Instead, it is as though experience and age has turned them into more rounded personalities ... in every sense.

They may be somewhat more grizzled and a lot plumper than they were in their less than lean middle years, but the Russian steppes of Opposition mean they are grateful for the kindness of strangers. As we coo over their brains, they could surely be forgiven for smiling wryly. John Bruton might have once been sneered at for his capacity to produce a policy document a week. Now a nation desperately seeking a road map out of the current debacle sighs seductively and says do tell us more when FG produces its 'New Era' policy document. Indeed, the thing is now so bad it is believed that some unfortunate souls are even reading Garret in the *Irish Times*.

And the comeback is not merely confined to the Grumpy Old Men. Up to two years ago it was still believed Labour's grey age profile was a problem. But the Tigers are in therapy and we want the folks from the previous war to see us through. Joan Burton and the old bluestocking wing may have been once mocked for their moral seriousness but no one now, however, cares about the pitch of Burton's voice. Instead, a nation living through the consequences of the collapse of the doctrine of moral hazard would almost accept the return of Ethics Eithne FitzGerald.

Sadly our new balding nurses will certainly have lots of cod liver oil to deliver when they get into power. Still, at least we can be comforted by one thing. When they come at us with the big needle this lot won't pick our pockets in the process.

Chapter 64

BRIAN HAYES, MIDDLE-AGED MAN RAMPANT

U p to the election of 2002 the career of Brian Hayes had been a study in the politics of perfection. From an early age the mannerly Mr Hayes had enjoyed the dubious delights of being John Bruton's 'special project'. But unlike other such 'pets', Hayes had displayed a tougher side to his character, for he had even carved out what appeared to be a safe seat in the difficult working class terrain of Dublin South West.

Then, just before that ill-fated election, the much-loved Olivia O'Leary was heard on RTÉ's 'Five Seven Live' issuing what almost sounded terribly like a tribute to the Sinn Féin candidate, Sean Crowe, in Hayes' constituency. Suddenly everything began to look terribly ominous, for the dulcet tones of Olivia were the clearest signal yet that the middle classes were abandoning ship. The Little Bo Peeps of Fine Gael had lost their quasi-constitutional status as the designated party of choice for the anti-Fianna Fáil electoral sheep.

On a closer, more forensic reading O'Leary's comments abut Crowe were more cutting than first appeared to be the case. But the subtext and the consequences were still devastating, for in its aftermath the ordinary voter could think only that Olivia felt it might now be all right for decent respectable people to vote for SF.

In Tallaght they did and that, we thought, was the end of that for Hayes. Back then the electoral monsters of SF simply did not lose seats and there appeared to be little enough road for Hayes to take out big dogs like Rabbitte and Conor Lenihan or even little 'uns like Charlie O'Connor.

In the end the most touching feature of the great comeback of Brian Hayes was that so many people were pleased. It was also slightly surprising, for in the aftermath of the great beheading of 2002, though he reached the safe mooring of the Seanad, it did look as though this was a deserved lap of honour that would simply serve to ease Hayes back into the civilian life of teaching.

So where had it all gone wrong? In truth, as is so often the case with Irish politics, the problem with Hayes was one of appearances. It is an article of faith amongst commentators on Irish politics that it is hard to love middle-aged, middle class men who are at ease with their station in life. If you are a middle class *Hot Press*-reading man infused with guilt and self-loathing about your comfortable status, then some degree of moral debt forgiveness can be allowed. The problem with Brian, however, was not just that he was a little too comfortable with his status as the advocate of middle Ireland.

Ultimately, the really unnerving thing about Brian's embrace of the middle class persona was that he was only in his early twenties. The TD who was once cruelly described as having been 'born wearing a waistcoat' was a 40-year-old hiding in a 20-year-old body. Of course, Hayes was clever in a self-approving sort of way but whilst his capacities were never doubted, least of all by himself, we are quite finicky about our politicians.

It is not enough for them to be smart, for they must be fun too. And it simply did not sit right that the young Mr Hayes appeared to think ecstasy was a freshly mown lawn.

It also didn't help that Master Hayes was simply too comfortable in the Leinster House milieu. This, after all, was a young man, yet here he was wringing his hands and performing on the Order of Business like some fawning barrister in a court. Within this context even his Dáil expertise was a dagger pointed at his future, for no one likes the child who is too clever.

He was also, on occasion, too cocky for his own good. One classic example of this occurred when the young Hayes instigated a Trinity Literary and Historical Society style debate on the need for a Council on the Status of Men. Sadly, though the best soldier the government could muster was Mary Wallace, young Master Hayes was blown out of the water as Ms Wallace went through two millennia of the exploitation of women and suggested we might sort out the issues concerning women first of all.

As the election approached in 2002, the similarity between Hayes and the ill-fated Tory leader William Hague intensified. This was not a good omen either for the bitter lesson Mr Hague also had to learn was that no matter how superior you are to your opponent, the most important quality a politician must possess is the capacity to ensure the electorate is at ease with them. In our case the failure of Hayes to secure that synthesis meant the man already being touted as the next leader of FG found himself being ousted from political life by a no mark from SF who could scarcely speak a coherent sentence.

And yet, ironically, failure was the making of Hayes for, as the sad tales of Brian Cowen reveal, the politician who has had the perfect career often evolves into a flawed pet. Failure, in contrast, inserts steel in the spine and a clever humility in the soul. As with all things in life, excesses of failure are not to be encouraged either but it is how you respond to disaster that defines character and surprisingly Hayes displayed true grit.

Up to the point where he had lost his seat, the doting eyes of John Bruton had conveyed Hayes through the vicissitudes of political life on a magical carpet of leadership approval. Now under the less benign gaze of Enda, Hayes did not spend the next five years bemoaning the cruelty of the electorate or the failures of the generals or attempt to parachute his way into one of the more genteel, easier Southside constituencies. Instead, he toughened it out, battled away in the council estates and, in what was a bit of a shock for some, despatched Sean Crowe back to obscurity. On this occasion in yet another straw in the wind that SF's time in the sunlight was done, Olivia did not go on a road trip with Sean.

Intriguingly, one of the more significant factors in the rehabilitation of Brian Hayes was that he was now a middle-aged candidate. The William Hague problem evaporated, for he was now of an age where punters would not wince if he was seen on camera wearing gloves and a scarf. The young tyro was now properly qualified to represent the concerns of Resident Association Man. He always had the support of the elderly blue-rinse brigade, who saw him as their darling boy. But he was no longer a precocious child imitating those who were more properly qualified to secure man's estate.

Failure has developed some other qualities. In the past there had been strong trace elements of the Mr Prim and Proper surrounding our man. Those who know him realise Hayes has always possessed a wicked sense of humour about the hypocrisies of political life, but an excessive sense of propriety deemed proper for a young man on the rise meant he downplayed those characteristics.

It also helps that suddenly the middle class virtues are fashionable again.

In the time when Ireland could be run on the fly, we admired the lads who could go out on the tear all night, hit the early houses, sleep it off for the day in the Department and then run the country. Or at least that is what we thought they were doing.

Now, however, we want our politicians to possess well-washed shiny faces and to be of the neat and tidy collar and tie variety. Our day of worshipping the vanities of the Tiger are over to such an extent that we want our public representatives go to the Dáil on the DART and own a semi-D that hasn't been done up via a suitcase full of cash from a Manchester bus company owner.

Of course, the adventures of young Master Hayes have not yet ended. Initially, under Enda, the darling boy of the blue-rinse brigade was a warm favourite for Cabinet preferment. But astonishingly, the same strange thing that happened to Deasy suddenly occurred to the ever-cautious young Mr Hayes. However, in the aftermath of the coup of the aristocrats it is a measure of how he has matured as a politician that Hayes was one of the few who salvaged any dignity. Other aristocrats snuffled, whimpered and, in one terribly embarrassing case, begged to keep their front-bench portfolio. In contrast, Hayes was sanguine for he is now mature enough to realise that when you play the great game and lose, all you can expect is the axe. Ironically that defeat in 2002 may also have helped, for it tends to give one a sense of perspective over the loss of front-bench privileges.

But though Richard and others may have shuffled back onto the front bench with all the vivacity of men wearing carpet slippers, the exile of Hayes may not be a long one.

You see, the one thing cautious ward bosses like Enda fear most is the spectacle of a turbulent priest with an independent conscience floating around the back benches.

And should Kenny fall down another political manhole, now Leo the Young Turk and Richard the Faint-hearted may be ahead in the pecking order. But for many, Richard is a broken reed whilst Leo may be hogtied by the instinctive preference FG have for safety rather than radicalism.

He may have had a terribly big fall in 2010, but should he play the political game correctly Brian Hayes may return to his former rampant state far more quickly than Enda would like.

Chapter 65 ∾

EVEN A GREEN CAN BE 'A FIERCE NICE FELLA'

One of the clearest examples of the differences between the various subsets of the political species occurred when the irredeemably rural Fianna Fáil TD Peter Kelly met Eamon Ryan on a foreign trip. As Kelly bewailed the variety of constituency issues—from sewage to questions as to the real identity of the deposed Emperor of Abyssinia—that he had to deal with, the FF TD noticed that Ryan was looking at him with some puzzlement. On being asked if he was worried about the Abyssinian thing, the then newly elected Green TD responded by asking Kelly to tell him more about 'these clinics' because he had never heard of them before.

Afterwards, in spite of their various differences, the FF TD made one critical point as he noted that whilst the Green TD was 'a bit strange', he was 'a fierce nice sort of a fella'. This observation cuts to the heart of Ryan's current political standing, for ultimately nothing in Irish politics—or in politics in any country throughout the world where you don't boil the heads of your defeated enemies before feeding them to the dogs—is more important than the acquisition of the reputation for being 'a fierce nice fella'.

Of course, mendacious politicians can survive for up to 20 years but the sad fate experienced by the not at all nice Ivor Callely indicates the electorate, even if it takes a while, eventually see through that. And rather like the 'Big Brother' reality show, once the voters come to the damning conclusion that you are not 'genuine', then your race is essentially run.

Outside of being a sort of 'fierce nice fella', Eamon Ryan possesses one other critical political trait. He is lucky. The Green Minister initially secured his seat in 2002 because of the implosion of Fine Gael and the stagnant state of Labour in Dublin South. Though FG recovered in 2007, his return was facilitated by the ongoing immobility of Labour and the disintegration of Liz O'Donnell into a parody of the politician her talents suggested she could

become. And when it comes to securing those transfers, it always helps to be
'a fierce nice fella'.

A figure who once claimed that one appearance a month in the *Irish Times*
would secure his re-election should be too naïve to survive the white heat of
Irish politics. However, we suspect there is more than a slight element of
playing to the gallery surrounding Ryan's Mr Smith Goes to Washington
public persona. And Ryan's success is down to more than the adoring gaze of
the yummy mummies of Dundrum who love Róisín Ingle and believe in
angels.

It does help that he has that clean-shaven other-worldly look that makes
women want to mother him but he is no sickly political child wandering
gauchely through a nest of vipers. When it came to the great post-2007 power
divvy up, Gormley may have made the unwise promise to resign as a Minister
in 2010 if he became leader in 2007. In contrast, quiet Eamon kept the powder
dry and made sure he was guaranteed a Cabinet seat for the duration. A man
who is the son and grandchild of a distinguished banking family knew that,
as in commerce, possession is nine-tenths of the law and that whilst
immediate gratification is nice, you must always look to long-term yield.

Ryan also picked up the knack of being a Minister fairly swiftly. So far in
his career he has had 'seven moments that were straight out of "Yes, Minister"
where the civil servants have said of some doomed initiative "Minister, that's
a very courageous decision, we must set up a review group."' It all taught Ryan
that whilst the media think power resides in Cabinet, top-level politics is 'like
"The X Factor" and the most critical audience is your own civil servants'.

This important political trait of luck was already evident courtesy of the
great escape when, for a brief window of time in 2004, the Greens were
touting Ryan as a potential candidate for the Presidential elections. That of its
own was bad enough but the even greater danger was that it was not beyond
the bounds of possibility that the 'fierce nice fella' might actually take on the
haughty incumbent and win.

The final decision was made at the beaches of Inchidoney where many
strange things happen. Fortunately, well, at least for Ryan, who was far too
young to become a political Miss Havisham wearing the ruined wedding dress
of a lost political career, the Greens for once lived up to their reputation and
lost their nerve.

The affair did, however, boost his profile to the extent where he was a shoe-
in for a Cabinet Ministry. Once there, Ryan swiftly stood out for the critical
reason that in a Cabinet of dyspeptic misanthropes he has the uncanny
capacity to create a sense of genuine hope. It is not, contrary to appearances,
an easy quality, for though all politicians have a certain capacity for insipid
varieties of rhetoric, no one ever believes them since they generally appeal

only to the idealism of the public when they themselves are in trouble.

In contrast, Ryan has the capacity to sound passionate but without doing so in a nagging, insincere sort of way. It is a difficult act but when you have that thing called 'it', then you can pull off this essential trick. And before you ask what this 'it' is, the best explanation we can give is that just as there are natural hurlers, or boxers such as Ali, who are born with perfect reflexes, some are just natural-born politicians.

The tragedy for the ordinary politician is that 'it' cannot be trained or coached for, like the playful id, the capacity to be a Blair or a Clinton or even a Bertie is a mischievous child of nature. Instead, all the envious rest can do is watch, wait, hope for the reflexes to go and then take those perfect fuckers down.

Nothing epitomised the capacity of Ryan to provoke an itch amongst the electorate that can only be scratched by the consummation of a first-preference more than the Green party launch of Lisbon II. Once we realised there wasn't going to be any foul language from Gogarty, we sank back into a state of boredom that was almost dissolute until Ryan began to speak. The metaphor he chose was an odd one. But as he spoke of how learning about Europe was like the experience he had when he got a cameraphone, bit by bit Ryan, by virtue of his enthusiasm and the simplicity of the metaphor, captured the attention of the entire room.

Of course, he is not perfect. Acute political observers have noted that even when he is apparently listening to you, Eamon is not short of the infamous Narcissus complex whereby he is all too aware that if you pretend to listen, you look even better.

The messianic thing can make people uncomfortable too, but whilst cynicism is understandable in a faithless land, even the driest soul secretly dreams of better times and Ryan is the first politician since Garret who is capable of conveying the false belief that with a little bit of communal effort 'things can only get better'. Now who was the other guy who used to say that? Oh yes, it was Mr Blair.

Intriguingly, the luck of the devil continues to stalk our man. After the triumph of George the Good it looked as though our Green goose was cooked. However, as FG began to count the days until George became the leader, Lee began to count the pennies and from thence the days until he could leave.

Still, there are limits to the luckiness of the Greens' 'fierce nice fella', for he has evolved into the political equivalent of a man trapped in a woman's body. If he were in any other party, and we suspect that might even include FF, there would be no limit to where he could end up. And were it FG, when it comes to the leadership crisis prowling around the dusty attic of the party's mindset, we suspect they would, if given the chance, clutch that lost Prodigal Son of Garret to its matronly bosom in a heartbeat. They are yearning, Eamon, for a clean-shaven man with a nice wife who works in the *Irish Times* to release them from the thraldom of overblown Mayo schoolteachers.

Sadly, for now at least, the capacity to fulfil the FG dream of replacing Garret the Good with Eamon the Optimist may be beyond the capacities of lucky Eamon. However, do not yet rule out the possibility the lost child Garret never had could yet engineer a most sincere escape from the political Tower of the Greens.

Chapter 66

LEO VARADKAR AND THE DANGEROUS POLITICS OF LADIES' HAIRDOS

O
ne of the few sure things we know in Irish politics is that the threshold for unacceptable behaviour is low. On a good day the Irish politician can get away with anything from perjury to gross incompetence and still receive a hero's greeting of bonfires and torch-lit rallies when he returns to his constituents. As with some odd religion there is, however, one obscure act that, if committed, is punishable by immediate excommunication—for the solitary thing you apparently cannot do is attack a woman's hairdo.

The first and most celebrated victim of this edict was Pee Flynn. After an unfortunate business with tapes the then Presidential election candidate Brian Lenihan had been on the cusp of mounting a vigorous comeback. Sadly for Fianna Fáil, and the country for that matter, this was derailed when the most vainglorious popinjay of the Haughey era Pee Flynn appeared on 'Saturday View' and tore into Mary Robinson and 'her new hairdo and interest in the family'. Pee might have got away with his critique of Ms Robinson's motherly instincts, but from the moment the man had criticised a woman's hairdo, the situation was so irretrievable even Bertie Ahern was ballyragged in the streets by posses of indignant women.

Two decades later a very different politician suffered a similar bruising experience. In the aftermath of election 2007 it swiftly became apparent that for once the nice boys of Fine Gael had acquired some politicians with a bit of bite. Outside of Lucinda there was Dr James Reilly, who possesses an unnerving resemblance to Brendan Grace's famous bad priest in 'Father Ted' who went by the name of Fr Fintan Stack.

None have, however, even come close to matching Leo Varadkar.

Normally the ideal new TD is a quiet, harmless fellow who is simply filled with gratitude just to be there. When it came to Leo, the impact our man made meant he swiftly acquired the nickname of Varad the Impaler. The trouble with Leo began when at the first post-election FG think-in Varadkar treated some of the more venerable FG TDs to the benefit of his views on the party's myriad failures over the last two decades. It all ended quite fractiously as distinguished elements of the FG ancient regime were accused of engaging in acts of 'crypto communism'. There were even some tears from the younger female element, but had events ever come to court, it is believed a strong defence could have been mounted on the grounds of the lateness of the hour and the taking of strong drink.

In fairness, Leo did not confine his ministrations to his own. Seeing as nobody believes more strongly than FF that, like good altar boys, once they have performed the vital art of voting, new TDs should be seen and not heard, you can only imagine the extent of the horror amongst the ranks when a new TD dared to speak his mind. It was all the more appalling when a TD who believes a Taoiseach to be corrupt openly says it, for that's just not the way we do things here.

Varadkar's cheek clearly discomfited Bertie Ahern, who had in his final imperial reinvention become used to a far more deferential sort of treatment. To the rest of the clubbable Leinster House inmates, it clearly indicated that Varadkar was that most unpleasant creature known as a 'man in a hurry' who was not afraid even of a Michelin-starred Taoiseach. This was one who would have to be taken care of and happily the much desired event occurred sooner rather than later.

The FÁS debacle, where Harney did the junketeering and poor Coughlan got the blame, appeared to be tailor-made for Varadkar. There was no shortage of scandal but one stand-out feature was the expenditure of what seemed to be a substantial sum of money on Ms Harney's hairdo. With the confidence of youth Leo led with his chin and demanded the immediate resignation of the Health Minister.

When it comes to the great book of reasons why Ms Harney should get the sack, the hairdo was pretty low down the list. Still, by the close of the incandescence one would have thought it was Varad the Impaler rather than 'Junket' Harney who had been gallivanting around the world at the expense of the taxpayers. It was bad enough that the great glass ceiling alliance of female journalists immediately united to defend the human rights of the women of the nation to a taxpayer-subsidised hairdo. But such, however, was the level of national outrage the women were joined by right-on commentators such as Vincent Browne.

Normally Vincent is a paid up member of the 'off with their heads sentence first, trial later' brigade. On this occasion Browne suffered from a fit of the vapours and raced to the defence of our void of a Health Minister. It all represented a new low for a nation that has never been distinguished by our capacity in politics to separate the woods from the trees. Eventually the ladies were appeased as Leo bowed to the national dislike of the sort of Tory Boy who has the cheek to stand out from the galloping herd and have a definitive opinion on anything.

Happily, after a brief exile amongst the massed ranks of the deliberate non-controversialists, the restoration of Leo to his old self was signalled when Varadkar asked the Tánaiste Mary Coughlan how she would respond to the claims that in international trips abroad there was a Coughlan 'cringe factor'. Once again there was an attempt to indulge in the politics of chivalry, but the world tends to be a little less kind when you have 450,000 people on the dole. And seeing as Ms Coughlan has a domestic cringe factor, it is difficult to believe things go any better when she's abroad schmoozing with the sheiks.

There were even better frolics to come courtesy of the Impaler's critique of Garret FitzGerald. The initial response by FG resembled what we could only imagine would be the case if in India you were to walk up to a sacred cow, whack it over the head with a mallet and start carving steaks out of the prostrate form. But the truth of the matter is that the dusty photographs of Garret in the FG HQ are an unquiet ghost whose presence saps the will of the living.

He may well be FG's designated living saint, but in spite of his status as a political special protection area the measure of a man lies in his legacy. Ultimately the clearest measure of the 'success' of Garret's reign was that the people were so desperate they even welcomed Haughey back in 1987. And since Garret they have never elected FG back into government again.

Whatever about the rights and wrongs of Leo's decision to fail poor Garret as a Taoiseach, the most important message to emerge from the furore was that a new generation were casting aside the shackles of the past. When Varadkar apologised it was in a manner that allowed him to retain some element of dignity, for it was an act that was definitely done with crossed fingers. And meanwhile back in the shadows Enda Kenny, who has little reason to feel any gratitude to FitzGerald, was grinning away happily for Dr FitzGerald has turned into the Thomas à Becket of FG.

The smiling stopped when the FG Impaler turned his attention to Cosgrave's child and suggested during the failed coup of the aristocrats that a deposed Enda would make quite the excellent Minister for Foreign Affairs. After the great debacle some were surprised by the survival of Varadkar. But for all of his flaws, Enda Kenny is a good judge of political horse-flesh. Kenny knew that, whatever about our broken reed of a Richard Bruton, the last thing he needed was an unbowed Varadkar prowling impatiently around the back benches.

Others may be puzzled that, unlike the visibly haunted Richard Bruton, his decision to abandon the lost group of regicides and nestle back in under Enda's wing did not take a feather out of Leo. Varad the Impaler, however, is the child of a different age. Unlike the ritually defeated ranks of old school FG TDS, who wander around carrying a perpetually haunted deferential air of a Departmental under-secretary, Varadkar walks tall.

He is part of the new breed of TDS, such as James Reilly or Lucinda, whose self-confidence has not been eaten away by the canker of constant defeat. More critically still, like all future leaders, he possesses an insouciant insolence that says that the normal rules do not apply to me.

It is a characteristic, oddly enough, that in politics is found only amongst those who are born to lead political parties.

Chapter 67 ∿

SOMETIMES WE NEED NECESSARY FICTIONS

If any journalist had said five years ago that Brian Lenihan would be the designated saviour of the country, they would have been put on compassionate leave.

It is strange but true that for the vast majority of his career Lenihan was an object lesson in how not to get on in Irish politics. The moment we realised Brian Lenihan did not walk with the ordinary occurred many years ago when some irrelevant Junior Minister was introducing an even more irrelevant bill to the Dáil. Suddenly everything changed utterly as the young Lenihan began his speech with a reference to the philosophical theories of 'the eminent Dutch jurist Hugo Grotius'.

As the Junior Minister almost fainted, for he knew little enough about the bill without having to factor in the views of seventeenth-century philosophers, one journalistic hack was sufficiently enthralled to write 'Goodness Grotius Lenihan is atrocious'.

It was a speech that we, alas, suspected would not endear the young tyro to Bertie Ahern and we were correct. As years passed in the fallow fields of the back benches, Mr Lenihan was far angrier about being denied his appropriate slot in the Cabinet of dunces than he let on. And of course, Mr Ahern was also far more aware of Lenihan's anger than he pretended to be.

The problem for Bertie, or more accurately for Lenihan, wasn't just that he wasn't one of 'the lads' or that he was the sort of dynastic creature a self-made man like Bertie secretly detested. The ward boss was an expert on character and an utter pragmatist like the Taoiseach was uneasy over the strain of pleasant madness that is stitched into the DNA of the Lenihans. It didn't stop Ahern from appointing Mary O'Rourke to the Cabinet but then, rather like the rest of FF, 'the Bert' was a bit terrified of Madame. But when it came to Lenihan, who could blame Mr Ahern if he decided to play cat's cradle with the big girl's blouse from the Bar Library?

It certainly was not a case of 'the life for Brian' as FF's brightest barrister was put in charge of non-events such as the Cabinet subcommittee into the children's crusade but time and the absence of much discernable talent within the ranks forced Ahern to promote him. Mind you, we are told it was a close run thing between Lenihan and Tom Kitt.

When the great apotheosis of the dynasts arrived and Mr Lenihan secured the ill-fated Finance Ministry, initially it looked as though Bertie's reservations were correct. You are indeed in trouble when the Finance Minister invites comparisons with the famous nursery rhyme about 'Little boy blue, come blow your horn, the sheep's in the meadow, the cows in the corn. But where is little boy blue? He's asleep in the meadow.'

In fairness to Lenihan, he was actually the victim of Mr Cowen's long sleep 'in the meadow'. But like all gaffers, BIFFO had slipped the hospital pass to his fellow dynastic scion just in the nick of time. The good or bad news, depending on where you stand on such things, was that after a wretched start Mr Lenihan's broad-brimmed ego swiftly repaired any uncertainties.

The bad news is that this has little to do with his fiscal abilities and everything to do with his profession as a barrister. The Minister's ebullient character did not change any of our economic fundamentals but, like a good Minister for Propaganda in some derelict fascist state, he has managed to put the best side out. However, if you step away from the rhetoric, anyone who actually believes Mr Lenihan is solving our crisis is a happy fool.

We do not wish to denigrate the man, for a politician combining the qualities of Adam Smith and Margaret Thatcher would struggle to control this crisis. But from the start Mr Lenihan floundered courtesy of a first Budget that ended with a call to patriotic duty. Oddly enough, rounds of applause were scarce on the benches of a FF party that has always been more into self-service than national service.

But as we now know, the trouble had started a lot earlier. When it came to the fateful night of the bank guarantee, we needed dealers like Ray MacSharry, who had experienced the hard days of being in the leper's corner of the manager's office. Instead, what we got was the politics of chaos theory being played out on the hoof by a gauche public schoolboy.

We could go on but it is Mr Lenihan's abilities rather than his weaknesses that are the source of our greatest concerns. The ability to put a good face on things is undoubtedly good for the morale of a psychologically destroyed people but is it in fact the very opposite to what is actually required right now. The unfortunate reality is that our barrister's clients are the same Department of Finance mandarins who, having squandered the Boom, have now been put in charge of the recovery. This is a recipe for hubris for it leaves our current most-loved Minister situated right in the middle of the great unvoiced conspiracy of our political elite, our mandarins and our bankers to avoid any element of moral hazard for their actions.

The truth of things is that if Ireland is to be reformed, we need revolutionaries rather than clever talkers. Seeing, however, that outside of being sophisticated spoofers the other defining feature of the Lenihans is loyalty to the elites of the state, the necessary revolution is unlikely to come from this quarter.

So why, given all these factors, is the Minister still riding so high?

If there is an argument for Darwin's theory of genetics it is that the Lenihan dynasty, for all of Ireland's best-loved political clan, from Brian Snr to Mary O'Rourke and Brian Lenihan, are eccentric but clever bluffers.

This is a pleasant but dangerous combination, for their eccentric unconventionality means it is easy to like them and their loquaciousness allows them to disguise any absence of expertise.

For now it is not just the public who are buying the bluff, for there was a double rationale behind Bertie's reluctance to promote the brightest barrister. Over the last year Mr Cowen has discovered that in giving Lenihan his head he may have fashioned himself a poisoned dart for his own back. The problem for bad BIFFO is that Mr Lenihan has also become quite the hero within a certain set of FF TDs. Of course, Mr Lenihan has been at pains to make it clear he is not running for the leadership of the party. But he is ending up near the scene of the anticipated crime far too often for Mr Cowen's comfort.

Mr Lenihan's love for the back-bench TDs is all the more intriguing for when he was a humble TD FF's new saint didn't appear to know that FF backbenchers actually existed. Happily these days the door of the Minister's office is open all hours should any desolate backbencher need to be comforted by the swaddling clothes of the Minister's 'concern'.

It does not, we presume, help Mr Cowen's mood that for good or ill the public have made their choice for Mr Lenihan to be the national designated hero. Amongst the insiders too, even though he sits serenely outside of FF's internal wars, the man who is not running for the leadership is, according to his supporters, 'in complete control of the party'. And even though Brian is not running for the leadership, apparently within FF the support is there without him asking for it ... which is nice.

In truth, BIFFO's Bash Street Gang should not be too upset about this set of events, for the Senior Counsel must remain true to their nature and gratitude for unexpected preferment is simply not in their DNA. Instead, each elevation is seen merely as a step towards a more appropriate recognition of their talents. This means Mr Lenihan and Mr Cowen are rather like the famous tale of the scorpion and the frog. At the edge of a lake a scorpion asks a frog to carry him across to the other side. Though the frog initially declines on the entirely justifiable basis that the scorpion will sting him, eventually he is persuaded to agree.

When, halfway across, the scorpion stings the frog and they begin to sink the frog asks the scorpion why he has doomed the two of them. The scorpion apologises but says with his last breath that he couldn't help himself because it is in his nature.

It is ironic that the fatal weakness in the Lenihan family gene may now be the source of their greatest strength. It would, of course, be wise if before it all goes too far we, and FF, checked to make sure Mr Lenihan is the real deal rather than just another great pretender. Such caution is unlikely, however, for Lenihan is the only figure within FF who has any concept of the great political art of conjuring up the sort of necessary fictions that can inspire a country.

Our society of political slow learners has discovered the hard, ever-expanding multi-billion euro way that a facility in the art of necessary fictions is a double-edged sword.

However, sometimes we need fictions more than the truth. And the sad truth of our current scenario is that, like poor Blanche DuBois and the kindness of strangers, the thing is now so desperate we'll even settle for a pretender so long as they sound a little plausible.

Chapter 68 ✦

THE PARTY THAT SECURES THE SUPPORT OF BREAKFAST ROLL MAN WILL WIN THE NEXT ELECTION

In the new land of zombie politicians, zombie banks, a zombie economy and a zombie people you would, in truth, miss Breakfast Roll Man. For a time he was as popular as Toad of Toad Hall but now it really is a case of come back, all is forgiven. Of course, were they to listen to 'Ireland's call', 100,000 of them would have to return.

The flight of Breakfast Roll Man may initially have been invisible but from late 2006 in a thousand rural pubs the smart guys began to realise that it was time to go. They, ahead of everyone else, knew that once again Fianna Fáil and our crepuscular mandarin class had turned the country into an economic wasteland where, like Steinbeck's sharecroppers leaving the American dustbowl, the only option for the young and the free was flight.

Of course, our obsession with scything down tall poppies like the Quinns and the FitzPatricks means we don't hear a lot about the deceased state of the former braying icon of the Tiger. The disinterest is all the more surprising for our man was once a ubiquitous presence in the Spars, the chippers, the pubs and the DIY centres of the land. But now as the rolls of dole fat gather around the tracksuited gut, rather like the returned soldiers of World War I, it is as though poor Breakfast Roll Man never existed.

In part the disinterest may be informed by our man's status as Ireland's latter-day Loads-a-money. Our baseball-capped soul had always attracted a certain element of distaste, for it was difficult for the former teacher of

Breakfast Roll Man to watch as the Muppet he regularly told would get nowhere powered past his stationary Ford Fiesta in a 2008 SUV. The self-regarding higher paid public sector worker could only look on in grim distaste as the plumber, chippie or spread sped past him in the earnings stakes. A revolution was going on where, suddenly, the lower orders were purchasing the sort of holiday homes in Croatia that used to be the preserve of our underpaid primary schoolteachers.

It was difficult to watch as the privileges formerly confined to a certain caste were democratised. This process was all the harder because the desires of Breakfast Roll Man were so limited. He knew nothing of art or culture whilst the politicisation of our hero in so far as it existed was limited to the vague recognition that Bertie was the boss, this was a good thing and Enda Kenny was a Muppet who was as exciting as a day-old spud in a fridge.

Of course, there is a reason why even the sort of Cedar Lounge socialist aesthetes who fret about the Iraqi working classes are indifferent to the fate of poor Breakfast Roll Man. In a very real sense, if Charlie McCreevy were ever given the chance to construct an electorate, our hero was the former Finance Minister's idealised voter. All politicians like to rule a stupid people with limited desires and our Breakfast Roll Men were the enlisted soldiers of the Celtic Tiger revolution.

In a country where anyone over 30 who was not of upper middle class extraction was deeply suspicious of expenditure, they took to limitless credit in the manner of lemmings racing joyously towards a cliff. Breakfast Roll Man and his 'partner' were the original designated habitués of the high street shop. The front on which they fought consisted of brand names like Hilfiger, Nike, and Brown Thomas for the posh ones. Rather like Indians seeing their first beads, Breakfast Roll Man and the 'bird' gazed in covetous awe at the pretty trinkets of multinational capitalism, took out their credit cards and did their duty.

Of course, everyone is now wagging fingers at them and saying in a po-faced manner that they should have been more 'careful'. But should we be so critical? We may now be in an iconoclastic rage of righteousness against excess but, like the scene where Gatsby weeps over the beauty of his shirts, are we being too merciless over their enchantment by the transient beauty of €500 stilettos?

You see, when it came to our gauche new aristocrats, everyone dipped their beak. In a country where it constantly rained they embraced the prospect of the sun, sea and sand three, four and even five times a year. And back in the day when the tax receipts were soaring, no one complained when they descended en masse on to the computer shops, or the open days for apartment sales where four grand bought you an option on the €350,000 duplex in Carrick-on-Shannon.

Instead, the banks and the finance mandarins and the politicians feasted on them in the manner of bears and spawning salmon. Emily O'Reilly could muse all she wanted about the virtues of tiptoeing back towards the chilly embrace of Mother Church. But our nouveau riche chippie who, on stopping work on a Friday, or maybe on a good week Thursday, would spend his weekend shopping, carousing and drinking was where it was at.

This happy-go-lucky fleshy soul might have inspired an insipid distaste in the minds of the *Irish Times* columnists, but the insatiable desires of these thoughtless consumers fed the property supplements of the same august institution. And if he could even escape for 15 minutes with our friendly local Lithuanian escort once the 'bird' had been given another 20 grand to construct an Italian crushed-stone kitchen, that was two and perhaps three sectors of the economy and two European countries that he was keeping ticking over.

And whether it was the pub or decking, he added to the sense of vitality, the buzz of the thing. The Labour-voting public sector worker might find their decaffeinated, skimmed milk, Fairtrade cappuccino turning sour in their mouth as our man swaggered by with a box set of 20 Budweiser, but the apotheosis of Breakfast Roll Man fed into the notion that we at last were an egalitarian society where anyone could succeed.

For decades a lack of faith in our capacities had not so much been a glass ceiling on aspiration as an old, rotten, corrugated tin roof that let in the rain and kept the place dark. But we had traded up now and we were the equal of … oh wait, we hadn't. Instead, we are back in the old shack for, as Ms Harney noted during her infamous three-week junket in New Zealand, the party is well and truly over. It is for some at least, dear, but certainly not you.

As Breakfast Roll Man's dreams disappeared like a leprechaun's pot of gold, the end of the party was epitomised by the rise of the head shop. Some tutted about the tabloid furores as the young flocked to sample the khat of the destroyed Tiger, but there was something shocking attached to the spectacle of a generation who are so demoralised they buy horse tranquillisers for kicks.

But what else are they to do, for the political consciousness of Breakfast Roll Man or of his fiancée is still not very acute. The tragedy for our man and his 'country girl' fiancée is that they are all still of the view that Enda Kenny is a Muppet. Breakfast Roll Man feels rolled over by Bertie, whom he now realises always thought he was a Muppet whilst BIFFO is of no solace to our man or his pregnant fiancée in a grubby tracksuit, waiting to be evicted from a house where both now live in a united state of hatred.

The problem, meanwhile, we as a society face is that the best elements of Breakfast Roll Men will leave. Those who stay, however, pose another difficulty, for few of those are designed to be part of the new shining castles in the sky smart economy. What happens, and who to an extent can blame them, if they turn feral?

We doubt it will come as much of a consolation to this poor peripheral creature but he is still of importance in one small regard. The political stenographers can write all they want of seismic shifts or ideological wars. The truth of things however, is that the party who can rescue poor Breakfast Roll Man will deserve to govern the country.

Chapter 69 ∾

HAVE YOU EVER THOUGHT IT MIGHT ACTUALLY BE US?

One of the most effective ways of gently ending a relationship that has become tedious is to sigh 'It's not you, it's me.' Of course, the real truth in such scenarios is that we are merely killing with kindness, for it always is you. We, you see, are never the boring, obsessive, perfectionist in the relationship.

Ironically, when it comes to the great game of politics, something quite similar is occurring to our once special relationship with Fianna Fáil. Sadly the bad news for our poor unloved BIFFO is that on this occasion everyone is definitively saying it is you. But whilst we are all united about the guilt of FF, have we ever thought that it might actually be us?

Seeing as FF set great store by never taking the lead on any issue, it would be utterly unfair to suggest they invented corruption or personal greed. Instead, like the perfect chameleon, they adopt the plumage of the people.

As we are now in the mood for truth it is time to admit the Irish electorate were not some modern version of Princess Diana who was seduced, impregnated and then betrayed.

We were always well capable of sucking our thumb, holding it up to the wind and deciding where it was our short-term interests actually lay. Of course, sometimes FF were genuinely idealistic, but whilst the peasants may have given a respectful ear to the Gaelic Twilight, we were more interested in abolishing the land annuities and seizing a few more farms. Pat, you see, even during the Home Rule and Catholic Emancipation eras, always voted with his pocket.

The truth of things is we walked into the current disaster with eyes wide open. Oh, we may talk the talk of purity and reform and the rest but, like

Milton and *Paradise Lost*, we have always secretly been of the devil's party.

So we voted for the party that was holding the party and we were not always wrong. Fine Gael used to appeal to our better nature but they became so politically debased the best alternative they could offer in 2007 was a lighter version of Bertie.

So it was that in election 2007 the only option we had was to trust the safe pair of hands that squandered the Boom to guide us safely through the recession. It was an offer that came straight from the ugly sister school of politics.

Now that the milk has been thoroughly spilt we are starting to hear all sorts of arguments about how we could reform our politics. The quaint figures from TASC and the *Irish Times* regularly speak of the virtues of a list system, for example. But how can it be that a selection of the fine academics, 'entrepreneurs', economists and regulators who led us to ruination would be any better than the current crew of politicians who merely stood idly by as they broke up the country?

The reality is that we were the partial authors of our own destiny.

It is only human that when asked about such acts of sin, we now adopt the famous line of Bob Hope's, when on being caught in bed with a starlet, he told his incandescent wife not to 'believe your lying eyes, honey'.

But we are the ones who tipped the wink to Bertie and who chuckled indulgently as we elected legislative clowns like Mattie McGrath and James Bannon. And whilst it is hard these days to find anyone who voted for Charlie or Rambo or Bertie, through some accidental miracle these gentlemen still topped the polls in every election.

FF may be a sloppy party, but we are a sloppy people.

We have been sloppy in the way we have treated our economy, our environment, our people and our politics.

It is never easy to look at the self with clear eyes, for how would Narcissus have fared if he looked in the water and saw a monster?

But as we cavil and mock poor Cowen and swear oaths of vengeance on his acolytes, it's time to remember we were the Frankenstein who created the current monster.

In the next election we should perhaps stop to smell the roses and seek out politicians of intellect and courage.

But if the voters really want to create a better place, we will need help from our politicians. For if the Opposition fail to step up to the mark, don't blame us if, like one of Roddy Doyle's victims of domestic violence, we return to the roguish old roués of FF.

It's up to you, Eamon and Enda.